Where Has Oprah
Taken Us?

Other books by Stephen Mansfield

The Faith of Barack Obama

The Search for God and Guinness

Never Give In:
The Extraordinary Character of Winston Churchill

Then Darkness Fled:
The Liberating Wisdom of Booker T. Washington

Forgotten Founding Father:
The Heroic Legacy of George Whitefield

The Faith of George W. Bush

The Faith of the American Soldier

Benedict XVI: His Life and Mission

Where Has Oprah Taken Us?

The Religious Influence
of the World's Most Famous Woman

Stephen Mansfield

THOMAS NELSON
Since 1798

NASHVILLE   DALLAS   MEXICO CITY   RIO DE JANEIRO

Published in Nashville, Tennessee, by Thomas Nelson. Thomas Nelson is a
trademark of Thomas Nelson, Inc.

Thomas Nelson, Inc., titles may be purchased in bulk for educational,
business, fund-raising, or sales promotional use. For information, please e-mail
SpecialMarkets@ThomasNelson.com.

ISBN 978-0-7852-3710-5 (IE)

Library of Congress Cataloging-in-Publication Data

Mansfield, Stephen.
  Where has Oprah taken us? : the religious influence of the world's most
famous woman / Stephen Mansfield.
      p. cm.
  Includes bibliographical references.
  ISBN 978-1-59555-308-9
  1. Winfrey, Oprah—Philosophy. 2. Winfrey, Oprah—Religion. 3.
Television personalities—United States—Biography. 4. Actors—United
States—Biography. 5. Religion and culture—United States. I. Title.
  PN1992.4.W56M35 2012
  791.4502'8'092—dc22
  [B]
                                                                    2011013385

Printed in the United States of America

11 12 13 14 15 QGF 6 5 4 3 2 1

To Annie Merle Williamson

Contents

Introduction ix

1. Oprah Rising 1

2. The Turning 35

3. The Age of Oprah 75

4. Oprah's Spiritual Family 117

5. Oprah's Favorite Things 171

Epilogue 213

Acknowledgments 217

About the Author 221

Notes 223

Index 233

Introduction

I t was September 23, 2001, and the nation's wounds were fresh
and bleeding. Twelve days before, Americans had endured the
horrors of a vast terrorist conspiracy as it spilled out upon their
shores. On that never-to-be-forgotten September 11, their proud
towers had collapsed. The stronghold of their military might had
been assailed. Valiant passengers aboard an airliner had wrestled
hijackers and then flown their plane into the ground. Thousands
had been killed. Millions more scarred forever.

Now, though, on this day, it was time to draw strength from
one another—and to heal. At New York's Yankee Stadium, an
event announced as "A Prayer for America" was to be held. It was
planned as an unapologetically religious affair, with the dignitar-
ies in attendance including representatives of nearly every major
faith in America. Cardinal Edward Egan, Imam Izak-El Pasha, and

Dr. Inberjit Singh, a Sikh leader, were to be present, as were dozens of other clergy from nearly as many traditions. Rabbi Joseph Potasnik, the chaplain of the Fire Department of New York, would also play a role.

It was sure to be emotional. Opera star Plácido Domingo would sing "Ave Maria." Singer Bette Midler would offer her near-classic "Wind Beneath My Wings." The conclusion would come with Lee Greenwood's stirring "God Bless the USA." Before that finale, survivors and grieving families of the dead would weep out their stories in testimonials that would fill the early autumn afternoon.

The hosts for the service were actor James Earl Jones and talk show host Oprah Winfrey. Jones was little surprise. Americans were used to his narrations—he was, after all, the voice of CNN—and to his dignified presence at national events. One broadcaster even quipped that his grand, sonorous voice was proof of the existence of God.

It was Winfrey, though, who caused some to wonder. A slim seven years before she had been merely a television talk show host. She had risen to fame on the strength of her astonishing gifts as an interviewer, her sparkling intelligence, her unflinching boldness, and her uncanny ability to make her audiences feel she was one of them. Yet in an effort to win the war for ratings, particularly against top-rated talk show host Phil Donahue, she had begun to traffic in themes from the dark underbelly of American life. Shows with titles such as "I Want My Abused Kids Back," "She Asked for It: The Rape Decision," "In Prison Having Teenaged Sex," "Little League Pedophiles," and "Married to a Molester" became commonplace.

The nation's moral guardians had grown outraged. Pulitzer Prize–winning television critic Tom Shales called shows like Winfrey's "talk rot" and said that she in particular specialized in creating "boob tube boobs." Consumer advocate Ralph Nader charged that Winfrey was media's worst moral "polluter" and wondered aloud if she and her producers must get "all their ideas from the *National Enquirer*."[1] When Vicki Abt, professor of sociology at Penn State, coauthored a stinging report for *The Journal of Popular Culture* titled "The Shameless World of Phil, Sally and Oprah," sophisticates took note and began looking askance at the Chicago-based program that had become one of the most successful in television history. Popular outrage rose. Even faithful viewers grew disgusted.

Winfrey and her producers felt the blows and knew a decision had to be made. It was time for a change. Before long, a new Oprah Winfrey emerged.

Both as a strategic repositioning of the program and as a product of Winfrey's read on the needs of the times, the popular daytime talk show turned to religion. The eclectic, nontraditional spirituality that had long been Winfrey's private source of inspiration now took center stage on her program. "I am defined by the world as a talk show host," she declared, "but I know that I am much more. I am spirit connected to greater spirit."[2] This connection to greater spirit now became the celebrity guest on every episode. Religious leaders quickly replaced the victims and victimizers who had long populated her programs. *Avant-garde* spiritual teachers such as Marianne Williamson, John Gray, Deepak Chopra, Iyanla Vanzant, Eckhart Tolle, and Gary Zukav were eagerly featured.

Viewers were encouraged to embrace their divine selves, to live in terms of the Hindu concept of *karma*, and to transform their reality through visualization. They were taught to create physical healing or to overcome poverty or to fashion success by changing and focusing their thoughts. To the delight of her fans,

Oprah herself began emerging from her interviewer's role to extol the benefits of her unique religious life. She taught her followers the techniques of "Remembering Your Spirit." She modeled the chanting of Hindu mantras. She invoked the spirits of her ancestors. On one program, she prayed for the needs of a viewer. She insisted that there is more than one path to God and enlightenment and she began to feature spokesmen for alternative faiths on her show. She spoke of a great awakening of vital spirituality wrung from the stony confines of traditional religion.

So influential was Winfrey's call to this novel brand of mysticism that pundits began respectfully speaking of her as "America's Pastor." The *New York Times* referred to her program as a "secular chapel."[3] Biographer Kitty Kelley would call her "a one-woman cathedral."[4]

By the time she took the podium at the "Prayer for America" event in 2001, she was no longer the slime queen of daytime television. She was the champion of a bold new religious movement, one that eschewed established religious categories and created a new faith out of the personally meaningful elements of any faith.

"When you lose a loved one, you gain an angel whose name you know," Winfrey proclaimed that day. "Over 6,000, and counting, angels added to the spiritual roster these past two weeks. It is my prayer that they will keep us in their sight with a direct line to our hearts. . . . Hope lives, prayer lives, love lives . . . [let not] one single life have passed in vain."[5]

Four days later, New York Mayor Rudy Giuliani visited *The Oprah Winfrey Show* to thank its host for her part in the touching ceremony. "People felt comforted" by her presence, he assured.[6] And so they did. Newscasters and bloggers exulted in the "spirit" and "vision" Winfrey brought to the event. It soon became obvious that the role an earlier generation might have granted to a Billy Graham or to a senior military chaplain or to a popular cardinal of the Roman Catholic Church now belonged to Oprah Winfrey. She had become the priestess of an innovative brand of spirituality, one that was even then reshaping the place and nature of religion in American life.

O

It is testament to her skills that during this time of religious transformation Oprah Winfrey never ceased to be the favorite girlfriend to millions of America's women. This was part of her appeal, part of the way she touched lives as counselor and friend. Survey after survey revealed that she was the celebrity American women most wished to invite into their homes. It was her warmth and her humor, her genuine interest in lives different from her own that made her so beloved. She was always there with the "Ooohh, girl!" or the "Oh, Lawd!" She was always eager to know. The bawdy and the off-color particularly thrilled her. Audiences had learned that these moments were when she would cut a glance to the camera as though to say, "Lean in close now, girls. This is going to be exciting!" She was the loud, crashing, hilarious, ever-present companion who sat at your kitchen table and told you that you were not alone, that your weight gain was nothing compared to hers, and that you would both get through it together.

So when she put her personal spirituality on display before her eager television audiences, she was like the friend down the street who had found Jesus or Buddha or Kabbalah or yoga and wanted to talk about it over coffee and cake. After all, everyone needs something to get through it all, don't they? Life is long and the days are lonely. Maybe this friend had something that worked. And so America listened.

Had she been just another spiritual seeker among the millions in her baby boomer generation, her story—and her spirituality—would have drawn little attention. Yet the fame and riches she dreamed of as a child had become hers; today she is one of the wealthiest and most visible women in the world. Her personal fortune is nearly $3 billion and her influence surpasses that of nearly any other contemporary. During the 2008–2009 broadcast season, before the nation switched to a digital television system, *The Oprah Winfrey Show* reached more than 110 million homes. Now, she commands nearly seven million viewers, down from twelve million a decade ago. The mere mention of a product on her program or the inclusion of anything from cars to frying pans to underwear on her list of "Oprah's Favorite Things" sends sales skyrocketing. Her influence extends even to politics. Her endorsement of Barack Obama for the presidency in 2008 was worth more than a million votes, according to analysts.[7] This has become known as the "Oprah Effect," the synergistic impact of Winfrey's fame and image upon markets, ideas, and behavior.

Much of the power of this "effect" arises from the public perception of Winfrey's character, of her bigheartedness and generosity. She is known to give hundreds of millions to charity. She has funded a girls' school in South Africa intended as a model for a new generation of female leadership in that troubled land. She seems ever to be about service, about making a difference, about investing in worthy causes that leave lives transformed. That her success seems in part to grow from her gracious giving appears to many of her devoted followers to be confirmation of her spiritual values.

Winfrey does not shy away from this connection and clearly

intends to place her irresistible "effect" in the service of her religious vision. Already she has propelled the careers of numerous prophets of alternative spirituality to unprecedented heights merely by granting them exposure on her talk show and podcast series. Retreats, enlightenment centers, conferences, seminars, and millions of CDs, books, and DVDs have resulted. In 2011, Winfrey launched the OWN network on cable television. Replacing the Discovery Health Channel, the network reached nearly eighty million homes the moment it aired.[8] There are, of course, the cooking shows and the home makeover episodes and reality shows with celebrities like Sarah Ferguson, Duchess of York. Yet some of the nearly ten thousand hours of programming a year is geared toward the alternative spirituality that has become Winfrey's central theme. Contracts are being negotiated with some of the nation's leading mystics and spiritual teachers. And money should be no problem. Automakers GM and Nissan committed to extensive advertising on OWN, while Proctor & Gamble signed a hefty $100 million ad deal that will range over the first three years of the network's life.[9]

The OWN network could play a transforming role in American religion. Consider that a single weekly religious program on OWN could well command an audience in the tens of millions. Meanwhile, Joel Osteen was the leading success among more mainstream religious broadcasters just before OWN launched, commanding a weekly audience of only seven million.[10] T. D. Jakes and Pat Robertson ranged well below that figure. Moreover, while these more traditional religious broadcasters appear on the air a few hours a week, Winfrey's spiritually oriented programming could amount to significant broadcast hours a year. In short, OWN could make Oprah Winfrey the most far-reaching religious broadcaster in television history.

Yet what will be the content of these hours of religious programming? Will they be the product of study and the counsel of experts? Will they draw from the wisdom of the centuries? Or will they be the product of pop spirituality and trendy mysticism?

It is a matter worth consideration. The content of Oprah's groundbreaking "Spirit Series," for example, was determined in a surprisingly casual way. Before Oprah departed for a lengthy vacation, an assistant handed her a suitcase filled with books chosen from the alternative spirituality best-seller lists. On some glistening beach or at a star-studded resort, Oprah digested the selections. If a book spoke to her, she instructed her producers to schedule the author for an appearance on her program. Soon, a spiritual teacher Oprah had never met received a phone call from Harpo Productions—usually from Corny Cole, one of Oprah's producers—and the arrangements were made. The teacher would appear on Oprah's podcast series, on her XM Satellite Radio program, or if among the fortunate few, on her network talk show. Most would not see Oprah until the day the interview was recorded and then would never have a chance to speak to her again. Yet entire careers were created from the power of this exposure with millions of Americans urged toward a form of alternative spirituality they likely would not have encountered in any other way.

It would all be reinforced by the strength of Oprah's personality, by the power of the Oprah Effect, and by her media appeal. Yet this was exactly what some feared. Was it possible that the Oprah Winfrey fame factor could entrench ideas in the souls of Americans they would never otherwise have taken seriously? It is a critically important question given that what Winfrey espouses on her programs challenges faiths that have existed for centuries, time-tested religions that have answered the soul's need for millennia before

Oprah Winfrey was even born. Could an informal, mystical, highly personalized religion of achievement and enchantment gain sway in the world simply because Oprah Winfrey proclaimed it and not because it gave any evidence of being true? In short, does fame trump truth when it comes to religion in our modern world?

It has happened before. One small example tells the tale. Consider the instance of Jordan's lovely Queen Noor and her best-selling book *Leap of Faith: Memoirs of an Unexpected Life*. Born Lisa Halaby, an American who graduated from Princeton and worked in the Middle East before meeting and marrying Jordan's King Hussein, Queen Noor is beautiful, wealthy, articulate, and often lauded for her benevolent work around the world. She is a member of the exceptional Jordanian royal family, represented most often in the West today by the striking Queen Rania, a favorite of television talk shows.

Because Queen Noor converted to Islam in order to marry, she took pains in her autobiography to explain her conversion to her husband's faith. In Islam, she says, she found "fundamental equality of rights of all men and women." She delighted in its call for "fairness, tolerance, and charity." She is drawn by Islam's emphasis on "simplicity" and its "call for justice," by the reality that "no Muslim is better than any other Muslim except by piety." These social values, along with Islam's teaching of a "believer's direct relationship with God," are the reasons she converted.[11]

There is no reason to doubt Queen Noor's devotion to Allah. In Islam she seems to have found her spiritual home. Yet whatever hold Islam has upon her heart, no informed observer could take seriously Queen Noor's claims about Islam's social teaching. It is no bigotry to state this. Not only are her claims found nowhere in the sacred texts of Islam, but even a casual survey of the world confirms that Islamic societies are among the most unequal in the rights enjoyed by men and women. As these words are written, the world watches while a woman charged with adultery faces stoning in one Islamic country, a woman who converted to Christianity faces the same in a second Islamic republic, and stories of women being beaten for as slight an offense as not having their hair properly scarved emerge from yet other Islamic nations. In Saudi Arabia, arguably the wealthiest and most West-friendly of Islamic societies, women lobby unsuccessfully for the mere right to drive or to go unattended to a mall. Equal rights? And who can doubt that Islamic societies are among the most intolerant on earth? Yet reviews of Queen Noor's book, a *New York Times* best seller, made almost no mention of these embellishments. And why? Because she is famous. Because she is powerful. Because she is wealthy. Because she is an attractive and well-spoken darling of the Western media.

Ideas have consequences, though—religious ideas in particular. How many young people were swayed by this pretty, sophisticated royal and her outlandish claims for Islam? What effect might this celebrity-powered homage to Islam have had on American foreign policy? On popular thinking in the West? On what is taught of Islam in our schools? Had a turbaned mullah made such claims on CNN, few Westerners would have taken him seriously. Yet when these same distortions come from a woman as impressive as Queen Noor, the medium overrides the message and ideas gain sway that never would have otherwise.

And so it is with Oprah Winfrey. Consider: If we were approached on the street by a stranger insisting that the world we see around us is not real, we would think him mad. If a coworker told us that our thoughts take on physical form outside of our bodies and shape reality the way we choose, we might think him imbalanced. If we saw a sick man being berated for allowing his flawed thoughts to make him ill, we would be disgusted and would rush to stop the abuse. Similarly, if a woman were raped and then told in our hearing that she had attracted her horrible experience through her thought life, we would be outraged. If we had a traffic accident and then learned that the person who hit us claimed he was innocent because the ancient pain of mankind actually caused the collision, we would laugh at the folly before referring the matter to our attorney. And if we were told that the only reason we perceive ourselves as separate from other human beings is that we believe we are and that in fact there is only one of us here in the world, we would dismiss the idea as silly and not worth our time.

Yet all of these ideas either have been extolled by Oprah Winfrey or have been proclaimed by spokesmen for alternative spirituality who have appeared on her show. And this returns us to our question: Is the sheer force of Oprah Winfrey's fame, money, and will urging a brand of spirituality upon the world that is unsound and unwise, that is damaging both to individuals and to society as a whole? In short, when it comes to religion, where has Oprah taken us?

O

A time-honored maxim suggests, "Great minds discuss ideas. Average minds discuss events. Small minds discuss people." This book is intended to address some of the matters of concern to great minds: ideas, theology, the power of religious truth. There is no intent here to descend into the small—to attack individuals or to plow the well-trod soil of Oprah Winfrey gossip. There will be no Stedman revelations in these pages, no malicious treatment of Winfrey's weight or family troubles. Here, there is no wish to wound or humiliate.

There is, however, the hope that religion may be discussed with an intelligence and openness that have not always marked our age. For too long we Americans have been a religiously ignorant people, cowed by a flawed understanding of the First Amendment into keeping religion at arm's length from culture. Our schools rarely teach the great religions. Even the knowledge of faith necessary for understanding world literature is often denied to our students. It has become as embarrassing as it is dangerous in our age of religious threat. Our foreign policies are often religiously ill informed. Our leaders routinely confess their ignorance of the religions that shape both the world and the country over which they rule. Our citizens stand mute before the most ludicrous of religious claims.

It is time, surely, to remove the blinding mystique and to explore faith with respect and yet with a level of reason that makes the discussion accessible to all. There is no compelling political correctness, for example, which ought to keep us from asking our presidential candidates what they believe about religion. In an age in which we are likely to know a presidential candidate's underwear preference and the name of his dog, isn't it appropriate to ask about beliefs that may shape his conduct in the Oval Office? In the same way, isn't it in keeping with wisdom to demand of our country's leading broadcasters that they defend their religious claims with intelligence and integrity? We live in an age that is at once too instant in communication, too global, and too dangerous to sidestep religious assertions by prominent figures out of an outworn sense of manners. We are all due our religious beliefs, and we are all due our religious privacy, yet we are all publicly accountable for our beliefs when they begin to impact society. So it must be in an Internet age, in an age of religious terrorism, and in a land of cultural diversity.

O

A Personal Word: *Try as they might, writers are seldom objective. There is bias, however slight, in their treatment of their topic, whether they intend it or not. This is particularly true of those who write about religion. An author can strain for objectivity and yet still slant his work by how he reports facts, by what facts he chooses to report, or by what he leaves unreported. This is not a matter of flawed character. It is a function of human beings not being God, of creatures being unable to stand completely apart from creation to see it as it is rather than from a limited and very human perspective.*

Perhaps the most that can be hoped for is that an author is aware of his bias and states it from the beginning. Accordingly, it should be said that I, the author of this book, am a Christian. It gets worse. I am also an evangelical Christian, one of that dreaded breed who believe their truth is a truth others ought to consider. Though I will attempt to approach this treatment of Oprah Winfrey's religious impact on our times from an objective point of view, it is likely, even natural, that my words will be shaded by my Christianity.

Still, since believing in Christianity is not tantamount to a brain bypass, it is possible for an exploration of a religious subject by an evangelical Christian to be written in such a way that it is instructive even to those who do not share his faith. This is particularly the case here, since the goal of this book is not to urge Christianity on unsuspecting readers. Instead, it is to attempt to understand and evaluate a recent brand of spirituality from the perspective of more traditional, historic faith. I am not God and cannot be completely without my vantage point. Yet I am aware of it, as are my readers now, and I will work to tame whatever evangelical temptations I may have in the interest of a perspective that is lovingly counter-pop-culture spirituality and lovingly in favor of the answers of historic faith for the human condition.

That said, though, there is some benefit to me offering my perspective in an acknowledged and unvarnished fashion. This is, after all, why a reader picks up a book: to hear what the author has to say. Therefore, from time to time in this book, there will be sections in which I provide a more unrestrained view of the topic at hand. These sections will be set off by italics, as this section is, to make clear when I am speaking more freely, more personally. This will allow me to express what thoughts I may have to offer—even when I agree with Oprah Winfrey—and yet allow the rest of the material, admittedly still riddled with the limitations of human nature, to be nevertheless somewhat more objective.

There. It is done. Bias acknowledged. Solution offered. Now, to the task.

1

Oprah Rising

Life is like a great big roller coaster. Everything in life
don't happen like it's suppose to.

—OUTKAST, "HUMBLE MUMBLE"

For those who wish to know the spiritual journey of Oprah
Winfrey, there is a fracture, a fault line, that must be recognized. It separates all that came before it in her religious life from
all that would unfold after. It is a partition in time of the kind historians delight in, a turning point like those in the novelist's tale,
and it is essential to understanding what would become the Oprah
Winfrey brand of faith.

This great divide occurred when she was in her twenties
and working as a reporter at Baltimore's WJZ-TV. She was also
attending Bethel African Methodist Episcopal Church in those
days, and it was there, on a Sunday morning as she sat listening to
a sermon by the Reverend John Richard Bryant, that the rupture
began. The theme for the day was the oft-repeated Old Testament

1

assertion that God is "a jealous God" (see Ex. 20:5). Winfrey later recalled the moment:

> I was just sitting there thinking for the first time after being raised a Baptist . . . church, church, church, Sunday, Sunday, Sunday . . . I thought, "Now why would God, who is omnipotent, who has everything, who was able to create me and raise the sun every morning, why would that God be jealous of anything that I have to say? Or be threatened by a question that I would have to ask?"[1]

Doubt settled into her soul. What she had been taught of God and Christianity all those years in church suddenly seemed uncertain. She began reaching for some broader, more accessible scheme of truth than what she had been told. Nearly by the end of Bryant's sermon, Winfrey had taken her first steps toward a new faith. "I was raised to not question God. It's a sin. But I started to think for myself . . . and that's when I really started, in my mid-twenties, my own journey towards my spirituality, my spiritual self."[2]

It was the kind of epiphany upon which destinies turn, and yet it is surprising that a single theme from a single sermon might lead to so much. It is particularly surprising given that Winfrey might easily have drawn far different conclusions about God being a jealous God from the ones that she did, as we shall see.

Obviously, other factors were at work in her soul. Undoubtedly, there were already fissures in her faith before that Baltimore Sunday morning. There had to be more than just one troubling sermon to account for the new trajectory of her spiritual life and for her discarding of much that she had taken as true before that day. Given the implications of this breach both for Winfrey and for the world, we should ponder her life prior to that critical moment for some understanding of how this turning point came about.

The Mississippi Years

Oprah Winfrey was born in Kosciusko, Mississippi, on January 29, 1954. A town of some six thousand at the time, Kosciusko was named for a Polish general who fought on the side of colonial forces in the American Revolution. Perhaps some of his heroism seeped into the people of the tiny Mississippi community. Its other famous citizen was James Meredith, the courageous civil rights leader who was the first African American to risk enrolling at the University of Mississippi.

There has been much debate and mythmaking about Winfrey's childhood, and it has obscured the hard facts and harder experience of black life in rural Mississippi in those days. It has also obscured the character and drive of the people who are the true heroes of the Oprah Winfrey story.

Young Oprah Gail was born to an unwed mother, Vernita Lee, but was raised in the arms of an extended family of such faith, generosity, and affection that it is not hard to understand how greatness might arise from it. At the heart of this family was Hattie Mae, Oprah's grandmother. A stern but loving and industrious woman, Hattie Mae was the granddaughter of slaves and possessed only a third-grade education. Her husband, Earlist, never did learn to read. Yet she would raise six children, and she would create such a gracious and virtuous culture around her that it would influence her famous granddaughter all her days.

We should remember that this was during the darkest season of the Mississippi story, when the state was the poorest in the nation, when racism roamed the night in white sheets, and when poverty crushed African American lives underfoot. For rural blacks, indoor plumbing was as much a dream as respect from white society. A black man faced with an approaching white on a town sidewalk was expected to step into the street when he passed. To vote was, in some parts of the state, to risk one's life. Lynchings were not unknown, and wise blacks taught their children to distinguish good whites from bad whites as a skill of survival. Faced with such conditions, blacks clung to their faith, to each other, and to the belief that character and righteousness would ultimately prevail. These certainties produced the nobility and determination that eventually became the bedrock of the civil rights movement.

Of character and righteousness Hattie Mae Lee knew much. She is remembered as the warm center of her family and an influence for faith and good works in her town. To help keep her family fed, she cooked each day for the local sheriff's office. She was also a skilled homemaker and had the devotion and discipline to transform a wooden house three miles outside the city limits into a thing of beauty, a gathering place lovingly remembered through the years. Katharine Carr Esters, Oprah's cousin, recalls that

> Aunt Hat kept a spotless house. . . . It was a wooden, six-room house with a large living room that had a fireplace and rocking chairs. There were three big windows with white Priscilla-style lace curtains. The dining room was filled with beautiful Chippendale furniture. And in Aunt Hat's bedroom she had this beautiful white bedspread across her bed that all the kids knew was off-limits for playing on.[3]

It is now well known that the unusual name "Oprah" came about as the result of a clerical error. Vernita, likely shaken and unsure at the birth of her first child, allowed her Aunt Ida to suggest the new baby's name. It would be "Orpah," Ida decided. This was an odd choice. Orpah was the obscure name of the sister-in-law of the biblical figure Ruth. According to the ancient story, the two women married brothers who soon died. Ruth decided to stay with her mother-in-law, Naomi, and care for her in her old age. Orpah, after much weeping and show of affection, simply left. She would become a symbol of showy emotion without commitment, and according to the Jewish historian Josephus, she would also become an ancestor of the fearsome giant, Goliath, nemesis of King David. Orpah was not a name that would have evoked noble themes for those who knew their Scripture, and perhaps this is what Ida intended. Fortunately, the midwife at the child's birth, Rebecca Presley, inverted the letters in the biblical name and entered "Oprah" instead.

There was another oddity on the birth certificate. The father of Oprah Gail Lee was listed as a man named Vernon Winfrey. Vernita had identified him as one of three men she had been with and the most likely candidate for father of the child. Vernon, a tall, slim, kindly man who worked as a coal miner, took Vernita at her word and accepted Oprah as his own. He would become the only father she would ever know, and he would do much to shape Oprah's character and thus the woman the world would one day celebrate. Years later he would realize that he was not the child's father. By then, it wouldn't matter. He had invested too much, loved too deeply. Oprah had already become his child in every sense that mattered.

Since Oprah's mother was an unwed teenager who worked off and on as a maid, mother and daughter lived in Hattie Mae's home and enjoyed the fruits of that kind woman's character and liberality.

The family was poor by nearly every standard, but hunger was always kept at bay and the home was filled with storytelling, laughter, and warmth. By all accounts, Oprah lacked for nothing. Her grandmother doted on her. Hattie Mae worked for a wealthy white family named Leonard, owners of the main department store in the area. Often Hattie Mae would return home from work carrying clothes, toys, and books the Leonards had sent along as gifts. Little Oprah had everything the Leonards' daughters had, family members recall, and this was an astonishing grace given the times and the vast economic chasm between black and white.

Besides providing richly for her granddaughter, Hattie Mae also fashioned her early character. "I remember when I was 4 watching my grandma boil clothes in a huge iron pot," Oprah has said.

I was crying, and Grandma asked, "What's the matter with you, girl?" "Big Mammy," I sobbed, "I'm going to die someday." "Honey," she said, "God don't mess with his children. You gotta do a lot of work in your life and not be afraid. The strong have got to take care of the others." I later came to realize that my grandmother was loosely translating from the epistle of Romans in the New Testament—"We that are strong ought to bear the infirmities of the weak" (15:1). Despite my age, I somehow grasped the concept. I knew I was going to help people, that I had a higher calling, so to speak.[4]

On Sundays, the child was dressed up and trotted off to Buffalo Baptist Church. It was there, as in Hattie Mae's home, that the essentials of the Christian faith were embedded in young Oprah's soul. Books and materials being in short supply, children

6

were encouraged to learn their "pieces"—memorized Bible verses and stories, favorite religious poems—and to recite them often before appreciative grown-ups. It was how a caring community assured that their faith lived on in the next generation. At home, Hattie Mae taught her granddaughter the Bible stories so dear to her. This was done with drama and devotion. Oprah took to it with zeal. In time, she perfected the story of Daniel from what she had learned from Hattie Mae and from the poetry of the black pulpit. She delighted in retelling the tale and was not beyond playfully hitting an adult to announce the start of a performance. She came to love Scripture, first its drama and later its meaning, and this early religious education served to awaken both her imagination and her gift for oratory.

It is touching to consider how devoted to learning Hattie Mae's family was. The common slur is that rural Mississippi negroes of the era were ignorant and happy to be so, that an innate practicality of mind kept them from valuing higher thought and literacy. It is a lie. Though Hattie Mae had only a third-grade education she taught Oprah the shapes of her letters as soon as the child would sit still long enough. An uncle then taught Oprah to read. In fact, she was so well taught at home in those early years that when she began school she had already learned sufficiently to bypass kindergarten and enter the first grade. This was fruit of the family's understanding—an understanding widely shared in the black community through the influence of Booker T. Washington and others—that education would empower the black man's rise. Oprah's cousin, Katharine, absorbed this belief and later became the first in the family to earn a college degree. "It took me twelve years of night school to get that diploma, but I finally did it . . . I bought a thesaurus and read it like a novel."[5]

Katharine's achievement could not have been made easier by the economic devastation that befell her community in the late 1950s. Apponaug Cotton Mill, the town's largest employer, closed and jobs became so scarce that many blacks in the area decided to move north in hope of work. They thus joined what became known as the Second Great Migration of southern blacks into northern cities like Detroit, Chicago, and Milwaukee. Already two million had moved north in the First Great Migration of 1920 to 1930. Now, for the same reasons as before—southern racism, northern economic opportunity, and hope—five million more made their way north from 1940 to 1970. Oprah's mother was among them. In 1958, realizing that there was no future for her as a maid in a declining economy, Vernita asked her Aunt Katharine to drive her to Milwaukee. Oprah stayed behind. She was four and a half and spent the next eighteen months of her life being raised by her grandparents.

Vernon, Vernita, and the War in Oprah's Soul

What the family recounts in hushed tones is that Vernita was soon swept up in the loose morals of a big northern city. She spent her money unwisely and gave her heart and her bed to a succession of men. She had a second daughter, Patricia, by one man in 1959 and then her first son, Jeffrey, by another man in 1960. She was in her mid-twenties, away from her moorings and caught up in a lifestyle she could not control. It would mark Oprah's life all her days that at this moment she rejoined her mother in Milwaukee. Her grandfather had recently died and this left sixty-year-old Hattie Mae to raise the child nearly alone. Soon in ill health, she could no longer bear the responsibility, and Oprah was shipped north.

It did not take long before all concerned realized that Oprah could not live permanently with her mother. Vernita and baby Patricia lived in a boarding house with rooms so tiny that Oprah had to sleep on the porch when she arrived. Having raced through a succession of low-paying jobs, Vernita was finally on welfare, and there was barely enough money to care for the two children, given their mother's habits. It was then that Vernon Winfrey reentered Oprah's life.

By 1959, Vernon was living in Nashville, Tennessee, and working for Vanderbilt University as a janitor. His life was pleasant. He had married Zelma Myers in 1958, a marriage that was happy and lasted until her death decades later. They lived in a brick house in East Nashville and were committed to their Baptist church and their community. Vernon had changed since those earlier, wilder days during which he had become embroiled with Vernita. He was more settled now, more dignified. He had become a man of genuine faith. Tall and lean with kind but somewhat sad eyes, he had come to understand the kind of character that was worth having, that would lead a man to better things. When he became a barber and opened his own shop, he hung a sign that proclaimed, "Live So the Preacher Won't Have to Tell Lies at Your Funeral." The words summarized the manner of the man.

When Vernita could no longer care for Oprah, the child was sent to live with Vernon. This began a season of shuttling her between Milwaukee and Nashville that left its mark. As Vernon later said, "It was a mistake. King Solomon taught long ago that you can't divide a child."[6] Still, Vernon gave it his best. As an antidote to Vernita's meager, unstable world, Vernon offered love, discipline, and rootedness. "We welcomed Oprah and gave her a proper home with structure—schooling, regular visits to the library, a little bit of television, playtime, and church every single

Sunday. I'd drive us to the Baptist church in my old 1950 Mercury and cover the seats to keep the lint off our clothes."[7] There were children to play with in the neighborhood, trees to climb, and a community that pulled together in adversity. Oprah thrived and became the sweet, responsive child Vernon knew she could be.

In 1963, though, she returned to Milwaukee to be with her mother. This devastated Vernon. He knew what had happened. Oprah had chafed a bit under his stern rule and had complained to Vernita. Nearly ten and longing for greater freedom, Oprah yearned in particular to watch more television than Vernon allowed. Vernita, seeing her opportunity, told her daughter that if she would return to Milwaukee she could watch all the television she desired. Oprah took the bait and returned to Milwaukee. "I never saw that sweet little girl again," Vernon lamented years later. "The innocent child that I knew in Nashville disappeared forever when I left her with her mother. I shed tears that day because I knew I was leaving her in a bad environment that was no place for a young child, but there was nothing I could do about it."[8]

Still, the years with Vernon had awakened Oprah's natural intelligence and instilled character despite her occasional resistance. Though she returned to Vernita's chaotic, neglectful swirl, she retained the habits her father had worked to embed in her. It paid off. One day at Milwaukee's Lincoln Middle School, Oprah pulled apart from the other students at the cafeteria to read a book. This was not unusual. She was often lost in that other, literary world Vernon had introduced her to. Fortunately, a nearby adult took note. His name was Eugene H. Abrams, and he was the director of Upward Bound, one of a number of programs that sought to elevate deserving black students as a strategy of the nation's War on Poverty. Abrams approached Oprah, got to know her, and told her what he had in mind. Before long, she was among five other black students sent to integrate into Nicolet High School in the wealthy, white suburbs of Fox Point.

In the lives of the prominent, seasons of heightened learning often prove the pivot to success. We think of Lincoln being given that famous barrel of books and reading late into the night by firelight. Perhaps Barack Obama comes to mind and his transforming acceptance into Punahou School in Honolulu. Then, too, there is Churchill on the Indian frontier or even Spike Lee and the reading his discerning grandmother insisted upon. For Oprah Winfrey, this move to Nicolet High School became a similar elevation. She not only enjoyed better teachers, books, programs, and facilities, but she entered a culture of wealth and advancement that changed her. She soon understood what hard work, wise spending, and cultivated habits could bring. She began to see what real wealth looked like and how the rich thought about prosperity as the fruit of long-term investment, even over generations. She was getting the education of a lifetime, not just in her textbooks but also as a guest in the lives of the successful.

Still, Vernon and Vernita warred in her soul. Out from under her father's heavy hand, she grew wild. She stole money, lied freely, and, when her adolescent body yielded to a voluptuous womanhood, drew men in droves. She, in turn, was drawn to older men and began living out the sexual mores of her mother. Hungry for male affection and, some family members insist, eager for the money she sometimes earned, she became a favorite of the neighborhood men.[9] Her excesses drove even the freewheeling Vernita to fear for her daughter's future. Finally, after a complicated deception in which Oprah managed to involve both Aretha Franklin and the family's pastor, Vernita tried to have Oprah committed to the juvenile detention center. There was a waiting period, though, and Vernita was desperate. Wisely, a family member contacted Vernon and begged him to take her back.

He was hesitant. He was weary of the back and forth that had marked the years. He would send off a fairly well-behaved young woman, a product of firm but loving church, school, and home, only to receive in return a hellion resentful of any intrusion upon her will. He would take her again, he determined, but this time only if she stayed. There were urgent phone calls between Milwaukee and Nashville, and finally it was agreed. Oprah would leave her tearful family in the North and live permanently in Nashville.

We should mark this moment. It is 1968, and by now Vernon has realized that he is not Oprah's biological father. Vernita had lied about paternity, or at best, had been woefully in error. At the necessary time, Vernon had been in the army and far removed from Kosciusko, Mississippi. He could have washed his hands of it all. He might have understandably chosen not to clean up Vernita's mess once again. Instead, he chose to take Oprah in. He had invested too much, had come to love this willful, vain girl too dearly. Having no children of his own, he had become her father. And his love, his steel in the face of her rage, his insistence upon the disciplines that would summon her best, transformed her from near prostitute in Milwaukee to the exceptional young woman she would become. It is this that makes Vernon Winfrey, perhaps alone alongside Hattie Mae, a hero of the Oprah Winfrey story.

The Anvils of Character

And so it began. Once Vernon, Zelma, and Oprah were gathered at the kitchen table of the Winfreys' Arrington Street home in

Nashville, the new order descended. Vernon told Oprah that she was through "making herself available to men." There would be no more bulging cleavage and exposed thighs. No more makeup befitting the streets. There would be curfews and clean clothes and chores. She would honor her God, her family, and her church. She would also study and get good grades. But there was more: each week she would go to the library and choose a book upon which to do a written report for Vernon and Zelma. "Not only did I have homework from school, but homework from home," Oprah complained years later.[10] It did not hurt her. She read books on dozens of great African Americans and the lessons stayed with her throughout her life. So did Vernon's philosophy. As if someone might miss his meaning, Vernon posted a sign on the wall of the little grocery store he had built beside his barber shop: "Attention Teenagers: If You Are Tired of Being Hassled by Unreasonable Parents, Now Is the Time for Action. Leave Home and Pay Your Own Way While You Still Know Everything."

Bombasts like this can make Vernon sound like a scold. It is only partly true. The truth is he loved this girl and would later say that "her company was a great joy to me" and that he knew the "promise" of her life.[11] Yet there is no denying that Vernon Winfrey was a disciplinarian of the kind driven by fear of what low character and foolish ways can bring. Vernon would not see this be true of Oprah. She was special and he knew it.

Always, though, there are the tests of destiny, and one arose not long after Oprah arrived in Nashville. She was pregnant. Initially she had tried to hide it with bulky clothes and distance, but that time had passed and her father had to know. The news devastated Vernon and Zelma, though the tale that Oprah told about how it might have happened was even worse.

In the summer of 1968, she had been driven from Milwaukee to Nashville by Trenton Winfrey, Vernon's closest brother. During the drive, the talk had turned to boys and Oprah's dating life. She complained that all the boys wanted to do was French-kiss. The conversation continued on this theme. Aroused, Trenton did the unimaginable. He pulled to the side of the road and asked her to take her panties off. Given Oprah's age, what followed cannot be considered anything other than rape. Sadly, when she told her father that she was pregnant, she also had to tell him that his brother might be the reason.

To Oprah's surprise, no one believed her. She had become something of a liar and it was not hard to imagine that the story about Trenton was a vile cover for her sexual antics of recent years. She had been with many men, and some recently. Any one of them might have been responsible. Besides, when confronted, Trenton denied any wrongdoing.

Oprah was stunned, and it was due to more than the sexual abuse and the pregnancy. She realized she lived in a world where her own actions had destroyed all trust. As she later recounted,

> Because I had already been involved in sexual promiscuity they thought if anything happened, it had to be my fault and because I couldn't definitely say that he was the father of the child, the issue became "Is he the father?" not the abuse . . . I wasn't the kind of kid who would persist in telling until someone believed you. I didn't think enough of myself to keep telling.[12]

So she endured the humiliation, and she was haunted by the look in Vernon's eyes.

The stress of it all likely led to an early delivery. Barely a week after her fifteenth birthday, Oprah was rushed to Hubbard Hospital at Nashville's Meharry Medical College where she gave birth to a tiny, struggling boy. Immediately, nurses whisked the child away to an incubator where he lived out all of his thirty-eight days in this world. His name was Vincent Miquell Lee and when he died he was given to Meharry for research. It was a sad and disturbing time. "I don't know what happened after the baby died," Vernon said years later. "I don't know what they did with the body—whether they used it in experiments or what. We tried to keep the fact of the baby quiet, even within the family. There was no funeral, no death notice."[13]

The facts of the abuse and the dead child were handled in a manner common in that age, one sure to leave shame and torment for years to come. Few were told and so there was no one for Oprah to confide in, no one to help her with her grief. As many a woman has done, she simply locked it all away. She would learn, though, that in time all trauma works its way to the surface. This would come years later, when Oprah Winfrey, the successful talk show host, would share her personal horrors with a watching world. For Oprah Winfrey the lonely and inwardly tormented fifteen-year-old girl, there was nothing to do but move on.

Fortunately, despite his understandable clumsiness with it all, Vernon summoned the words his overwhelmed daughter needed to hear. After tenderly telling her of the death of her child, he said, "This is your second chance. We were prepared, Zelma and I, to take this baby and let you continue your schooling, but God has chosen to take this baby and so I think God is giving you a second chance, and if I were you, I would use it."[14]

He had offered her hope. In her broken state, she returned to school a week after the death of her child and determined to be different. As biographer Kitty Kelley writes, Oprah

> began to reinvent herself. Gone was the sullen student with swollen ankles crouched in the back row wearing a baggy sweater. In her place was a bright-eyed, energetic sophomore with relentless confidence who demanded to be recognized beyond the confines of her school and her church.[15]

One sign of a change was her deeper devotion to her faith. A boy she dated at length recounted years later that the two never had sex because "it was a matter of our Christian upbringing and our determination to make something of ourselves as adults."[16] This was new in Oprah's life, not the faith but the understanding of a connection between faith, ethics, and the future. Clearly, she not only shared her Christianity openly but also understood that it came with moral demands. Friends came to regard her as a serious Christian with a meaningful devotion to Jesus Christ. Evidence of this comes from something Oprah wrote in a friend's yearbook, a friend who reports that the friendship was based on "the same strong Christian beliefs": "You have showed me more by your actions, by the way you live from day to day, that there is only One Way, Jesus Christ! And that without Him taking control, without Him running the whole show, life is just an endless go-round with no meaning."[17]

The Talent and the Ambition

Yet this deeper faith merged with a new force in Oprah's personality: a brash and unapologetic ambition so fierce that intimates would comment upon it all her life. In the spring of 1969, just months after the tragic end of her pregnancy, she announced herself to Andrea Haynes, the speech and drama teacher at Nashville's East High School. "I'm Oprah Gail Winfrey," she proclaimed. Then, moments later, she assured, "I'm going to be a movie star." She had obviously believed Vernon's words about a second chance and had embraced them with a grandiose, adolescent sense of destiny.

Under the tutelage of Ms. Haynes, she began to flourish. The teacher gave her a copy of *God's Trombones: Eight Negro Sermons in Verse*, by James Weldon Johnson, and she mastered them, blending in her big voice, her gift for mimicry, and her own emotional range. After thrilling performances at school assemblies she performed some of the sermons for her church and then at churches throughout Nashville. She was an inspiration and her reputation grew. She traveled widely to give presentations and even ended up in Los Angeles at the request of area churches there. While there she made her way to Grauman's Chinese Theatre and the famous Hollywood Walk of Fame. It set her imagination and her sense of destiny aflame. Returning home, she told Vernon, "Daddy, I got down on my knees there and ran my hand along all those stars on the street and I said to myself, 'One day, I'm going to put my own star among those stars.'" Later, Vernon said, "That was the foreshadowing I had that she would one day be famous."[18]

Assured of her gifts, Oprah joined the National Forensic League, which allowed Ms. Haynes to coach her more thoroughly. In 1970, when she was seventeen, she won a first-place trophy for her now refined reenactment of a *God's Trombones* sermon on the theme of judgment. "I prayed before I competed," she told her school paper, "and said, 'Now, God, you just help me tell them about this. They need to know about the Judgment. So help me tell them.'"[19] It was the mixture of theatrics and spirituality that would define her life.

She was on fire as a performer. She won competitions sponsored by the Black Elks Club of Nashville and by the Freemasons. At the Tennessee State Forensic Tournament, she won first place, and this sent her to the nationals at Stanford University. She did not win, but her rendering of a selection from Margaret Walker's novel *Jubilee* was stunning. She was discovering the reach of her gifts. Her classmates elected her Most Popular Girl and she was inducted into the National Honor Society.

Time and chance grace the lives of all who rise to greatness, and Oprah was no exception. While collecting money for the March of Dimes as part of a school charity effort, she ventured into WVOL, the sole black radio station in Nashville, and asked for support. John Heidelberg, a disc jockey and later owner of the station, pledged to help. When Oprah returned to collect the money, Heidelberg noticed her grammar, bearing, and rich voice and asked if he could make a "demo" tape. She agreed, and when the management of the station heard both the tape and Heidelberg's eager proposal, they offered Oprah a job. She accepted and soon found herself playing music and chattering over the airwaves on Sunday evenings.

Timing continued to favor her. Not long after Oprah joined the station, the manager's house burned down. In gratitude for the care of the fire department, the manager decided to participate in the Miss Fire Prevention contest, a beauty and talent contest respected in those years. Oprah decided to compete. Buoyed by the station's support and the citywide reputation she was earning through radio, she won. This was days before she graduated from East Nashville High, a successful student in every respect.

Vernon was proud and looked back with gratitude that his daughter had achieved so much, had risen above the tawdry Milwaukee years. He was not satisfied, though. She must go to college. Oprah resisted. She had hoped to parlay her experience on radio into a television career. She dreamed of being the black Barbara Walters, she said. Vernon believed she was meant for better things and insisted that she enroll in Tennessee State University, a historically black college. He might have chosen the famous Fisk University for her—it was also in Nashville, and some called it the "Black Harvard"—but it was four times the cost of TSU, and expenses were being paid by the profits from a barbershop.

Her college years would not live brightly in her memory. She loved her job at WVOL and her $115 paycheck, but she found the school dull and spoke so disparagingly of it in later years that she offended TSU alumni and friends. Still, there were bright spots. She won the Miss Black Tennessee contest in 1972. It came with no scholarship money, but it was a boost to her confidence and confirmation of the career she hoped to create. With mounting success she grew bolder in her manner and opinions. She even took on professors at TSU when she thought them in error. Entire class sessions were consumed with her challenges. Yet some professors took note of her intelligence and saw that she was particularly skilled in the field of broadcasting. Dr. W. D. Cox recalled her as exceptional: "I knew her from age sixteen to about twenty-one. I taught her in stage lighting, scenery, and the history of the theater. She was a very likeable student, carried a full load and took responsibility seriously."[20]

Ideally, college years are when a student's gifts and interests coalesce with an opportunity to learn in a field with a future. In this, Oprah was exceptionally fortunate. Broadcasting was obviously her calling. She had good looks, a big personality, and a full voice that commanded attention. She was also quick-witted and funny, with a piercing intelligence. As important, she was genuinely interested in people. This translated over radio waves as it would later on television. She had an imagination and a needling curiosity that made her want to know what it was like to be someone else, to live lives far different from hers. This all came naturally to her and made her a fascinating interviewer. Other broadcasters had to work hard to feign interest on the air. Not Oprah. For her, interest in the stories of others was part of how she approached the world. Professors and station managers saw this and sensed she might have the gifts to become something special.

That she was black helped her win her first television job. In the early 1970s there was a push from civil rights activists around the country for television personalities to reflect the racial makeup of their audiences. The FCC weighed in as well and began urging stations to diversify. Nashville was 80 percent white and 20 percent black in those days, but this was certainly not reflected on TV screens. The local NAACP had made racial equality in Nashville's television programming a frontline cause, and soon station managers were being pressured to put blacks on the air.

Once again, fortunate timing graced her life. She was proving herself a valuable talent at WVOL just when the tide of public opinion created a demand for black and female faces on television. Also fortunate was the fact that Chris Clark, the news director at the local CBS affiliate, WLAC, was committed to change.

When I was coming up in television in the 1960s, it was a white-bread world—no room for blacks, women, Jews, or Greeks like me. My real name is Christopher Botsaris, but I had to change it to get a job on the air. By the time I got to WLAC, Nashville had been through the really rough civil rights battles, but we still needed to show that we were committed to integration.[21]

Clark met with Oprah at the urging of WVOL, liked her immediately, and then made the risky and historic decision to hire her to anchor his station's premier news broadcast. In one move, Clark had hired the first female anchor in Nashville history, had hired the first black anchor in Nashville history, and had launched the broadcasting career of one of the most successful television personalities in history.

This meeting of talent and opportunity has often been disparaged in the retelling. Critics and the resentful have seen Oprah's hiring as, in Kitty Kelley's words, "a big wet kiss from the affirmative action fairy." Even Oprah has seemed embarrassed in recalling her good fortune: "No way did I deserve that job. I was a classic token, but I sure was one happy token."[22] As she tells it, once hired, "I announced to everybody there, 'This is my first day on the job, and I don't know anything. Please help me because I have told the news director at Channel 5 that I know what I'm doing. Pleeeze help me.'"[23]

It is an easy, if insulting, interpretation of events, but it belies the facts. The truth is that had Winfrey not already proven herself a solid on-air talent she would never have been hired. There were other black female newscasters available, even in the Nashville area. The job did not fall to her automatically. She was hired because, though she was inexperienced, she was engaging and bright. As important, her prior achievements—Miss Black Tennessee, her success as a speaker—made her popular in the community. Executives sensed that what she didn't know she would learn quickly. She did. The evidence is in the astoundingly successful broadcast career that followed.

What is often overlooked is how tough she had to be. Nashville was just a few years beyond the lunch counter violence that had became so famous as part of the civil rights struggle and that David Halberstam chronicled in his moving history, *The Children*. The Ku Klux Klan had begun its sordid history just ninety minutes away in Pulaski and it took courage to be a black broadcaster in a city where the word *nigger* was still casually used. During one early assignment, Oprah introduced herself to a shopkeeper and offered her hand. "We don't shake hands with niggers down here," the man angrily retorted. "I'll bet the niggers are glad," she fired back, unflinching.[24]

Her battle to be courageous has become the stuff of office legend. To this day an audiotape is circulated around the offices at WTVF-TV, the new name for WLAC, which captures Oprah summoning the boldness for one particular assignment. There had been a rumor that the Symbionese Liberation Army, the leftist organization that had recently kidnapped heiress Patty Hearst, was hiding in an East Nashville house. Oprah and her cameramen were assigned the task of confirming the story. The audiotape, recorded accidentally by one of the crew, records Oprah's fear and yet her determination to do her job well. As she and her crew approach the house in their car, Oprah grows nervous. "Go slow! Okay, here, right here. Oh no! What's that? Oh, God! Go around, go around!" It turned out that the SLA was nowhere to be found, but WLAC's new anchor forced herself to knock on the door of a suspected terrorist hideout to be sure. The recording has wrung many a laugh, but it is tender evidence of a twenty-year-old news anchor trying desperately to be the intrepid reporter her dreams demanded.[25]

She worked hard to overcome her weaknesses—she was a poor writer, for example—and what she lacked in polish she made up for by being genuine and compelling on the air. Her appeal was that she cared, she was concerned, and this was in remarkable contrast to the disinterested manner of most broadcasters. Oddly, one of the criticisms most often heard of her in this period is that she was "too compassionate." Chris Clark insists, "Her downfall as a journalist was that she could not be detached. She'd be sent to cover a fire, come back to the station, and work the phones trying to get help for the burnt-out family instead of writing the story for the evening news."[26] If this gift for sympathy made her less professional in the eyes of her colleagues, it also endeared her to the public.

It was not long before she became one of Nashville's most celebrated women. She won awards—Woman of the Year from one organization, Outstanding Broadcaster from another—and this bolstered her confidence. She thought nothing of taking over an assignment from an incompetent producer or experimenting with camera angles to see if she could capture a story more powerfully. She was clearly in her element and drew admiration for her suggestions about makeup, about lighting, and even about the thematic progression of a major news special. It all felt destined to her, as though her gifts and success somehow flowed from being rightly positioned, from having the chance to do what she was made to do.

The Moral Revolt

It was a thrilling season, but it was also a season of broken moorings. Now a local success, Oprah decided to move out of her father's house and take an apartment miles away in the Hickory Hollow section of Nashville. This infuriated Vernon. He feared she would recede into the immorality of her earlier years. He was right. Already the availability of drugs at WLAC had snared her. It was hard to avoid. Cocaine was snorted before broadcasts, LSD was sold in production booths, and marijuana was so abundant that management had to have a vending machine removed when they discovered it had been modified to dispense the beloved weed.[27] An anchor was given a "coke spoon"—a device for snorting cocaine— as an office gift. No one thought it odd. There would come a day when Oprah would speak of these excesses with regret, but in the mid-1970s this was the style of the smart set, and Oprah wanted more than anything to be seen as part of it. There were also the men. Freed from her father's control and plunging herself into the currents of the sexual revolution, she took lovers. In this she was cautious because she was so visible, but men who ranged from old college boyfriends to John Tesh, then an Adonis-like anchorman in Nashville, have spoken of intimate lives with Oprah.[28]

It may have been that this moral change was about more than merely blending into a hedonistic entertainment industry. She may also have been hurting, medicating her soul with sex and drugs when her inner agonies could not be quelled any other way. Harry Chapman, a revered Nashville figure, coanchored the weekend news with Oprah in those days.

"There was an undercurrent of sadness about her," he recalls. "She was sweet and fun with all of us, but you could never get away from the idea that she was grieving. Something drew her downward and it was always there. Whatever she did, from work to romance to partying to downing the junk food she loved so much—you got the impression she was trying to silence a pain, a darkness that was always just behind her eyes.[29]

Perhaps it was the loss of her child. Perhaps it was that she had tasted success in television and it had not been all she had hoped. Perhaps it was that she had a mother she had not seen in years, a biological father she had never met, and was raised by a man so strict she told friends she had grown to hate him. Perhaps she was, at the end of the day, alone. So she worked and she drank and she put white powder up her nose to help her rise above it all. And she took men to her bed to feel what passed for love to her damaged soul. But the undercurrent of sadness Harry Chapman felt from her was always there.

And what of her faith? She was now twenty-one, and in the manner of her young professional tribe, she began distancing herself from her Baptist church, if not from belief. She still attended church services but largely because it was tradition, what African Americans are supposed to do. So she went, but it was obvious to all that her faith did not define her as it once had. The words she had written in a high school yearbook those years ago—"there is truly only One Way, Jesus Christ . . . without Him taking control . . . life is just an endless go-round with no meaning"—might have been confirmed by her experience, but they were no longer the truth of her heart. She was in moral revolt. A religious revolt was soon to follow.

The Baltimore Debacle

Whatever her spiritual condition, it did not diminish the quality of her work. By mid-1975, barely eighteen months into her television career, her reputation became such that large stations in Atlanta and Baltimore began recruiting her. Nashville had become too small; it was merely the thirtieth television market in the country.

She had promise of greater things, particularly in large cities with sizeable numbers of African Americans. It was not an easy decision, but after counseling with friends and weighing her other options, she chose WJZ-TV in Baltimore. They were offering forty thousand dollars a year and they intended to make her a star. They had won her by appealing to her dream. She had never let go of her plan to land in a top-ten market and then become the black Barbara Walters. WJZ-TV owned five stations, was close enough to New York for her to draw attention from her profession's top tier, and it was far away from Nashville, a town that had begun to suffocate.

It is easy to see in retrospect what Oprah, in her eagerness and ambition, could not perceive at the time: the new role in Baltimore was a setup for failure. There were a variety of reasons for this. The first was her coanchor. WJZ-TV had decided to create a one-hour news program, and this required more than the traditional single anchor. There would have to be a coanchor, someone just as capable in handling the news and yet of complementary personality and style. Thus the hiring of Oprah.

Yet, unwisely, she was to be paired with Baltimore legend Jerry Turner. On the air for more than a decade, Turner was the epitome of the sophisticated, incisive news anchor common in that era. He drew better numbers in the Baltimore market than even Walter Cronkite and was beloved throughout the region. General manager William F. Baker has said that

> Jerry Turner was as superb an anchor as you could find anywhere in the business. He was appealing, authoritative, and most importantly, he was adored by the Baltimore community. Absolutely worshipped. He was the reason WJZ ranked number one in the market for years, and as you know, news is the jewel

of the crown in television, and determines how a station fares in terms of money and prestige.[30]

By comparison, Oprah had worked in television for just under two years in a city half the size of the Baltimore area. It was a pairing of the elder statesman with the upstart; the distinguished white man with the young, hip, African American woman; the seasoned newsman with the popular personality from some place back in Tennessee.

Making matters worse was the way in which WJZ-TV introduced Oprah to her new audience. Management had not learned the fine art of underpromising and overdelivering. Instead, they promoted their new coanchor in nearly messianic terms. An amateurish series of television commercials showed confused people on the street being asked, "Do you know what an Oprah is?" "Offrey?" puzzled Baltimoreans would ask. "What's an Oprah?" The ads were clumsy and raised more questions than they answered, as did print ads and billboards of the same caliber. By the time Oprah arrived, people were intrigued, uninformed, and a bit irritated. "The whole thing backfired," she later said. "People were expecting The Second Coming and all they got was me."[31]

The most destructive ticking time bomb under Oprah's coanchor chair, though, was her own lack of preparation to report international news and her unfamiliarity with the English of the political elite. Baltimore is less than an hour's train ride from Washington DC, and it is essential that news anchors in the area be conversant with world affairs and articulate in the speech of East Coast sophisticates. WJZ-TV's new coanchor was nowhere near ready for prime time. Once the new program was launched, the embarrassments began. As Kitty Kelley has perfectly summarized,

Oprah "read the word *Canada* from the teleprompter as 'Ca-NAY-da' three times in one newscast. She later mispronounced *Barbados* as 'Barb-a-DOZE.' She read a report about a vote in absentia in California as if 'Inabsentia' were a town near San Francisco. A few nights later she characterized someone as having 'a blaze attitude,' not knowing how to pronounce blasé."

Turner grew apoplectic. He was astonished that she allowed staffers to write her copy and was speechless when she once broke the rhythm of the broadcast by commenting after one story, "Wow, that's terrible." On another occasion, probably trying to compensate for her inexperience with humor and banter, Oprah teasingly told Turner, "You're old enough to be my father." The newsroom froze. Management knew the clock was ticking on this new arrangement. Ratings had plummeted.

It was only eight months before Oprah was removed from her anchor role. It happened on April Fool's Day, 1977. From the second most powerful position at the station, she was demoted to doing "cut ins" for the early morning talk show. This was the lowest role at the station for an on-air personality and Oprah knew it. She had failed and failed publicly. All of Baltimore witnessed her humiliation. Had her contract not guaranteed twenty-five months of pay and had she not needed the money, she would have left in shame and likely returned to Nashville to lick her wounds and rebuild. It was a horrible time. "I did mindless, inane, stupid stories and I hated every minute of it," she said, "but thought even while I was doing it, 'Well, it doesn't make any sense to quit because everyone else thinks this is such a great job.'"[32] It did not help that WJZ-TV paired Jerry Turner with Al Sanders, an experienced black newsman at the station, and the two were so successful together that they dominated the Baltimore market for another decade. Oprah was left to watch and to consider what might have been had she been more capable.

The entire agonizing experience drilled down into Oprah's soul, tapping unacknowledged reservoirs of self-doubt and insecurity. In her diary, she wrote, "I wonder if I'll ever be able to master this so-called success!"[33] A local reporter later revealed, "After her string of successes, Oprah was devastated. . . . She feared her career was grinding to a halt, and thought briefly about leaving town. Her hair fell out, leaving great bald patches; she had to keep her head wrapped in scarves while working."[34]

Reinventing Oprah

It was the crucible of her life thus far and to answer it she turned almost unthinkingly to the religion that had begun to define her: achievement. "I was always frustrated with myself, thinking I wasn't doing enough," she later said of this period. "I just had to achieve."[35] Sinking, she reached for words she had first heard from Jesse Jackson at a Nashville appearance years before. They had meant so much to her then that she had taped them to her mirror and recited them each day: "If you can conceive it and believe it, you can achieve it." Jackson had borrowed the sentence from the motivational teachers of the day and had used it to inspire inner-city audiences. The sentiment captured Oprah, hungry as she was for an inspiring philosophy to authenticate her ambitions.

She had long envisioned herself as a glowing success and now, despite her failures, she forced herself to believe it could all still be true. She set about achieving the dream once more. While doing the degrading bits and pieces of reporting she was assigned to do by her station's management, she began to reinvent herself. She started by investing in the community. She organized a fund-raising rally for Jesse Jackson's Operation PUSH and this helped to restore her tarnished reputation in Baltimore. She also deepened her commitment to Bethel A.M.E., her church, and out of this came an opportunity to be part of a dramatic presentation called, "To Make a Poet Black and Beautiful and Bid Her Sing." This took her back to her speaking roots. The centerpiece was an excerpt from Margaret Walker's *Jubilee*, a selection Oprah had performed many times. She was, again, spectacular in the role, and each performance was met with numerous standing ovations. Her confidence returned, particularly when presentations in Nashville—with her father in the audience—and in New York City were met with critical acclaim and appreciative audiences.

She was beginning to rise, if not professionally at least personally, and she was finding a new source of strength for her life. It was a kind of soul force and it was summoned by visualization, by her ability to picture in her mind the person she yearned to be. Hadn't Reverend Jackson said it? "If you can conceive it and believe it, you can achieve it." Perhaps this was not what she had learned during all those hours in Sunday school, but it was working for her now. The naysayers had tried to make her doubt herself and play the fool. She knew what she was meant to be, though, and would not let them steal her inner certainty, the image of her destiny that had dimmed but was coming back to her.

○

It was just at this time, as she was nursing these thoughts, that the great divide occurred in her life. As the meaning of her failure was flooding in upon her—and yet just when she was beginning to fight back because she believed that her life's purpose depended on it—she went to Bethel A.M.E. that memorable Sunday morning and heard Reverend Bryant teach. And he had taught about how God is a jealous God. And it had not seemed quite right. "Now why would God, who is omnipotent, who has everything, who was able to create me and raise the sun every morning, why would that God be jealous of anything that I have to say? Or be threatened by a question that I would have to ask?"[36] And so she set herself on a new path, on "my own journey towards my spirituality, my spiritual self."[37]

What is intriguing in retrospect is how much the genuine truth of a "jealous God" might have meant to her in that season of her life. The biblical meaning of God being "jealous" is not what it appears on the surface. Had Oprah applied her reporter's investigative skills or simply asked her pastor, she might have learned that the Hebrew word for jealous—*qanno*—has at its root the concept of "zeal or yearning." The jealousy attributed to God is not akin to the petty human emotion, but is rather the fruit of love. It means not that God is jealous in the manner that Winfrey concluded, but rather that his love gives him a passion and zeal for his creatures which resents all other gods and despises anything that attempts to destroy those dear to him.

What might this have meant to Oprah Winfrey in her twenties, a young woman who had failed at her first major-market broadcasting job and was so stressed by the experience that her hair was falling out? What might this have meant to her searching soul, hungry as she obviously was for a vital spiritual life? How might she have been changed by the knowledge of a God passionate in love and fiercely possessive of his children?

But no. This God—the God of her father, the God of tradition, the God of her youth—she now found wanting. He had let her down, left her in despair and humiliation. She decided he was too small, too petty, for her and certainly for her ambitions. And so she decided to find meaning elsewhere and, in time, she would take that meaning to an eager and attentive world.

Vernon Winfrey would watch it all. On the television in his Nashville barbershop and in conversations with his famous daughter, he would come to see what he had hoped was not true. In an unguarded moment with an interviewer, he would later say in sadness what many like him had already concluded: "She no longer believes in Jesus Christ as her savior. That's just not how I raised her."[38]

○

There is a revealing dynamic to Winfrey's decision during the "God is a jealous God" sermon and it prefigures much that would come after. It is not that she questioned a biblical truth. No, uncertainty about the claims of the Bible is normal. It is part of the process of seeking, part of the journey that leads to faith. No one can blame Oprah for having her doubts.

Instead, the important revelation from her turning at Bethel A.M.E. is not as much what she decided or why, but how.

Consider: She is confronted with a truth that has been believed for centuries. It comes from ancient texts and it brings good news to mankind—"God is eager for you, even yearning for you in the manner of a lover; draw near to him."

Yet Winfrey considers almost nothing outside of her own feelings and her quickly formed thoughts. There is no research, no consulting of authority, no humility before a great and time-honored body of truth. There is no consideration of tradition or the tested scholarship of centuries. She did not even open a reference book in the church library or make an appointment with the pastor—a man of great scholarship—to seek a deeper understanding.

Instead, that God might be in some way a jealous God does not feel right, does not seem on the surface to be true. And Oprah believes she is qualified to decide the matter—instantly. So she concludes right then and there that the Christian faith is wanting, that there is some better scheme by which to understand the world and through which to gain power for living.

We will see this way of making decisions in spiritual matters again and again in Winfrey's life. She draws life-altering conclusions quickly, informally—based on her feeling in the face of an idea and the most casual of reasoning. Experience— the way an idea feels or settles into the soul—is ultimate. In fact, she evaluates most all spiritual information in terms of what experience it produces, by how it leads to a change in feeling or energy or emotion or success. She does not seem to be primarily interested in what is ultimately, eternally true. She seems instead to be interested in what appears to work for her in this present life.

But this raises an important question, and it is one of the great questions in the study of philosophy: How do you know what you know? How do you know what is true? Scholars call this the question of epistemology. It literally means "the study of knowledge" and it concerns itself with what knowledge is and how we can be sure of it.

For Winfrey, certainty comes from feeling and from immediate thought. There is no authority outside herself. There is no check or balance or confirmation or legacy of elders pointing to what is true. Truth is felt. Truth is immediately grasped. Truth always leads to heightened experience. And truth is always an individually determined thing. This is the epistemology of Oprah Winfrey's brand of faith.

And what about those who choose to follow her? I have enough trouble choosing from a restaurant menu or deciding how I feel about political candidates. Choose among religions based on how they feel to me? No, I need ancient words. I need elders. I need wise ones who have gone before. I need the confirmation of a community of faith. My emotions are too fickle, too human, to be a judge of spiritual truth.

The conclusion is simply this: if history is not our guide, if written words are not our guide, if elders in faith are not our guide—and we are only to be led by our experience and thoughts—then we are left to create spiritual lives of our own on the strength of our limited minds and our screwed-up emotions.

What I know is this: I am not capable of deciding my own path to salvation. I doubt any of us are. And the thought that I am left to seek out "my spirituality, my spiritual self on my own" makes the universe a lonely, fearful place.

2

The Turning

When you believe in things you don't understand then you suffer.
Superstition ain't the way.

—STEVIE WONDER, "SUPERSTITION"

I t is 1978. Oprah Winfrey is twenty-four years old. And life is
not what she had hoped.

She was a local radio star in Nashville during her college years
and then became the first black female television anchor in that
city's history. Her talent lifted her. She was celebrated, recognized
on the streets. Longing for greater heights, she took a job as a
coanchor at Baltimore's WJZ-TV and was welcomed like a media
goddess. But eight months later she was dropped. She had proven
too rough, too unknowing, too unsophisticated. Now, she has
been forced to content herself with cut-ins during the morning
news program. She interviews a parrot this week. It is an improvement. Last week she tried to make a piece about snow tires into
something of interest. But she is finished, they say. Office wags are

taking bets on how long it will be before she turns tail and runs back to whatever southern town she came from.

But they do not know Oprah. This fun, sassy, big-personalitied black reporter whom some call Opie is more than she appears. Beyond the jokes about her oversized backside and the junk food and her flirtatious ways is a woman of flaming ambition. She will tolerate their dismissal of her for now because she knows who she really is. She will be famous one day. She will rise to such heights that they will forget the day of her humiliation. She has seen it. She can conceive it. She believes it. She will achieve it. And so she paces her Baltimore apartment and sounds out her dreams and speaks the truths behind the meaning of her life. She reads books about becoming rich and taking hold of potential and she makes their language and their culture her own. And she waits, enjoying the joke on all of them. She will fulfill her destiny. She will be what she was made to be. The doors will open. It is meant to be.

People Are Talking

It is 1978. Oprah Winfrey is twenty-four years old. And destiny has come calling.

While she is busy with the story about the new cockatoo at the zoo and the cinnamon bun that looks like Jimmy Carter, a new general manager has come to WJZ-TV. His name is William Baker, and he is riding high on his reputation as the creator of *Morning Exchange* in Cleveland, Ohio, the highest-rated local morning show in America. Baker is smart—a rare TV executive with a PhD—and he is well connected. His assignment is to do in Baltimore what he has done in Cleveland: build a top-rated daytime talk show.

He has decided to call his new creation *People Are Talking.* As he tells reporters, "This show will be the ultimate refinement of every morning talk show that has ever been presented. . . . Housewives are bright, intelligent people. They are deep-thinking people. . . . *People Are Talking* will be the biggest studio morning show this city—or any city—has ever done."[1] Clearly, he intends to take on all competitors, even the revered Phil Donahue. When the staff at WJZ-TV hear what Baker has in mind, they know what he will need: an ad-libbing, fun, big-hearted black woman to make viewers look up from their coffee and take notice. He will need Oprah Winfrey.

She would not be easy to win to the idea, though. It was daytime television, after all, and it sounded to her like the snore it often was. Making it worse, she would have to master the often silly "dialing for dollars" segment in which the host dialed the phones of people selected electronically to win cash. It was one step up from carnival work and to a woman of Oprah Winfrey's ambitions—a woman who spoke openly of being the black Barbara Walters—it was early death.

Baker offered Oprah the job, plying her with promises and begging her to realize she was a perfect fit. Oprah objected, Baker countered, and finally, painfully, she agreed. She would be the new cohost of *People Are Talking* in Baltimore, Maryland. Baker recalls that she left his office in tears. She thought it was the final humiliation before the end of her career.

When the show launched on August 14, 1978, Oprah's fears seemed to be confirmed. The *Baltimore Sun* headline read, "A Breath of Hot, Stale Air." The accompanying article was scathing: "*People Are Talking* sputtered into life yesterday like some sort of souped-up car with a rookie driver who had never used a clutch before." The only bright spot was Oprah. She was "well polished" and survived the dialing for dollars episode "with unusual grace, giving this tacky little gimmick about as much class as possible." Then, a warning: "A long run at this and Oprah's image as a news reporter is not going to be helped."[2]

It was an uncertain start, but the production soon found its pace. What critics and perhaps even Oprah herself did not understand at first was what the shift from news to free-for-all talk show offered her. For the first time, she could unpack all her gifts on the air: her innate interest in people, her love of fun and laughter, her insatiable curiosity, even her crassness. Some of the very facets of her personality that had caused her to fail as a straitlaced anchor of nightly news now made her, in time, a hit on daytime television.

The women who were the target audience for the show quickly fell in love with Oprah. When sex became the topic, she often gave a side-glance to the camera with a wicked gleam in her eye. It was her way of saying, "Come on, girls. This is what we really want to know." On other occasions, she would bake brownies on the air and then cram three into her mouth, just as most of her viewers wished to do. She once got the entire studio audience to get up and dance while cameramen scrambled to capture the mayhem. When an embarrassing moment occurred, she would laugh, make a narrator's comment to the audience, and then return to a difficult guest with a look that said, "It's you they think is the fool. Just keep on this way and they'll only love me more." She came to understand that an interview did not have to be flawless to be a success. She just had to connect to the crowd. Guests could fend for themselves if they tried to make things hard for her.

It worked. Even the critics came around. Bill Carter of the *Baltimore Sun* soon wrote, "Oprah is rapidly proving that she was an excellent selection for a morning talk show host. She simply looks very good in the morning talk format. She is low key but bright and attractive, and that combination works well over a morning cup of coffee."[3]

Over the next five years, *People Are Talking* increased its market steadily until it surpassed Phil Donahue's audience in Baltimore. With success came bigger stars as guests. Oprah met and interviewed Muhammad Ali, Pearl Bailey, Jesse Jackson, Maya Angelou, and Dick Cavett among others. She worked hard to master her art—often preparing late into the night—and soon gained a reputation as a tough, informed, engaging interviewer. She remembered her on-air stumbles during her early days at WJZ-TV and practiced eagerly to rise above them. Management was thrilled and began talking about syndication.

Turmoil of Soul

The spiritual transformation she had begun on that Sunday morning at Bethel A.M.E. continued during these years. Exposed to the wider world through her successful talk show, she took on more cosmopolitan values. Of her cohost, Richard Sher, she later said, "He taught me how to be Jewish. He also taught me to swear." Already in doubt about the moral judgments of the Christian faith, she now found herself sympathetic with the alternative lifestyles of her guests. She once interviewed a quadriplegic transsexual who had adopted a child created from the artificial insemination of her boyfriend's sperm into her sister. Afterward she said, "It was just a moving thing. I thought, 'This child will grow up with more love than most children.' Before, I was one of those people who thought all homosexuals or anything like that were going to burn in hell because the Scriptures said it."[4]

She was abandoning her former faith, and the surest evidence of it was the long-term affair she had with a married man. She had become obsessed with a tall, athletic disc jockey named Tim Watts. That Watts was married with a wife and young son and that everyone at the station knew of the affair did not dissuade her. In time, it did not even matter that Watts had yet a third lover while he was stealing around town to secretly meet Oprah in hotel rooms and the apartments of friends. Blowing past moral restraint, concern for her reputation, and even regard for her own sanity, Oprah gave her heart to Watts with a passion she would come to regret.

The affair led to some of the worst years of her life. True, there was the thrill of stolen hours and the excitement of sexual tension and invading the forbidden. To feel wanted, to feel desired—to know that somewhere someone ached for you as you did for him— was an addiction Oprah could not break. Yet the emotional crashes were violent and damaging. She knew the man she loved returned to the arms of a wife and a child and she was tortured by cycles of shame and rejection. She demeaned herself. She often threw tantrums when Watts tried to leave and once even dropped his keys in the toilet to make him stay. She stalked him. She begged. She even tried to win him with gifts. Always, there was the loneliness. An affair makes life about one person, and when that person is gone there is no one left except those who have been set at a distance by the secrecy and the hiding. Oprah found herself alone on holidays, alone on her birthdays, and alone even at remote, romantic locations when at the last minute Watts couldn't make a planned rendezvous.

Depression set in and then thoughts of suicide. Fantasizing about her death, Oprah wrote a note to a friend about where her

will was and asked her friend to water the plants. It was pitiful.
Years later Oprah would confess to her television audience,

> I was in love; it was an obsession. I was one of those sick women
> who believed that life was nothing without a man. . . . The more
> he rejected me, the more I wanted him. I felt depleted, power-
> less. . . . There's nothing worse than rejection. It's worse than
> death. I would wish sometimes for the guy to die because at least I
> could go to the grave and visit. I have been down on the floor on
> my knees crying so hard, my eyes were swollen . . . then it came to
> me. I realized there was no difference between me and an abused
> woman who has to go to a shelter—except that I could stay home.[5]

In 1986, she told *Cosmopolitan* magazine,

> If I start to talk about it, I'll weep on the floor. But I tell you, I
> will never travel that road again. The next time somebody tells
> me he's no good for me, I'm gonna believe him. I'm not going
> to say to myself, "Well, maybe I'm too pushy, or maybe I don't
> talk enough about him, or maybe, maybe, maybe. I'm not rac-
> ing home to meet him there and then not hear from him until
> midnight. Uh, uh. Too painful."[6]

What is missing from these reflections on the affair is any
moral concern. She regrets the lost years for the damage they
did to her but not for the betrayal of a faith or a moral code.
At no time is she concerned that a displeased God is watching.
Clearly, Christianity was no longer the spiritual vision of her
life. She had seen too much, done too much. The lessons of her
sleepy church in Nashville could not sustain her now. Instead,

her religion became whatever maxims and practices lifted her to her destiny. To accomplish, to rise. This was the defining determination of her life.

Still, on her twenty-eighth birthday, she wept for hours because she realized just how alone she was.

In this state, in 1983 she was forced to make a critical decision about her career. It was time to renew her contract with WJZ-TV but one of her favorite producers, Debra DiMaio, had moved on to WLS in Chicago and was begging Oprah to reconsider. An opening had come available and it was a perfect fit for Oprah. The show was called *A.M. Chicago*, and one of its hosts, Robb Weller, was leaving. At DiMaio's urging, Oprah sent a tape and a résumé and then agreed to an interview in Chicago. The managers at WLS were captivated. Oprah was perfect. She was just the joking, self-deprecating, always curious black personality they needed. They offered her two hundred thousand dollars a year, a car, and an apartment. They were also offering a lead role on a flagship program in the third-biggest market in the nation.

Oddly, Oprah later recalled the decision to leave Baltimore for Chicago as having been largely determined by race: "I made a deliberate choice about where to go. Los Angeles? I'm black and female, and they don't work in LA. Orientals and Hispanics are their minorities. New York? I don't like New York, period. Washington? There are thirteen women to every man in DC. Forget it. I have enough problems." Chicago fit the bill. "It's a big little town, sort of cosmopolitan country. The energy is different than Baltimore. It's more like New York, but you're not overwhelmed like in New York."[7]

Whatever her reasons for the move, Oprah Winfrey and the city of Chicago were right for each other. From the moment she went on the air at WLS, the city that poet Carl Sandburg had dubbed "the city of big shoulders" seemed to fall in love with its big, brassy new television star. Once again, timing favored her. It was the moment of African American media ascent. Bill Cosby ruled evening television on *The Cosby Show*, Bryant Gumbel ruled morning television on *The Today Show*, and Oprah believed the daytime was waiting for her. She was right. Her success would prove historic.

Oprah on Oprah

What is intriguing about this time in her life is how central Oprah became to Oprah. She had long been an exaggerated personality, but much of this was shtick. She had known, too, her failures and her disgraces. Prior to Chicago, despite her ambitions, she seems to have held both the public, expanded Oprah and the flawed, insecure woman in balance. But with the move to Chicago, she began to extol herself in such unguarded terms that the words *arrogant*, *boorish*, and *vain* might have been used of her. They weren't. The press bought her portrayal of herself nearly without comment. But this was more than public relations. It was the blend of chosen woman on a divine mission and insecure, self-absorbed woman that would mark her for years to come. An interview with the *Philadelphia Inquirer* from this period makes the case:

> I'm very strong . . . very strong. I know there is nothing you or anybody can tell me that I don't already know. I have this inner spirit that directs and guides me . . . I'll tell you what being interviewed has done for me. It's the therapy I never had . . . I'm always growing. Now I've learned to acknowledge and accept

the fact that I'm a kind person. I really like me, I really do. I'd like to know me, if I weren't me. And me knowing that is the most important thing.[8]

In fairness, it is not hard to understand how her rapid success in Chicago made her the center of her own narrative. She began hosting *A.M. Chicago* in 1984 and thus began her ascent. Within months, she had surpassed the ratings of talk show king Phil Donahue in the Chicago market. This led to her first national exposure in *Newsweek*, which in turn led to an oft-recalled January 29, 1985, appearance on the *Tonight Show*, hosted by Joan Rivers. That same year—in yet another astounding gift of destiny—she was chosen to play Sofia in the Steven Spielberg film *The Color Purple*, a role for which she earned an Academy Award nomination. Then, in 1986, she joined with leading Chicago attorney and agent Jeffrey D. Jacobs to form Harpo, Inc., which gave her control of her brand and marketing. This came at the same time that she entered national syndication and just as *A.M. Chicago* was renamed *The Oprah Winfrey Show*. She had been in Chicago just over two years and in that short time had become famous, rich, and positioned for the media empire of her dreams. It is no wonder she had become her own favorite topic of conversation.

Still, her messianic sense in this period is astounding, and it is central to understanding her evolving spirituality. She had believed since childhood that she was made for something unique. This had been a certainty since that moment with Hattie Mae by the pot of boiling clothes when Oprah, age four, had sensed she was made to help other people. Throughout her life, no matter her failures, she always returned to her unshakable faith that she was made to do great things. She got pregnant at the age of fourteen and lost the baby the next year, and yet within weeks she was announcing herself at her high school as a future movie star. She blew her first major-market anchor job through ignorance and lack of preparation, and yet within months she was rebuilding her life, confident of a destiny others could not envision. Even in the dark days of her affair with Tim Watts and the humiliating cut-ins on morning TV, she believed. She spoke the words. She confessed, prayed, and chanted the motivational mantras of success.

It all might have seemed the desperate grasping of a wounded, uncertain soul except that once Oprah Winfrey moved to Chicago, she rocketed to success. It happened so suddenly it all seemed prior, as though it had already happened in some other realm. At this moment, she had a choice. She could lean to the biblical concept of destiny, which meant that a loving God had determined a lofty fate for her that she could never have deserved and that she ought to receive in humility and gratitude. Or, she could choose to believe that she was inherently an exceptional creature, one whom the laws of the universe conspired to elevate. She chose the latter, and whether this was base vanity and ego or not, this sense of self-importance was so powerful in her that it pulled all in her life into its wake.

TV Guide's R. C. Smith asked Oprah during this time if she would give up her talk show for her acting career. Her response is telling:

> I intend to do and have it all. I want to have a movie career, a television career, a talk show career. So I will do movies for television and movies for the big screen and I will have my talk show. I will have a wonderful life. I will continue to be fulfilled doing all of those things, because no one can tell me how to live

my life. I believe in my own possibilities, so I can do whatever I feel I'm capable of doing, and I feel I can do it all.[9]

It was hard to understand why a woman who had been so fortunate needed to assert herself as though she had somehow been denied advantages. When *The Color Purple* did not win even one of its eleven Academy Award nominations, other actors in the film, like Whoopi Goldberg, spoke out about the misdeeds of the Hollywood NAACP, which had protested the movie as a slur against black men. Oprah spoke out about herself and in such vaunted terms that reporters were left mystified: "When you mention great actresses, you'll have to say my name: 'Meryl . . . Oprah,' 'Hepburn . . . Oprah.' That's what I want. What I am is an actress. I don't get paid for acting. But I was born to act."[10]

To a *Vanity Fair* interviewer she declared,

I transcend race, really. I believe that I have a higher calling. What I do goes beyond the realm of everyday parameters. I am profoundly effective. The response I get on the street—I mean Joan Lunden [former host of *Good Morning America*] doesn't get that and I know it. I know people really, really love me, love me, love me. A bonding of the human spirit takes place. Being able to lift a whole consciousness—that's what I do.[11]

Oprah's New World

It was during this time that money entered her life in such huge amounts that it seemed affirmation of her exaggerated beliefs about herself. We should remember that she had been offered a salary of two hundred thousand dollars a year to host *A.M. Chicago* in 1984.

Eighteen months later, when *The Oprah Winfrey Show* signed a syndication deal with King World, she received a one-million-dollar signing bonus and called her father to say, "Daddy, I'm a millionaire!" It was only the beginning. The next year, in 1987, industry estimates were that she had earned more than thirty-one million dollars. Three years later, she earned fifty-five million dollars. Each year after, the story was much the same, with Winfrey earning massive sums of money, often above a hundred million a year.

To her credit, she was extravagantly generous. She sent staffers on foreign vacations, turned producers loose in the best New York stores with instructions to buy anything they wanted, and was not beyond giving entire houses as gifts to friends. Critics said she was a rich, insecure woman buying affection. Still others said that she had come to symbolize the soul-killing materialism of the age. She didn't care. She lavished houses, Mercedeses, and Jaguars on herself, bought mink coats for mentors and even for reporters who treated her kindly, and settled Vernon and Vernita in luxury.

It was during this time that she also began the relationship with Stedman Graham that would prove so controversial. He was a tall, athletic, light-skinned African American businessman and model whom Oprah adored. After they met and had dated for a while, Oprah took Stedman to Nashville to meet her father. Everyone expected that they would marry. It soon became obvious, however, that Oprah had no intention of binding herself to a man or putting at risk what she had. She did want Stedman in her life, though. They soon lived together, vacationed together, and Oprah had no hesitation about telling her television audience that each night the two knelt together by their bed to pray. This offended many African Americans in her audience, who are, in general, liberal politically but conservative theologically and morally and could not understand Oprah's insistence upon being public about living with a man she would not marry. It was the first indication to many of her fans that her religious life was not what they had imagined, that it was actually whatever Oprah proclaimed it to be, needed it to be. In truth, Oprah simply perceived herself to have grown beyond the traditional boundaries, both in her profession and in her religion.

What many in her vast audience did not understand was how Oprah Winfrey's religion was primarily Oprah Winfrey. Having discarded a God who could be jealous, she had replaced him with the lesser god of achievement. This goal, this magnetic force, this deity was the spiritual center of her life. To become more, bigger, better, happier was the goal, and any belief or practice that made this possible became part of the new religion Winfrey was daily fashioning. Even her relationship with Stedman was rooted in the worship of personal improvement. As Kitty Kelley writes, "Oprah and Stedman were melded in their devotion to the gospel of self-help."[12] They read books like *Creative Visualization*, *Psycho-Cybernetics*, *The Nature of Personal Reality*, and *The Road Less Traveled* and found in each of these the keys to crafting their own spiritual reality, to becoming deities in their own created order. Traditional religion and traditional morality had little role to play.

The Price of Fame

Whatever Oprah was creating spiritually, professionally she was also engineering one of the great success stories of entertainment history. In the decade from 1984, when she moved to Chicago, to 1994, when she turned forty, Oprah Winfrey's ascent to international acclaim was breathtaking. She broke records for audience

size, advertising, and profits. She won nearly every award she qualified for, sometimes repeatedly. *The Oprah Winfrey Show* became
so influential that it was a cultural force all its own. Presidents
made appearances to clean up tarnished reputations. Prime ministers appeared to plead the cause of their countries. Movie stars
wept out confessions of wrongdoing.

Yet all was not noble on *The Oprah Winfrey Show*. From the
beginning, Winfrey had worked to pass her competition in the ratings by surpassing them in the grimy and the depraved. She knew
she could never be as learned or as penetrating as Phil Donahue,
her prime competitor, whose show the eminent historian David
Halberstam had once labeled "the most important graduate school
in America."[13] An hour of the Donahue program might explore a
foreign policy crisis or a Supreme Court ruling or a religious fault
line in American culture and in a manner that was both elevating
and entertaining. Even if the topic was a rock star's addictions or
sexual abuse in the workplace or the Ku Klux Klan, the subject
was treated with dignity and with an eye to improving society
through dialogue. Oprah knew she could never be as smooth or as
wise as Phil Donahue.

Unable to go around Donahue's lofty themes, she went
beneath them. She knew sex would sell and she did programs on
rape, on molestation, on penis size, on transgender sexuality, on
date rape, on clergy sexual abuse, and, incessantly, on the sexual
abuse of children. If there was a hot new sexual practice making
the rounds, she covered it. She did one show on the autoerotic
asphyxiation practices of teenage boys and another on group sex
in prisons. Beyond sex, and realizing that the bloodier the topic
the wider the appeal, she did programs on satanic cults sacrificing
babies and kids that kill. There was seemingly no sexual oddity,

act of violence, freakish deed, or lurid practice that she would not put on the air.

What galled many observers was that while *The Oprah Winfrey Show* spewed filth from America's cultural sewers, Winfrey continued to speak of herself in terms that would have been overstated had she been Mother Teresa. At the same time the *Wall Street Journal* described her program as "Nuts 'n' Sluts" and "Freak of the Week,"[14] Winfrey spoke of herself as an incarnation. To the *Chicago Sun-Times*' Robert Feder, she once said, "I had been looking at pictures of Rosa Parks and Leontyne Price and I believe I am the resurrection of a lot of my ancestors. I am the resurrected life for them. I am living the dream. Please, please quote me correctly, 'cause I don't want people thinkin' I'm Jesus. All my life, I have done dramatic interpretations of black women. Harriet Tubman, Sojourner Truth, Fannie Lou Hamer are all a part of me. I've always felt that my life is their life fulfilled, that they are bridges that I crossed over on. They never dreamed it could be this good. I still feel that they're all with me, going, 'Go, girl. Go for it.'"[15]

For some, this was all too much. The *Sun-Times*' Daniel Ruth could not restrain himself. He wrote that Oprah's ego had gone on "a Falstaffian, gluttonous binge":

> Don't worry, Oprah. Just because you can turn pap into cash, you needn't fret too much about comparisons to Christ . . . I have a hard time believing Sojourner Truth spent a lot of time wrestling with subjects like "Victims of Freeloaders" (Oprah show: July 5, 1988), "Soap Opera Stars and Their Fans" (Oprah show: June 29, 1988) or "Dressing Sexy" (Oprah show: July 28, 1988). . . . Please, dearest Oprah, don't presume to place yourself in a class with genuine intellects, leaders and such pioneering black women as Sojourner

Truth, Harriet Tubman, Fannie Lou Hamer, Leontyne Price, and especially Rosa Parks, who earned their rightful acclaim through commitment, quality, and courage.[16]

Winfrey seemed oblivious to the tension in her life. On the one hand, she believed she was an instrument of "spiritual awakening." She insisted that she was "highly attuned to my divine self." She had made mistakes, she admitted, only because she had temporarily failed to hear "the voice of God." She thought nothing of rebuking Nobel Peace Prize–winner Elie Wiesel because he did not believe that his surviving the Holocaust was a divine miracle. She listened to spiritual gurus like Shirley MacLaine and Marianne Williamson and came to believe even more firmly that she was divinely appointed. As she once reported, "Stedman thinks I'm one of those chosen people. You know, hand-picked by the universe to do great things." This was more than the kind encouragement of a boyfriend. It was a certainty in Oprah's mind. "God is with me. That's why I always succeed . . . I am God-centered."[17]

Meanwhile, the themes of her daily show were drawn from the dark side of human existence. She explored prostitution by taking cameras inside Utah's Bunny Ranch brothel, made famous in an X-rated HBO series. She dwelt so long on child murders that some viewers complained and stopped watching. Always, there was the favorite theme of cheating, violent, lying, unworthy men. Oddly, it was while doing a show on just such a theme that she felt the first pangs of guilt for the direction of her show:

The day I felt clearly the worst I've ever felt on television was in 1989, when we were still live and we had the wife, the girlfriend, and the husband, and on the air the husband announced to the wife the girlfriend was pregnant. And the expression on her face . . . I looked at her and felt horrible for myself and felt horrible for her. So I turned to her and said, "I'm really sorry you had to be put in this position and you had to hear this on television. This never should have happened." That's when I said, "We cannot do this anymore." I can't say we never did another show with conflict, but that's when I first thought about it.[18]

Whatever regret Oprah may have felt, it led to no change in the program. This was 1989. The twisted and the perverse continued to inform *The Oprah Winfrey Show* for another five years. Ratings soared.

The New Vision

The turning began in 1994 with Oprah's fortieth birthday. She had been looking forward to a grand celebration of her four decades of life, and plans had long been in the making for a dazzling series of events. Dubbed "Forty for Oprah's Fortieth," the merriment would begin with forty of Oprah's closest friends flying by private plane from Chicago to Los Angeles to stay in thousand-dollar-a-night suites at the Hotel Bel-Air. Dinner would be a fifteen-thousand-dollar affair at L'Orangerie with guests including Steven Spielberg, Tina Turner, Julius "Dr. J" Irving, Quincy Jones, Nastassja Kinski, Maria Shriver and Arnold Schwarzenegger, and Sidney Poitier. The next day all would lunch at The Ivy and then be chauffeured to Santa Monica for a shopping spree, a favorite Winfrey pastime and gift. Later in the afternoon, there would be tea at the home of the Schwarzeneggers, and finally, that evening, the women would prepare for a sleepover at Oprah's bungalow. It was all sure to be glorious.

Still, there was a dark cloud, and it had been hanging over Team Oprah for quite some time. The criticism of her shows had increased. Though she saw herself as a gift to her generation, as a force for spiritual renewal, she was being lambasted as an evil influence, as the Slime Queen of daytime television. Universities held symposia on the "Oprafication" of America. Psychologists wrote papers warning of the harm that could come, particularly to the young, from making extreme sex acts and lifestyle choices objects of fascination. Even William Bennett, former secretary of education, weighed in, arguing shows like Winfrey's deformed the American psyche and made entertainment of the despicable and the dangerous.

On the second evening of Oprah's birthday celebration, as the women settled down to champagne and conversation at the bungalow, talk turned to the mounting criticism and to what might be done. Each one in attendance adored Oprah and believed she was an "anointed one," an "apostle of truth." As Kitty Kelley writes, "Each believed that Oprah was a blessed disciple, a special messenger sent from God to do good."[19] Maya Angelou, who attended the party, later explained to *Vogue* magazine,

In a queer way . . . she holds a spiritual position not unlike Norman Vincent Peale once did. Each culture and each time has its spiritual nattering nabob. At one time it was Peale, and for some Republicans it was Barry Goldwater. These are moral mountains that we looked up to, some of us. For others, it's the Dalai Lama and there's always the present and future and past pope. And these are people who, to lesser or greater degrees, are really the lights, the pinnacles of what is right and kind and true and good and moral. Well . . . she's sort of that.[20]

Convinced of Oprah's mission, the women began discussing how Oprah might best be a blessing to her generation. Someone suggested and all agreed that she should join with the pope to lead the world in a weekend of prayer. His Holiness would certainly welcome the opportunity, it was thought. A staffer would pursue it. Then, another suggested that she should interview Mother Teresa, who had won the Nobel Peace Prize for her ministry to the poor of Calcutta. Oprah was dubious. "I don't think she's much of a talker," she objected. "That would be a long hour on television."[21] The suggestions continued throughout the evening. Little of practical use came of it but there had been a determination. Something had to change. *The Oprah Winfrey Show* had clearly failed thus far to rise to the level of Oprah Winfrey's purpose on earth.

The cause of a course correction was helped by the fact that Oprah sensed 1994 was destined to be a transforming year for her. As she had been telling the press, it was intended to be a year of "profound change for me, emotionally, spiritually, and physically."[22] Then, too, she was tired of the worn-out themes on the show and had been for quite some time. "I have to move on," she told *Entertainment Weekly*. "We're not gonna book a show where someone is talking about their victimization. . . . The last time I did a show on women being stalked, they said how hard it is, and I recognize it is. But five years ago I would have been more sensitive to it. Last year I said [to the stalked women], 'So move. So move!'"[23] As she told *Redbook*, "I cannot listen to other people blaming their mothers for another year."[24]

This yearning for a change in spirit had led to a critical change in staff, as well. In the May ratings sweeps of 1994, *The Oprah Winfrey Show* suffered the blows of heated competition and "dropped to the lowest point they had been in three years."[25] This led to near panicked discussion among Oprah's producers—and to a contest of wills. Debra DiMaio, Oprah's friend since Baltimore and her longtime producer, argued for a return to basics. She wanted to focus on the controversial, sometime gritty programming that had launched the show to stratospheric ratings in the first place. The hard-edged and the titillating would rescue the sinking ship. Oprah disagreed. She could not go back to the early days. She had changed too much. Now, she insisted, spirituality, the meaning of life, and how to better the world would be her themes. It was a new day for *The Oprah Winfrey Show* and her team should embrace it. DiMaio could not. On June 22, 1994, she abruptly resigned, leaving Oprah free to pursue her new sense of calling for her flagging program.

In hopes of discovering a new path, on September 12 and 13, 1994, Oprah invited leading television critics to join her for a two-part series called "Are Talk Shows Bad?" The decision to confront the topic had come in the wake of Penn State professor Vicki Abt's scathing article for the *Journal of Popular Culture*, "The Shameless World of Phil, Sally, and Oprah: Television Talk Show and the Deconstructing of Society." Oprah's guests spared her nothing. Abt believed, as she later wrote, that talk shows like *The Oprah Winfrey Show* had "rapidly eroded the boundaries that we have established to control behavior and to make sense of our life."[26] Other guests offered equally cutting criticism, all of which Winfrey absorbed graciously. Finally, as the second episode neared its end, Oprah asked about suggestions for change. Tom Shales offered what many took as a blueprint:

> I'd like to see more smart people on TV. Fewer ordinary people
> and more extraordinary people. . . . In the '50s NBC did a series

called 'Wisdom.' And they would interview Bertrand Russell and Frank Lloyd Wright and Carl Sandburg. . . . The very median level of the talk show, this one perhaps notwithstanding, has sunk very, very low. And I think it's got to be brought up somehow.[27]

It is testament to Winfrey's emerging worldview that several months later, on December 14, 1994, she introduced her longtime personal spiritual advisor, Marianne Williamson, as "one of the wisest people I know." Symbolic of changes to come, dysfunctional guests from earlier Oprah Winfrey shows were invited back so that Oprah's new theme of spirituality could impact their lives. As she explained in introducing the show, in past programs "the therapists did all they could" but had failed. Now, she had invited back some of the seemingly hopeless cases "to help them in a way that we feel is more effective than any expert in the world." The theme of the show was prayer, with Winfrey and Williamson dispensing advice to the hurting: "prayer enables us to take the power of God and bring it down to the plane of our actual earth experience"; "a little bit of violence in the mind . . . is contributing to the violence of our times"; through prayer "the mind is lifted up to a new kind of thinking."[28] At the show's end, Winfrey led her audience in the prayers included in Williamson's latest book.

It was the beginning of the fulfillment of Oprah's birthday dream. She had sensed 1994 would be a year of change and it was. Eager to move on from the dispiriting themes of the past, she had insisted upon a shift in focus, rejected DiMaio's vision for her show, and sought the counsel of her most heated critics as to how she might change. Then, certain of what must happen, she turned her show—which she had often called "her ministry"—to just that: to ministry of the nontraditional religion she had long made her own. That December show with Williamson was only a start, but in its wake would come hundreds like it. It was the first movement in a turning, a realignment.

Beloved

Yet it was not the turning itself. The full transformation of the television program would come, but only after a further transformation of Winfrey herself. By all accounts, this occurred during the making of the film *Beloved*, based upon the acclaimed Toni Morrison novel of the same name. A Pulitzer Prize–winning masterpiece, Morrison's story is a tender, agonizing, supernatural journey through the horrors of slavery of a kind that seems almost intentionally designed to capture Winfrey's heart. It did, and it would fashion her spirituality for years to come.

Inspired by the true story of Margaret Garner—an Ohio slave remembered for killing her daughter rather than allowing her to be returned to slavery—*Beloved* imagines the post–Civil War world of the ex-slave Sethe and her daughter, Denver. Sethe, too, has killed a child rather than allow her to return to slavery. This was long before, though, and now Sethe has endured prison and then made a life for herself and her second child. It is a troubled life, though. The spirit of the slain baby haunts their home and torments both mother and child. In time, Paul D, a former slave who has known Sethe in the days of bondage on a plantation called Sweet Home, appears. Quickly realizing the hold the slain baby's haunting presence has on Sethe and Denver, Paul D drives the spirit out in a rage. It works. There is peace for a short time, but then the baby, whose tombstone bears only the word *Beloved*, appears as she would have been had she lived. Now, amidst recollections of the brutality of the slave experience, Sethe must confront the meaning of the choices she has made, navigate her love for Paul D, and decide how to live between spirit and reality, past and present, living daughter and dead daughter incarnate.

Oprah had read the novel when it first appeared in 1987 and it had been an epiphany for her. "I was taken in," she later wrote.

> The book took me in. I felt absorbed by it. I felt I was in the interior of the words. The words resonated with me in a way that doesn't often happen. There's a difference between reading a book and enjoying—even loving—the story, and having the feeling that the words are somehow connected to some part of you, that then becomes your story. I felt in some way it was my own remembering. I knew it, I knew Sethe when I encountered her. I felt that she was in some way a part of myself . . . I was overcome with the idea of bringing her to life.[29]

Sensing that once again destiny was at play in her life, she sent staffers scurrying for a way to reach Morrison. When she did, she gushed out her intention to make the movie of *Beloved*. "How can you be serious?" Morrison replied. "How could this ever be a movie?" Winfrey assured her she knew how, offered Morrison a reported one million dollars for the rights, and set about the odyssey of making the film.[30]

It was not a smooth journey and it would take nearly a decade. She had asked Jodie Foster to consider directing the film, but Foster said the book was too complex for a movie. Jane Campion, director of *The Piano*, was also asked but begged off, saying that she knew too little about the black experience. It did not help that

Oprah felt destined to play Sethe herself. When she asked Peter Weir, famed Australian director of films like *Witness* and *Dead Poets Society*, he was willing but couldn't envision Oprah in the lead role. This enraged her and she later recounted their conversations with bitterness: "And would I please just trust him and if he felt that I could be in it he would certainly make every effort. You want me to give you my script and you decide if I can be in it? Okay. Bye-bye."[31] Finally, she settled on Oscar-winning director Jonathan Demme, famous for his iconic *The Silence of the Lambs*, who was thrilled for her to play the role of Sethe.

Typically, Oprah soured attitudes toward the film with her inflated claims. She had made no secret of her desire to be a famous actress and she now resurrected these hopes before a disbelieving Hollywood press. "It will be my *Schindler's List*," she exulted, comparing herself and her film to one of the most poignant portrayals of genocide in movie history. "It's my history. It is my legacy," she insisted. "It is the capital WHO of who I am."[32]

This bravado betrayed her insecurity before the acting challenges at hand. Danny Glover (*Lethal Weapon, Witness*) had been chosen to play Paul D. Kimberly Elise (*Set It Off*) had been asked to play Denver. And British actress Thandie Newton (*Jefferson in Paris, Interview with a Vampire*) was given the task of making Beloved, the resurrected baby spirit, live on the screen. Oprah knew she had work to do.

She prepared for the role of Sethe with intensity. She read slave narratives, stared into the eyes of slaves in photos, and kept slave ownership papers with her during shooting to remind her of the evil drama she had been chosen to portray. She even submitted to a reenactment of the experience of a slave on the Underground Railroad.

This undid her. Blindfolded in the woods, she was given the name Rebecca and told "your story is that you live in Baltimore as a free woman. You were captured overnight and brought to this place. Men broke into your home, they brought you here, and now this is where you live." Oprah accepted this and sat in silence for several minutes before a man with alcohol on his breath accosted her.

"Where are you from?" he demanded after learning her name.

"I'm a schoolteacher in Baltimore with three children, and now there's been this horrible mistake."

"You're a nigger gal," he screeched. "Doesn't matter to me what kind of school you teach in. You're one of those smart niggers, ain't you? You don't know nothing, gal."

The man left and Oprah found herself weeping uncontrollably. Then a black woman approached who said she worked in the big house on the plantation and then began to explain the rules. "But you don't understand," Oprah protested. "I'm a free woman."

"No, no, you don't understand, child, you ain't free no more, you belong to Mr. So and So, just like all of us do."

Again Oprah wept, unable to contain her grief and her fear. The utter despair and helplessness of the slave washed over her. Afterward she concluded, "And what it felt like was death with no salvation. And that became my definition of slavery: death with no salvation on a daily basis. Darkness with no hope. Just pretending to live."[33]

This experience had cracked open her soul to the slaves' misery and now she wanted to become their embodiment, to feel them living through her as she performed. It was not hard for someone who already thought of herself as a "resurrection" of African American heroes past and who felt in touch with her "divine self" to envision how the still-living souls of slaves might indwell her. She began to seek possession.

From the slave ownership papers she kept with her, she evolved a ritual: "I brought one of these to my trailer on set. And I would literally call out the names—Joe and Bess and Sara and Emily and Sue and Dara—from that list every morning. I lit a candle, spoke their names and attempted to honor their spirits." Eager for a supernatural connection that transcended time, she explained, "I was striving to create a life that, in ways you cannot articulate, will be felt in the spirit of the character. I ask my body to be the carrier for the spirits of those who have come before me."[34]

For Oprah, filming *Beloved* was a supernatural experience. During one of the first days on the set, an older actress said to her, "We're on assignment. The Ancestors have called this one up. It's so strong. So strong." Oprah agreed. The next day she recorded in her journal that she "awakened early, and did my daily prayer to the Ancestors." Later she wrote that while acting she was "carrying the Ancestors in my heart, hoping, but also knowing, they, too, carry me . . . the power of the spirits whose lives went unnoticed, demeaned and diminished by slavery. Calling on you. Calling on you . . . I'm counting on them."[35] Frustrated in not having perfected a scene, she pulled aside and prayed, "If y'all are coming, come now."[36] She was speaking, again, to the ancestors in whom she had placed her trust.

Having brought her spirituality to her art, she began to see great acting as yielding control to the spirits. After watching Thandie Newton's stunning portrayal of Beloved during one day of filming, Oprah later wrote, "Channeling at its finest!" Frustrated with herself on another day, she demands, "Channel. Channel. Channel. Where are you, Sethe?" When yet another scene goes badly, she later comments, "I got so caught up in the day I forgot about channeling."[37]

It is significant given what would follow that while Oprah was filming *Beloved*, she was also pondering the future of her television show. Rumors had begun circulating that her devotion to the film signaled that she was bringing her talk show days to an end. It is clear from her journal that she was wrestling. When a dolly grip operator remarked one day, "You were on the news this morning. They say you're quitting your show," Oprah was surprised that her deliberations were public but then wrote, "I hear it's the buzz—I'm quitting! Before I started this movie I felt strongly that I could end the show. I've surprised myself with the revelation to go on and see what the end will be. Now I believe this movie and the preparation for this movie has given me the strength and insight to continue."[38]

The inspiration had begun to flow in the early days of the filming. "This thought came while making coffee," she wrote nearly two weeks in.

> I am a descendant of slaves. I came from nothing. No power. No money. Not even my thoughts were my own. I had no free will. No voice. Now, I have the freedom, power and will to speak to millions every day—having come from nowhere. I would be a fool to give up *The Oprah Winfrey Show*. I must figure out a way to make it work. To surround myself with people who are enthusiastic, who want to do it, who are not burned out, who understand the worth of this extraordinary time and opportunity to change people for the better.[39]

Yet she grew unsure. Just over a month later, she wrote,

> The time is approaching. I'm beginning to feel real pressure about the decision to continue or not continue the show. Just

read from *Even the Stars Look Lonesome*, Maya Angelou's book. Here's the reason to continue: "We were stolen and sold from the African continent together. We crouched together in the barracoons, without enough air to share between us. We lay, back to belly, in the filthy holds of slaveships in one another's excrement, menstrual blood and urine. We were hosed down and oiled to give sheen to our skin, then stood on the auction blocks and were sold together. We rose before sunrise from the cold ground, were driven into the cane field and the cotton field together. We each took the lash that pulled the skin from our backs. Each of us singled out for the sexual enjoyment and exploitation of those who desired our bodies but hated us. . . . We may yet survive our grotesque history."[40]

Oprah continued to struggle and pray but finally, the spirit of *Beloved* filling her soul, she decided the work must go on. "So this is where I've come from," she wrote, her course clear. "How dare I even think of quitting. Now I have a voice that can be heard around the world. I must find a way to say what needs to be heard. May the Ancestors and all the power that is God abide with me. Direct my path. I am not afraid."[41]

Though Oprah drew strength from the experience of the film, audiences did not. *Beloved* was released on October 16, 1998, supported by one of the most expensive marketing campaigns in movie history—thirty million dollars. Oprah had once said, "I don't care if two people come to see it or two million."[42] It wasn't true, but critics reminded her of the two-person audience when the film proved a box office failure. Six weeks into release, *Beloved* had fallen behind *Bride of Chucky* in attendance. The film earned only $22,843,047 but had cost $83,000,000 to make and market.

Beloved's collapse left Oprah in depression. She ate to excess. She wept. She raged. Friends urged a psychiatrist. Making matters worse, while she was grieving *Beloved* she learned that she had lost her number one talk show slot to Jerry Springer. Still, the despair forced her to her core, where she recovered the strength she had acquired during the shooting of her movie. She was not the same woman she had been. The ancestors lived in her now. They were a bridge for her. She had a calling, not perhaps from a divine source but from the souls that summoned her through time. Collecting herself, she began telling her producers what she envisioned. *Beloved* "changed my life," she explained. "I want to bring meaning to people's lives."[43] To remind herself and her staff of what the *Beloved* experience should mean, she had a huge photograph of her as Sethe—scars from her whippings exposed—hung outside her office. Mounted next to it was a huge whip—to make certain that the searing pain of the past was never forgotten.

It was clear that Oprah intended a massive change in direction, but the exact path was uncertain. Her staff was reminded of an unsettling conference call from the set of *Beloved* in which she had called for new thinking about the show but had offered more questions than certainties.

> The gist is being how do people lead their lives? How can we help them do it better? In every aspect of their lives, how can we lead them to their truth? First, we must be led to our own. Who are we? What do we stand for? What do we believe? How can what we say be an influence for the good, the better? All of this so called "power" means nothing if we don't share it. Use it for the good. How do we do that? That is the only question to be answered. The shows will follow that answer.[44]

By the start of 1999, Oprah had decided to renew her contract with King World for two years. *Beloved* may have fallen far beneath her hopes, but her appeal as a talk show host was undimmed. As was her power to gain wealth. She had once said, "Money just falls off of me. Just falls off me."[45] She was right. She received thirty million dollars in cash advances for signing and 450,000 King World stock options. This was in addition to the 1,395,000 stock options she already had from earlier deals. And once again, timing favored her. In 1999, CBS took over King World. Oprah, who was already worth over $725 million, gained options on 4.4 million shares, worth a hundred million dollars.[46]

The Ministry

The confluence of her determination to make something noble of her show and the new stream of spirituality she had tapped into while filming *Beloved* led to a transformation of *The Oprah Winfrey Show*. She had new confidence, new wealth, and a new source of spiritual power. She also may have had a dose of anger after the film that was to be her *Schindler's List* failed and failed embarrassingly. She decided that it was time to expose the world to the eclectic spirituality that had privately empowered and inspired her through the years. No longer would she honor her divine self through meditation, chanting, candle lighting, and ancestor worship in the morning and then later in the day tape a program about children being murdered or about women and their vibrators. It was time to lead a spiritual revolution, to begin the awakening. The vision born the night of her fortieth birthday party was about to be fulfilled.

For the 1999–2000 season, she announced a campaign called

"Change Your Life" television. Women who had tuned into her show to learn about the latest thrilling household appliances or about Oprah's favorite fragrances or to hear celebrity gossip or to revel in disgust at the nasty underbelly of American society were now introduced to a religious revolution. Insisting that religion and spirituality are two different things—"religion is what you belong to but spirituality is what you do"—Oprah began to lead her audiences into an alternative stream of supernatural living of a kind that had seldom been aired on television and certainly not before a daytime audience. Suddenly, women who attended their Baptist church on Sunday mornings or their Methodist Bible study on Tuesdays or who carried pictures of the pope and wore crucifixes—or who watched T. D. Jakes or Pat Robertson or Joel Osteen nodding with approval—were immersed into a way of seeing themselves and the world that was unlike anything they had known.

They were also introduced to an Oprah Winfrey they had not met before. The Oprah they had known was the black Baptist woman who had risen above poverty, prejudice, and sexual abuse to carve out a media empire. Their Oprah was rich and certainly among the elite, but she was also one of the girls. She could talk about girdles and boyfriends and bras like she was sitting on the floor by their closet while they tried on clothes. She was the ultimate girlfriend—weight rising and falling, openly lusting for Brad Pitt like all of them were, finding the world an interesting but funny place, and making all the other girls feel like they weren't alone. Oprah was the friend you met for wine on the way home from the office. She was the one you told that the kids were draining you dry and that your husband was getting weird in bed. She could laugh. She could be naughty. She was moved by what moved you.

The new Oprah was, well, spooky. She obviously had another

life few knew about, a well of power and beliefs that she hadn't been willing to expose before now. Oh, there had been the occasional reference to "higher power" or "my spiritual self." But there was also talk of Jesus and church and the oft-shouted "Lawd, hep me!" that wrung a laugh and that felt familiar to blacks and whites alike. This new version of Oprah, though, used words like "energy" and "spirits" and "focus" in ways that were new to most of her audience. Things were happening on stage that weren't usually seen on television and it felt like Spooky Oprah was trying to reach through the TV screen and rearrange each viewer's soul.

Then again, it wasn't Oprah who did the heavy spiritual lifting; it was her guests. One of the most popular books in America at that time was *Men Are from Mars, Women Are from Venus*, a marriage guide that urged strong relationships grown from deeper understanding of the differences between men and women. Those in Oprah's audience who had read the influential book probably expected Gray to talk about how to relate to their spouse better. Instead, the best-selling author instructed viewers about how to meditate and chant the words, "O glorious future, my heart is open to you. Come into my life." Later, in a discussion of how past emotions shape behavior, Gray told a weeping woman in the studio audience, "I'd like you to go back to your inner child. I want you to imagine Mommy and Daddy coming to you, and I want you to express your feelings to them."[47]

This was tame. Along with Gary Zukav, author of *The Seat of the Soul*, Oprah devoted an entire program to the Hindu concept of *karma*. "Energy is energy," Zukav said assuringly. "Your feelings are the force field of your soul." Another guest, Iyanla Vanzant, author of *Acts of Faith*, urged viewers to "surrender to the god of your understanding," promised "total and complete peace" if they did, and thought this was best done by "getting naked with your-self."[48] Financial advice superstar Suze Orman built on a favorite Oprah theme by telling the audience, "money is a living entity and responds to energy, including yours."[49] Then, in a statement that would have created a firestorm of controversy had it been made by a television preacher, Orman assured, "Your self worth equals your net worth."[50]

The "Change Your Life" shows ended with a segment entitled "Remember Your Spirit," during which Oprah, accompanied by low lights and New Age music, insisted, "I am defined by the world as a talk-show host, but . . . I am spirit connected to the greater spirit."[51] It had all proven too popular to end, though, and the pro-grams devoted to alternative spirituality continued. In one episode, Oprah introduced a psychic with whom she had consulted. The woman had previously—and correctly—sensed that Oprah was worried about joint pain and this led immediately to an invitation to be a guest on the show. She described herself as a "medical intui-tive" and gave diagnoses to any member of the audience willing to stand and give their name and age. To one man who suffered with migraine headaches she said, "Life owes me an explanation. That thought is in your liver and so it's burning. And what happens from the liver is there's an energetic circuit and it goes right up to the brain channel. And that starts the fire neurologically and that's why you have migraines."[52]

Rumors began to spread that Oprah had become unbalanced. Stories of her odd behavior circulated. Her visit to L'Enfant Gallery in Washington DC to consider buying some John Kirthian Court paintings is a storied example. Owner Peter A. Colasante had been contacted by staffers at Harpo to arrange for a viewing of Court's paintings while Oprah was in town on other business. It had not been an easy event to put together. Finally, when the day arrived, Colasante recalled, Oprah "walked through the front door and started waving her hands over her head like she was doing a very slow St. Vitus' dance." "I just don't feel it," Oprah began shouting, shaking her head. "I just don't feel it. The vibrations aren't right . . . they're not speaking to me . . ." Colasante and his staff were stunned. This wasn't what they had expected. With Winfrey still trying to feel the right vibrations, they tried to show her the other paintings they had assembled for her at great cost. It wasn't to be. A gallery staffer said the wrong thing and, as Colasante remembered it, Oprah "flounced out of the gallery, and I followed her down the street to her limousines. She yelled at her pilot. 'Get the plane . . . Get the plane. We're leaving.' And that was the end of Oprah Winfrey and her spirits and her vibrations."[53]

It would go on like this for years. Audiences were enthralled. Oprah's conservative Baptist family members were disappointed. The press was disgusted. Richard Roeper of the *Chicago Sun-Times* quipped, "As I stand in the eye of this latest hurricane of national [self-] worship, may I point out one thing: She's getting really goofy with all the spiritual questing. . . . It seems to me we're watching a woman go through an almost frantic search for spiritual bliss and higher consciousness."[54] Another journalist called "Change Your Life" television "a fairly skin-crawling thing."[55] Jeff MacGregor of the *New York Times* charged that the new direction of Oprah's show was "host worship" filled with "mind numbing clichés of personal improvement. . . . Like many gurus and circuit riders before her," he said, "Oprah has found a way to shamelessly market the history of her own misery and confusion as a form of worship."[56] Late-night comedians told jokes about "Deepak Oprah."

These criticisms stung. Asked if she was a "New Ager," she

fired back, "I am not a New Age anything and I resent being called that. I am just trying to open a door so that people can see themselves more clearly and perhaps be the light to get them to God, whatever they may call that. I don't see spirits in trees and I don't sit in the room with crystals."[57] Denials aside, the television shows on spirituality continued and were supplemented by a podcast series and an XM radio program along the same lines. Alternative spirituality as advocated by Deepak Chopra, Marianne Williamson, Iyanla Vanzant, Roger Kamenetz, Gary Zukav, Elizabeth Lesser, Carolyn Myss, Reverend Ed Bacon, Eckhart Tolle, Wayne Dyer, Byron Katie, and Andrew Weil, to name but a few, became the unrelenting theme of *The Oprah Winfrey Show*.

The Secret

By 2007, Oprah's spiritual crusade had taken on a messianic tone. Nothing reveals this as much as her gushing support for the popular book *The Secret*. The work of Australian television producer Rhonda Byrne, *The Secret* had been released in March 2006 and had achieved huge sales, largely through viral marketing. By year's end, the book and DVD package set was in the top five of Amazon's Christmas week best sellers. On February 7 of the following year, Oprah introduced Byrne to her audiences, having already told them that as she opened the book and DVD set, "I took God out of the box." Now, she proclaimed, "You can have it all. And, in fact, you already hold the power to make that happen."[58]

In the interview with Byrne, Winfrey was giddy. "This is a happy, happy day for me," she exulted. "I've known 'The Secret'—I didn't call it 'The Secret'—for years. And for years on this show, this is what I've been trying to do, is to get people to see it."[59]

But what was this secret? As Byrne revealed, the secret was otherwise called the Law of Attraction and meant simply this: thoughts become things. "So what you're saying," Oprah asked, "is that we all . . . create our own circumstances by the choices that we make and the choices that we make are fueled by our thoughts. So our thoughts are the most powerful things that we have here on Earth."[60] Byrne said yes. Turning to her audience, Oprah summarized: "It means that everything that happens to you, good and bad, you are attracting to yourself. It's something that I really have believed in for years, that the energy you put out into the world is always gonna be coming back to you. That's the basic principle."[61]

In a second program devoted to the book and its core concept, Oprah explained how closely her vision for her show aligned with the ideas in *The Secret*. "It is what this show is all about, and has been about for 21 years, taking responsibility for your life, knowing that every choice that you've made has led you to where you are right now. Well, the good news is that everybody has the power, no matter where you are in your life, to start changing it today."[62]

The outcry against this mystical message was instant. Salon .com's Peter Birkenhead called it "minty-fresh snake oil." HBO's Bill Maher called it "insane." *The Washington Post* slammed it as "slimy." And Richard Roeper—upon hearing an ad for a seminar on the book's themes in which Winfrey says, "You only have to believe that you can succeed, that you can be whatever your heart desires, be willing to work for it, and you can have it"—screamed,

Only if you live in Tinkerbell's world. In the real world, of course, there are millions upon millions of people who have tried the believe-desire-work portion of that equation and yet will NEVER have what they want. They will experience an entire life arc without escaping from poverty or despair, without ever finding love or happiness or wealth of material things and-or spirit.[63]

Oprah was undaunted. She had found her spiritual voice and embraced the ministry to which she was called. She would still do her shows on Spanx undergarments or Carol's Daughter beauty products or her favorite Key Lime Bundt Cake. She would have the best and the brightest and the richest on her show. But always there was the theme of the invisible path to peace, achievement, money, and fulfillment, always there were the empowering of the ancestors and the connection to the greater spirit that had long defined her life.

She had carved out her own unique spirituality just as she had carved out her own one-of-a-kind media empire. She defied the rules, in business as in faith, and the contradictions did not seem to bother her fans. As Kitty Kelley writes, Oprah

> quoted the Bible but did not attend church. . . . On family values she covered all the bases: she applauded motherhood but for herself she had chosen a career over children [and] life with a man outside of marriage. . . . She preached self-improvement (makeovers and cleansing fasts) and self-empowerment (believe it and achieve it) sprinkled with the New Agey piffle of *The Secret*. . . . Contradictions aside, Oprah became a towering presence in America, a one-woman cathedral.[64]

And so she had perceived herself to be. And so, for millions worldwide, she had become.

O

That Oprah Winfrey has engineered an amazingly successful broadcast career is certain. She is gifted and her achievements should be celebrated. She has, as she has often said, changed the history of her profession. Yet what her stunning career urges her to believe about herself ought to be different from what her faith tells her. In Oprah's case, though, the two seem to be nearly exactly the same thing. And this is the problem.

Most of the great religions of the world teach that man achieves his greatest spiritual heights by seeing himself as small in comparison to God and creation. Islam makes it a virtue to be Abdullah—a "slave of Allah." Judaism urges a man to see himself as "small in his own eyes." Christianity calls a man to "humble himself under the mighty hand of God." The lesson seems to be much the same: man sees most clearly and climbs to his loftiest heights when free of the burden of himself.

Yet Oprah Winfrey's faith seems to be a confirmation of her own greatness. Every experience, every message from the invisible realm, every form of power she accesses is about her and her well-being. And she believes the same of every human being on earth: for the willing, the universe brings only good, only comfort, only personal peace and affluence.

It is just here at which Oprah's faith is most suspect. If a man were to publicly reject God and then set about the task of fashioning his own religion, we would naturally expect him to create a religion of himself, about his own well-being and his own blessing or enchantment. It is not likely he would go out and fashion a faith of extreme self-sacrifice. Instead, we would naturally expect a humanly derived religion to mean only good for human beings. We would know his religion is man-made because his religion is all about man.

This seems to be exactly what Oprah has done. She believes that the spiritual powers in her life mean her only good. She even distances herself from those who do not walk in the same blessing from "spirit" that she has known. She is almost at a loss to explain evil in the world and, in fact, she seems confused by it. What she does believe is that she is special, anointed, chosen, created for a purpose, and a unique vessel for the blessing of mankind. Indeed, she and the pope will lead the world in prayer.

It makes us wonder if the religion of Oprah Winfrey is nothing more than a religion about Oprah Winfrey and how she is special in the world. It also makes us wonder if what she is urging us to believe is that we, too, can access the powers of the universe to be as special, as blessed, as successful, as happy, and as fulfilled as she is.

I do not find in this, though, the complexity and the variations that I expect of truth. I do not find an explanation for good and evil, a call to compassion, or a worldview that helps me contend with my biggest problem—the darkness in my soul. Most of all, I am certain I have seen Oprah Winfrey's faith before, that it has taken the form of a taunt that I have encountered in another place.

I remember now. The call to Oprah Winfrey's kind of faith is very much the same as another summons I once heard: "Ye shall be as gods."

3

The Age of Oprah

You're telling all those lies about the good things that we can have if we close our eyes.

—George Harrison, "Think for Yourself"

Every life is in some way a reflection of its age. Yet some lives are more. Some—and this is particularly true of the great and the famous—are embodiments of their times. They symbolize and capture the meaning of the broader flow of their generation. This is part of what moved the Scottish historian Thomas Carlyle to insist that "the history of the world is but the biography of great men." It is an overstated sentiment, of course, but it shows how much a period, a nation, or a people can be understood through the life of a single notable individual. In our own day, and particularly in the matter of popular religion, of no one is this more true than Oprah Winfrey.

Yet it might not have been so. Had Oprah remained within the confines of the traditional Christianity of her early years, the focus of her heart would have been drawn away from the styles and beliefs of her times. This is because unswerving, orthodox, unapologetic Christianity stands against the prevailing culture. It calls its followers to be in the world but not of the world, to embrace a kind of engaged monasticism. To not be conformed to the age is as much expected as devotion to God. This makes a believer otherworldly and tethers his religious vision to a source that is outside of human history, outside of contemporary culture.

This was not to be the faith of Oprah Winfrey. Instead, by her mid-twenties, she had turned from the faith of Sunday mornings and a Jesus in whom alone is salvation. She had turned from that brand of faith that calls a soul out of society and bids it live in the light of the age to come. Instead, she had embraced a secular faith, meaning one "of the age." This new, informal religion kept the language and forms of Christianity but replaced it with meaning drawn from the spiritual explorations of her times, from the ideals and poetry and experimenting of her generation. To understand her religious journey, then, it is essential to understand the spiritual currents of her day and to discern how she navigated those currents toward her own unique form of supernatural fulfillment.

Scanning the course of her generation will naturally remove us a bit from the story of Oprah herself. We should not be unsettled by this. In order to understand the age of Oprah we have to lift our gaze from Oprah to peer for a while into the events that shaped her life and beliefs. We will return to mentions of her from time to time, if only to locate her life on the timeline of her age. The benefits of this, though—the insight it will give us into the woman she has become—will be more than worth the journey away from home.

A Generation of Seekers

It is important to recall that Oprah Winfrey was born in 1954. This makes her part of that eighty-million-strong reproductive surge called the baby boomers who would inherit a world they found wanting and who would then set out to remake that world in their own image. They would be a transformational generation, then, and would leave almost nothing of morals, politics, art, and pleasure unchanged. As a result of their reconstructive efforts, religion in America would never again be the same.

The society their parents bequeathed them was broadly Christian. It had always been so. When the U.S. Supreme Court stated in an 1892 case that "our civilization and our institutions are emphatically Christian," no one thought this at odds with what the man on the street believed.[1] Nor was it thought odd when President Franklin Roosevelt and Prime Minister Winston Churchill worshipped together during World War II and then summoned the "Christian nations" to oppose totalitarianism. This was simply the way the Western world understood itself.

By 1954, though, the age of Eisenhower had dawned. Despite the efforts of men like Billy Graham and Oral Roberts, American religion had become an insipid brand of conformity, a sanctifier of cultural norms, too loosely woven through society to be of much redemptive good. In this, Eisenhower himself symbolized the times. Ike had once movingly called for a national day of prayer and fasting, yet when that day came he spent it playing golf. He boldly proclaimed his belief that religion is essential to a republic, but then added "and I don't care what that religion is!" Though it was during the Eisenhower administration that the phrase *In God We Trust* became the national motto, this was more a statement of opposition to the global communism of the day than it was any indication of the state of the American soul.

That soul had been captured by a vision often described in the popular *Life* magazine as "the good life." We should recall that the World War II generation had endured sixteen years of deprivation and hardship brought on by the Great Depression and then by a bloody global war. By 1945, the United States was the mightiest nation on earth, owned 90 percent of the world's gold, and was eager to turn inward and revel in her abundance. An era of triumphant materialism dawned. For a war-weary people, the American dream became bound up with a frame house in the suburbs, cars with huge fins, and 2.1 beaming children. Bowling, backyard grilling, and vacationing via the nation's new superhighways became the rage, the symbols of a satisfied nation rewarding itself. We perhaps remember the values of this age best from the June Cleaver–type housewife proudly displaying her modern, space-age kitchen, the promise of a strong and noble society reflected in every shiny appliance.

But all was not well. The baby boomers grew up in this materialistic age and found it stifling. They could look down the long highway of their lives and see themselves living out the patterns their parents' generation had set for them. College and then a good job. Marriage and then children. Decades of labor to pay for the best schools for their children and then hopefully enough left upon which to retire. And why? So that their children could in turn go to college, get a job, and start the cycle over again. This was what the American dream had become.

But what of the soul? What of the meaning of life? What of the restless heart and the yearning for something beyond what the eye can see?

The Beats

As early as the mid-1950s, just as Oprah Winfrey was coming into the world, signs of discontent began to surface. We tend to remember that era as popular entertainment encourages us to do: as a time of poodle skirts and sock hops and milkshakes at the diner and ducktail haircuts. That 1950s was there, too, and it was as naïve and sweet as it is often portrayed. But there was a harder-edged version and it arose in the dissatisfaction of a generation. Students gathered in coffee shops to commiserate. Young men grew beards and wore berets, anything to be *other*. Poetry readings became the rage and all to the accompaniment of bongo drums and guitars. The point was to begin to question, to push back, to slow the conveyor belt of expectation as it carried you to a soul-numbing fate.

At first a style, it soon became a movement. Authors like Jack Kerouac and Allen Ginsberg had already named it the "Beat Movement" before most Americans knew it existed. Originally Kerouac, whose travelogue *On the Road* would define a generation, had said, "To be Beat was to be at the bottom of your personality looking up."[2] As early as 1948, he wrote, "The word 'beat' originally meant poor, down and out, deadbeat, on the bum, sleeping in subways." By 1954, though, Kerouac insisted that the word was related to "beatific," to the sounds that accompanied "the rumblings of a new soul."[3] It was, said historian David Halberstam in his magnificent treatment of the era, *The Fifties*, a word used "to describe those who went against the prevailing tide of materialism and personal ambition."[4]

The Beats were bohemian and nomadic. They were, in the words of editor and critic Malcolm Cowley, "looking for something to believe, an essentially religious faith that would permit them to live at peace with their world."[5] They tended to drop out of school, travel, smoke marijuana, and read poetry. They were early hippies, but they were more. They were the vanguard of the great surge of discontented youth who would create what we know as the 1960s counterculture. They were pretentious, yes, with their cigarettes and self-importance and their almost laughably abstract poetry. Yet Kerouac's *On The Road*, written on a hundred-foot roll of shelf paper, was a masterpiece, as was Allen Ginsberg's "Howl," written while the author was high on peyote. In fact, Ginsberg's reading of "Howl" at Gallery Six in San Francisco on October 13, 1955, has become one of the notable moments in American literary history, its famous opening line nearly a cultural call to arms: "I saw the best minds of my generation / destroyed by madness / starving, mystical, naked / who dragged themselves thru the angry streets at / dawn looking for a negro fix . . ."[6] These were serious themes being pondered by serious minds in people striving to appear unserious.

The Lure of the East

For our purposes here, it was the Beat Movement's reach to the East that is important. The Second World War had introduced American society to the religions of Asia. Soldiers raised Baptist in Texas found themselves admiring prayer at Buddhist temples on Pacific islands. A cup of tea with a Buddhist priest or perhaps an invitation to a Buddhist home and soon a soldier might return home, if not converted, at least sympathetic with the wisdom of the East. Then there were the many marriages of soldiers to Asian women that brought the religions of Asia to neighborhoods in America. Soon the religious mysteries of the East, which had once been removed and exotic, now began to offer themselves in answer to the gaping spiritual void of the West.

What appealed most about the religions of the East was their view of reality. Hinduism taught a concept it called *maya*: the reality we see is only real as a dream is real—it actually exists but it is not ultimate reality. Our existence is a tissue-thin lesser reality we should try to escape in order to become one with ultimate consciousness. Buddhism built on this view and taught men to rise above suffering through detachment and meditation. Taoism taught that the dichotomies of the West—good and evil, light and dark, pleasure and pain—were all part of a whole that ought to be embraced as the natural flow of life. To a young American generation who felt themselves welded to the material and to the moral pronouncements of an older generation for whom they had no respect, the East with its gentle, mystical, otherworldliness issued a call.

When American churches seemed more infused with the spirit of the age than with the spirit of God, religions of the East began to look attractive to the young. Beat ideals were blended with Eastern concepts to produce what was later called "Beat Zen." One Beat writer described this as "one-is-all-and-all-is-one-so-what-the-hell."[7] The Beats were taking the mood of a religion—or perhaps more specifically the spiritual detachment from daily life—and making it both their style and the basis for their understanding of the world. What should not be missed is the choice Beats made. Rather than reacting to the rationalistic, moralistic American religions by turning to atheism, they chose mysticism and Eastern mysticism at that.

In fact, Kerouac mocked the mechanistic worldview so prevalent at the time: "So you people don't believe in God. So you're all big, smart, know-it-all Marxists and Freudians, hey? Why don't you come back in a million years and tell me all about it, angels?"[8] Instead, he urged the Beats to celebrate faith—all of them: "I want to speak for things, for the crucifix I speak out, for the star of Israel I speak out, for the divinest man who ever lived who was a German (Bach) I speak out, for Mohammed I speak out, for Buddha I speak out, for Lao-tse and Chang-tse I speak out, for D. T. Suzuki I speak out . . . This is Beat! Love your lives out!"[9] This was not the first time in American history that the varieties of world religions were viewed as of equal value, as on parallel paths to enlightenment, but the Beat Movement was the channel through which this belief became cool, entered the youth counterculture of the 1960s, and thus entered the pop culture of later decades.

This Beat fascination with Eastern spirituality was not lost on religious leaders in the East. For nearly a century, Indian gurus had been calling for the worldwide spread of Hinduism and even for Hinduism to become the mother of all other religions. In the Beat emphasis on informal spirituality over formal religious institutions, on experience over creed, the gurus saw their opportunity. Even then, at the dawn of the 1960s, psychologist Carl Rogers was sounding out the spiritual insistence of his generation in *On Becoming Human*: "Neither the Bible nor the prophets—neither Freud nor research, neither the revelations of God nor man can take precedence over my own direct experience."[10] This was the certainty the Beat Movement carried into the critical next decade of their lives and it gave the gurus of the East their gateway.

In the minds of a rising generation, the East offered experience, while Christianity offered conformity to a superficial American culture. The East offered transformation, while Christianity offered little more than condemnation of the new, freer morality. The East offered oneness with God. American Christianity offered the promise of God one day—if you behaved.

And so the East came. A Hindu guru named Mahesh Prasad

Varma was already in the United States before the decade of the 1960s began. A graduate of the University of Allabad in the field of physics, he had rejected science for spiritual pursuits and begun to study and meditate with the legendary Guru Dev. There followed two years in a Himalayan cave for meditation and nearly as many months traveling alone in the forests of India. His experiences in meditation convinced him that he had developed a new approach to an ancient Hindu discipline. He was also convinced that he should carry his message to the West, to America, where the spiritual hunger of a rising generation had drawn the attention of the world. Mahesh Prasad Varma thus repackaged himself and his message for Western consumption. He became the Maharishi Mahesh Yogi. The Hindu practice of meditation became Transcendental Meditation, a more "scientific" version of practices designed to merge the soul with what the maharishi called "cosmic consciousness."

The Wounds of the 1960s

The maharishi would likely never have been known to most Americans had it not been for something that happened in February 1964, the year that Oprah Winfrey turned ten years old: the Beatles landed in America. Their story would merge with that of the Maharishi Mahesh Yogi, and the result would forever change the spiritual vision of the rising baby boom generation.

First, though, the opening progression of the 1960s. In January 1961, John F. Kennedy became president of the United States. To the baby boomers, Kennedy was an inspiration. The other presidents they had known—Roosevelt, Truman, and Eisenhower—had all been distant grandfather figures to them. Kennedy was young, handsome, witty, a war hero, and a Pulitzer Prize–winning author. His wife was beautiful and urbane. His children mischievous and sweet. In his inaugural address, Kennedy had warned the world of a new tribe on the rise in America:

> The torch has been passed to a new generation of Americans— born in this century, tempered by war, disciplined by a hard and bitter peace, proud of our ancient heritage—and unwilling to witness or permit the slow undoing of those human rights to which this nation has always been committed, and to which we are committed today at home and around the world.[11]

For the young of America, Kennedy was indeed—in Jackie Kennedy's later, telling phrase—the king of Camelot. And the generation born in the fifteen years since World War II wanted desperately to be Kennedy's knights of the Round Table. He made them believe that the world need not remain as it was but could be changed. He also made them believe that they were destined to do it. He lifted them, then, from their disillusionment with the world their parents had handed them to a fiery confidence that they could refashion that world into what it should be.

What Kennedy offered, though, was a secular vision. He quoted Scripture more than any president up to that time, but he changed the quotations to speak of democracy, freedom, and the American way of life. He spoke religiously of America's "calling" to venture into outer space, conquer poverty, win against communism, and take global responsibility through a program called the Peace Corps. Youth. Idealism. The New Frontier. Camelot revisited. Kennedy's vision, naïve and humanistic though it was, caused young America to believe they could change the world by their own strength—and they never saw the world or themselves in quite the same way again.

As though in confirmation of this secular vision, in 1962, the U.S. Supreme Court ruled in *Engel v. Vitale* that it is unconstitutional for state officials to lead prayers in public schools. This ruling was based upon a mounting legal consensus that the meaning of the First Amendment—"Congress shall make no law respecting an establishment of religion, or prohibiting the free exercise thereof"—was that there should be a "wall of separation between church and state," Jefferson's famous phrase. Thus, thirty-nine million schoolchildren were forbidden to pray the standard incantation: "Almighty God, we acknowledge our dependence upon thee, and we beg thy blessings upon us, our parents, our teachers, and our country." The meaning was more important than the forbidden practice. The discerning realized that the Christian consensus that had once bound American society to the will of a loving God was eroding, helped along in the process by a court-ordered process of secularization.

This was bad timing, for the next year America would need that loving God as much as ever. On November 22, 1963, President John F. Kennedy was shot in Dallas's Dealey Plaza. The images are seared into our cultural memory. Breathless announcers interrupting the broadcast day. The final announcement from Parkland Hospital. A tearful Walter Cronkite unable to utter the words. Jacqueline's pink bloodstained suit and her pillbox hat. The shock of a nation. The confusion. The chaos. Later, little John-John tearfully saluting his father's casket as the caisson rolled by. The live televised assassination of the president's assassin.

The much-debated question of who shot John Kennedy in Dallas is not nearly as important as what it did to the nation. It was a collective trauma on an unprecedented scale, as though the whole nation had experienced a violent accident with all the fear, the uncontrollable emotion, and the desperate search for normalcy that follows such horrors. The gaping national wound the death of Kennedy left on the American soul meant the loss of the troubled innocence that had characterized postwar society. Now, the young knights of Camelot were set adrift.

Though we do not tend to connect the two events in memory, just ten weeks after the assassination of Kennedy, the Beatles landed in America. The young were desperate for distraction. From the beginning, the Beatles electrified young America, as films from their historic concert at New York's Shea Stadium depict. Screaming, weeping, contorting youths were moved by forces beyond the music. Sixteen-year-old girls charged the stage, flattening policemen twice their size, while others simply passed out and had to be carried from the field. No one seemed more stunned by the commotion than the Fab Four themselves, but their music had touched the mourning hearts of Camelot's lonely young knights.

They would become the pied pipers of a generation, moving from innocuous offerings like "Please, Please Me," "She Loves You," and "I Want to Hold Your Hand" in 1964 to the darker *Rubber Soul* album in 1965 and finally to the epochal *Sgt. Pepper's Lonely Hearts Club Band* in 1967. On the much-discussed *Sgt. Pepper's* album cover, psychedelic Beatles take center stage, replacing images of the original Beatles who appear to be in mourning. Standing around the "new" Beatles are depictions of the band's many heroes, including the Maharishi Mahesh Yogi.

They had met the maharishi in London in 1967 and had, like many in their generation, been captivated by the religious vision of the East. They studied with the maharishi first in Wales and then at his ashram in Rishikesh in India early in 1968. It had not gone well. Ringo Starr left after ten days, disgusted with the vegetarian diet. Paul McCartney left three weeks later. George Harrison and John Lennon left two weeks after that when they learned that the maharishi had made sexual advances toward some of the women who traveled with the Beatles, Mia Farrow in particular. Lennon told a *Tonight Show* audience several months later, "We believe in meditation, but not the maharishi and his scene."[12] Associating with the maharishi, he said, was an "error in judgment."[13]

Transcendental Meditation

Though the Beatles had known the maharishi for barely two years, they had propelled him to global visibility. In 1968, the guru announced that he would put all his efforts into training leaders for his Transcendental Meditation (TM) movement. This was little more than a Westernized name for an ancient Eastern religious practice, as a U.S. court would determine in 1977.[14] Still, because the maharishi called his practices Transcendental Meditation rather than simply the Hindu meditation that it was, because he labeled it "scientific," and because he billed himself as guru to the stars, TM gained access where it never would have otherwise. It was encouraged in public schools, YMCAs, businesses, and even churches. It became so popular that the Illinois House of Representatives passed a bill in 1972 urging its public schools to encourage TM in its programs. California passed a similar law soon after. TM was funded by a grant from the National Institutes of Health, taught for credit in high schools and colleges throughout the nation, and even employed by the U.S. Army in treating alcoholism and drug dependency.

By the mid-1970s, a high school football player in an American public high school could find himself required to sit through a TM class and then meditate while chanting the name of a Hindu deity if he was to be allowed to remain on his team.[15] Patients in hospitals, and sometimes Roman Catholic, Baptist, or Presbyterian hospitals, were encouraged to meditate and chant as part of their recovery. TM rooms were arranged in corporate headquarters, on U.S. Navy ships, and even on Capitol Hill in Washington DC. The maharishi had succeeded in embedding TM where no traditional religious organization, under ban of the First Amendment, would have been permitted.

Beyond the success of the Transcendental Meditation movement was the success of the Eastern ideas out of which it grew. Since most people absorb ideas viscerally rather than through study, breathe them in from the culture around them rather than receive them from formal presentations, Eastern concepts and terms oozed into the American worldview. Friends sat in living rooms discussing the idea of reincarnation, for example, and wondering aloud who they might have been in a previous life. They had learned only the pop version of this Hindu belief, though. It was cool to think about whether one had once been Abraham Lincoln or Catherine the Great. It did not occur to those who adopted this belief that in Hinduism, reincarnation (or *samsara*) is not a gift but a punishment. Orthodox Hindus believe themselves trapped in a constant cycle of existence, and this cycle might not be upward. A soul might take the form of a horse in one life but fail in that incarnation and find itself a dung beetle or a flea or a lizard in a next life. In each incarnation, if *karma* is not fulfilled, the progression of existence is downward, not upward. What was hellish and feared and a prison in the East became a comfort and a matter of eager imaginations in the West, thanks to the sanitizing public relations work of the maharishi.

Karma, too, received a makeover. In Hinduism, *karma* is the moral law that must be observed in any incarnation a soul might take. It must not be interfered with or the soul will regress to a lower state in the next incarnation. A horse must fulfill the *karma* of being a horse or the soul that inhabits that horse might find itself a lesser being in the next life, in a new incarnation. In India, for example, the brutal state of the untouchables, the lowest class, is protected by religious Hindus. Charity for these beggars and poverty-stricken beings is opposed. When Mother Teresa first began ministering to the sick and the dying of Calcutta, she and her Sisters of Mercy were often beaten and resisted by Hindus who believed that a diseased man withering away in a gutter was fulfilling his *karma* and must not be helped. He must suffer and perhaps die unaided because this was what it meant to fulfill *karma*.

In the West, under the tutelage of the maharishi and those gurus who followed his example, *karma* was made into something akin to luck. It was understood to be the good fortune that came from doing positive deeds. Baby boomers who had learned this redefined version of the ancient concept would make sure they threw a dollar to the homeless man on the street while commenting to a friend, "I need all the *karma* I can get. I have a big presentation to make today." This was, of course, exactly the opposite of the Eastern concept of the term and gurus in India protested the distortions, but Western culture was ripe for the deceptions and so made the reworked language of Hinduism into a fad-driven faith of its own.

As deeply as Eastern concepts took root in American soil, they were still alien plantings. Scientists who programmed computers or who worked to put men in space would speak of their reality as a thin veil masking the greater "oneness" beyond. Couples who sang of the amazing grace of Jesus Christ in church on Sunday mornings would join others in the fellowship hall of that same church midweek to chant the names of Hindu deities and seek union with *Brahma* while sitting in yoga positions, unaware of the inconsistencies or that the very word *yoga* means "union" and is intended for that purpose. Terms and concepts like *reincarnation, meditation, karma, mantra, yoga, urna* (the "third eye"), and *guru* entered the daily language of Americans and indicated a shift eastward in cultural moorings. This shift was aided by the many movies that treated Eastern themes in the decades that followed. Films like the *Star Wars* trilogy, *E.T., Gandhi, A Passage to India*, and *The Razor's Edge* embedded Eastern concepts even more deeply into the American psyche.

Americans would do with these ancient concepts what they would. In self-help and business motivational seminars, attendees were taught the Eastern concept that what men perceive as reality isn't genuinely real, but with the novel addition that it is possible to fashion the greater ultimate reality by words, by action, and, most of all, by believing the desired state into being. This became a secret of success, the invisible power behind corporate achievement. It is this view that led to Jesse Jackson's insistence that "if you can conceive it and believe it, you can achieve it," the words Oprah Winfrey kept on her bathroom mirror and said to herself over and over again each day.

Television preachers would, often inadvertently, veer into Eastern provinces when they told their audiences that by giving money they could amass cosmic goodwill that would in turn grace their lives. The Bible in their hands did indeed teach generosity as a path to prosperity, but not in terms anything like the karmic teaching of Hinduism. And many a movement would teach that the key to physical healing was the choice to disbelieve that the troubling sickness was real. This practice was centuries old and had entered American religion through the Christian Scientists of the nineteenth century, but the idea gained new currency through the counterculture of the 1960s and the various spiritual therapy streams that sprang from it.

Of course, a classic Western reworking of Eastern ideas would be found in the book *The Secret*, the book Oprah described as "God" to her television audience. While the Eastern concept of *maya* is, as we have seen, that the present reality is a thin veil to be escaped in pursuit of a merging with another, ultimate reality, Westerners transformed this into something altogether different. The refashioned belief became that if the present reality is wanting, then the ultimate reality could be created by the will of man. If man would only think differently, he could attract the reality he desired, thus the Law of Attraction: "thoughts become things." This was, of course, little more than an Eastern view of reality coupled with Western willfulness and hunger for power, but it was an enticing concept for the tens of millions who bought the book and DVD or who attended *The Secret* seminars.

Rise of the New Age

By the late 1970s and 1980s, this merging of Eastern and Western themes was called the New Age movement. The term was at least as old as nineteenth-century Romantic poet William Blake's famous line "when the New Age is at leisure to pronounce, all will be set right," but it was also used by those who believed that a new age of spirituality had been ushered in by the religious forces unleashed in the 1960s. There was a messianic sense to this, a belief that a great liberation of mankind was about to occur. The old religious order of saviors and doctrines and creeds and structures had been overturned, New Agers believed. No loss. It had only stood in the way of man's religious evolution anyway. Now, with the Protestant consensus cast aside, the world was free to break into new spiritual territory, to unite with the cosmic power—however defined, however pursued. This was how the West and Americans, in particular, had made use of the Eastern ideas newly come to their shores.

We should remind ourselves once again, though, that the New Age movement in all its forms took Eastern ideas and turned them precisely upon their heads. While in the East *maya*—the view that the present world is not ultimate reality but a thinly veiled lie—was horrible news, in the West this was taken as a call to create a new, often materialistic reality through confessions and deeds and supercharged belief. While in the East reincarnation was the worst of imprisonments to an unmerciful cycle of incarnations, in the West it was almost a parlor game in which the faithful imagined for themselves who they might have been in a previous life. Sometimes this was done through "regression therapy" in which a therapist helped his client discern who he or she had been in a prior incarnation. This bordered on ancestor worship but it was nothing akin to the Eastern concept of *samsara* or reincarnation. Then, finally, there was *karma*, which in the East was the moral law of fulfilling whatever incarnation a soul found itself experiencing, but in the West was a kind of "good deeds in exchange for good fortune" arrangement that was exercised even by those who believed in nothing beyond the material, beyond what the eye can see. In short, the West took the ideas of the East and created an entirely new religion of self-empowerment and enchantment, which was new in history and unrelated to anything a traditional Hindu or Buddhist or Taoist might have believed.

As important as these refashioned Eastern concepts were in the decades that came after the 1960s, they were not the only spiritual forces to flourish in that tumultuous season. At a time when courts were disentangling traditional faith from American public life, when John Lennon was correctly claiming that the Beatles were "more popular than Jesus Christ," and when an "anything goes" approach to religious experimentation prevailed, other, darker forces surfaced too. These arose not from the ancient religions of the East but rather from the ancient pagan religions of the West that had prevailed prior to Christianity. With Christianity being pried off of society by a matrix of forces during the 1960s, old faiths made new by counterculture trendiness announced themselves.

The Evil Side of Beauty

An example is the movement that was begun on April 30, 1966, by Anton Szandor LaVey. The son of a San Francisco liquor salesman, LaVey was a gifted, intelligent youth consumed by fascination with the occult. His talents led him, at the age of eighteen, to play keyboard for a carnival, and this is when he began to question the power of traditional religions. As he later recounted,

> On Saturday night, I would see men lusting after half-naked girls dancing at the carnival and on Sunday morning when I was playing organ for tent show evangelists at the other end of the carnival lot, I would see these same men sitting in the pews with their wives and children asking God to forgive and purge them of carnal desires. And the next Saturday night they'd be back at

the carnival or some other place of indulgence. I knew then that the Christian Church thrives on hypocrisy and that man's carnal nature will out no matter how much is purged or scourged by any white light religion.[16]

After years with the carnival, LaVey became a San Francisco police department photographer, and this introduced him to the corrupt, seamy, bloody side of life. He again questioned the idea of a Christian God. How could a horrible death be attributed to God's will, as so many suggested at times of tragedy? How was anything like the Christian God involved in the filth and gore LaVey was photographing day after day? These questions continued to stir in his mind as he left the police department and began playing the organ in nightclubs. He sought answers and began studying the black arts, the ways of the occult through the centuries. Finally, he found what he had been looking for. He found the worldview to explain what he had seen in his short thirty-six years.

On *Walpurgisnacht*—the ancient springtime festival of Europe—or April 30, 1966, LaVey summoned the press to proclaim what he called "the age of Satan." He had shaved his head, put on a clerical collar, and trimmed his Mephistophelian beard. He announced the dawn of a new religion—the religion of Satan, a religion suited for the age. Its agency would be the Church of Satan, and he, LaVey, would be its Black Pope. In the manifesto of this new movement published in 1969, *The Satanic Bible*, LaVey offered his creed in the Nine Satanic Statements.

1. Satan represents indulgence instead of abstinence!
2. Satan represents vital existence, instead of spiritual
   pipe dreams!

3. Satan represents undefiled wisdom, instead of hypocritical self-deceit!

4. Satan represents kindness to those who deserve it, instead of love wasted on ingrates!

5. Satan represents vengeance instead of turning the other cheek!

6. Satan represents responsibility to the responsible, instead of concern for psychic vampires!

7. Satan represents man as just another animal, sometimes better, sometimes worse than those that walk on all-fours, who, because of his "divine spiritual and intellectual development," has become the most vicious animal of all!

8. Satan represents all of the so-called sins, as they all lead to physical, mental or emotional gratification!

9. Satan has been the best friend the church has ever had, as he has kept it in business all these years![17]

LaVey propelled his new church into national visibility through his gifts for showmanship. Typically, he invited the media to watch as he conducted a Black Mass. This involved LaVey feigning intercourse with a nude woman on a black-clad altar. A year after founding his movement, he baptized his daughter Zeena into the Church of Satan and sold recordings of the ceremony. Always ostentatious, he kept a full-grown lion in his home until neighbors complained. By the end of 1967, media from around the U.S., Europe, and even Japan had been assigned to report on the latest news from the Church of Satan.

It might all have been a stunt befitting Halloween had LaVey and his church not become so surprisingly influential. *The Satanic Bible*, LaVey's creation, was a best seller. The church drew tens of thousands of followers at its peak. LaVey became a favorite of talk television and even appeared on the *Phil Donahue Show* to articulate his views. Among his disciples were Sammy Davis Jr. and Jayne Mansfield. He served as a consultant on demonic matters for the 1968 film *Rosemary's Baby*, a box office success starring Mia Farrow and John Cassavetes. LaVey's movement achieved such mainstream legitimacy that it was recognized by the U.S. armed forces, whose chaplains were required to learn the skills of ministering to a military member of the Church of Satan.

What was obscured by the media feeding frenzy surrounding LaVey was that Church of Satan doctrine was little more than humanism dressed in occult garb. *The Satanic Bible* made clear that Satan was viewed as a symbol but not as a living being. The central force in the religion was the human being and his drives, desires, and passions. In fact, the highest holy day for a member of the Church of Satan is his own birthday. As one expert has written,

> The Church of Satan worships Satan, most clearly symbolized in the Roman God Lucifer, the bearer of light, the spirit of the air, and the personification of enlightenment. Satan is not visualized as an anthropomorphic being, rather he represents the forces of nature. To the Satanist, the self is the highest embodiment of human life and is sacred. The Church of Satan is essentially a human potential movement and members are encouraged to develop whatever capabilities they can by which they might excel. They are, however, cautioned to recognize their limitations—an important factor in this philosophy of rational self-interest. Satanists practice magick, the art of changing situations or events in accordance with one's will, which would, using normally accepted methods, be impossible.[18]

Clearly, the innovative, creative, experimental culture of the 1960s had taken even ancient pagan religions and done to them what it had done to the ways of the East. Rather than worship a pagan god or Satan himself—a natural expectation for a movement called the Church of Satan—the narcissistic counterculture had made Satan little more than a symbol and had placed man at the center of its system of worship. What would have been devotion to a deity and accompanying spirits in the pre-Christian era had been resurrected as devotion to self in the name of a deity in the 1960s. In this tumultuous, transforming era, both the religious ideas of the East and of ancient pagan Europe were kidnapped and refashioned as "human potential" movements by a self-centered humanism that consumed religions to remake them in its own image.

And what of the supernatural? What of spirits and demons and angels and gods? Did they actually exist? If so, did they have a role to play in these counterculture religions? Did the humanistic reworking of ancient faiths leave any room for spiritual beings, the supernatural realities that the ancients would have held certain?

The answers began to come, if they had not already, in 1969—as the counterculture wound down and the evil side of beauty began making itself known. On December 6 of that year, the Rolling Stones performed at a free-of-charge concert at the Altamont Speedway near San Francisco. More than three hundred thousand attended. Dubbed "Woodstock West," attractions included bands like Santana, Jefferson Airplane, and of course, the Stones themselves. In an ironic and ill-fated decision, the Hell's Angels motorcycle gang was hired to serve as bodyguards. As a result, violence mounted during the earlier performances and reached a crescendo when the Stones took the stage.

When the group that described itself as "the greatest

rock-n-roll band in the world" launched into one of its signature songs, "Sympathy for the Devil," a flurry of violence broke out. It was so disrupting that the Stones' lead man, Mick Jagger, ceased his gyrating and tried to calm the crowd. It was too late. A member of the Hell's Angels had knifed a black man just beyond the edge of the stage. Both the knifing and what came after were captured for posterity by cameras filming the movie, *Gimme Shelter.* Desperate to save the moment and talking on in his nervousness, Jagger said, "We always have something very funny happen when we start that number . . ."[19] As Stones' biographer Philip Norman later wrote, "There, at last, was the crucial moment at Altamont in the red-spotlit dark, as Mick Jagger stood, helpless among the real demons his masquerade had summoned up."[20]

This seemed of a piece with what Americans had already been witnessing on their televisions over the previous months. On August 9, actress Sharon Tate and a group of friends had been brutally murdered in their Los Angeles home. The next night, on August 10, Leno and Rosemary LaBianca were viciously stabbed to death and left for their children to discover. The senselessness and cruelty of the killings stunned the nation. Sharon Tate had been eight months pregnant when she was killed, her belly slashed open, her body stabbed sixteen times. Her friend, Voytek Frykowski, was stabbed fifty-one times, shot, and pistol-whipped until the gun's grip broke against his skull. The killers wrote messages on the walls of their victims' houses in blood.

These murders took place only a week before the nation turned its attention to Max Yasgur's farm in New York. There, a concert that later came to be called Woodstock was just taking place. Los Angeles police were grateful for anything that distracted the press. The Tate/LaBianca murders were so heinous it took months to determine what had happened, much less who was responsible. Finally, on December 1, less than a week before Altamont, the Los Angeles chief of police began making the story public. Attention centered upon Charles Manson and his dune buggy–driving band of followers. Manson was likely insane, but he was also, by all accounts, a master manipulator adept at appearing to be more than he was. He had befriended rock stars and even had one of his songs recorded by the Beach Boys. He had also taken what was meant to be the glory of the counterculture movement and used it to control his pitiful gang of misfits. As one historian has written, Manson "turned out to be a vicious con artist who used drugs, mysticism, occultism, Beatles lyrics, Hermann Hesse's pop classic in Eastern mysticism, *Siddhartha*, sexual debauchery, and other mind-altering techniques to create a dedicated little band of revolutionaries and murderers."[21]

If the details of the murders and Manson's Hitleresque rants were not tantalizing enough, there was also an intriguing backstory to the killings. Sharon Tate was married to Roman Polanski, director of the groundbreaking and financially successful occult film *Rosemary's Baby.* As we have seen, the spiritual advisor for that film was Church of Satan founder Anton LaVey. Yet LaVey had also befriended Charles Manson, who looked to the Black Pope as an inspiration. The Tate/LaBianca murders proved to be more than merely the deeds of drugged-out thieves. In Manson's troubled mind, it was the beginning of a revolution inspired by the values of LaVey and a "Sympathy for the Devil" counterculture.

Occult America

As these realities reached a weary American society in late 1969, the year Oprah turned fifteen, disillusionment set in. The dream had been betrayed. Hopes for a new world fashioned by cosmic unity, New Age consciousness, free love, mind-altering drugs, and a revolutionary social order collapsed. The deaths of counter-culture heroes marked the death of the age. In September 1970, legendary guitarist Jimi Hendrix died of a drug overdose. Within weeks, Janis Joplin, the raspy-voiced, blues-singing sweetheart of her generation, was dead. By the next July, Jim Morrison, lead singer of the Doors, had died mysteriously in France. As though intending to provide the perfect symbol of an era's end, Paul McCartney filed a suit for the dissolution of the Beatles on December 31, 1970.

By 1974, then, the year Oprah Winfrey turned twenty and was the first black news anchor at WTVF-TV in Nashville, the political and social vision of the 1960s had died, but the spiritual and religious vision lived on. Watergate, an economic depression, the antics of Richard Nixon, and the dishonorable end to the Vietnam War had killed the former. But the latter survived. Christianity had been challenged as the primary religious force behind American culture. The spirituality of the East had prevailed throughout much of American culture. There was a newfound ease with the occult. And all was put in the service of a uniquely American self-help/personal achievement/human potential vision. This eclectic force would continue to shape millions of lives in the unfolding decades.

As Mitch Horowitz has written in his essential *Occult America: The Secret History of How Mysticism Shaped Our Nation*,

> In the mid-'70s, the monthly *New Age Journal* had solidified the name for this new spiritual movement. There was no longer an easily discerned "occult" or "Eastern" or "yogic" subculture; rather, America experienced the rise of a vast metaphysical

culture that appeared ever-expanding, ever-accommodating, and perpetually ready to adapt to any foreign or homegrown influence that met the needs of those who yearned for self-discovery or personal fulfillment.[22]

What emerged from this era and at this time—the 1970s—was more than "a softheaded jumble of spiritual-therapeutic remedies or bromides," Horowitz insists.[23] Instead, there were five firm beliefs that were at the same time revolutionary in terms of the previous American experience and yet increasingly accepted in terms of American culture at the time. Spirituality in the United States was defined by:

1. A belief in the therapeutic value of spiritual or religious ideas.
2. A belief in a mind-body connection in health.
3. A belief that human consciousness is evolving to higher stages.
4. A belief that thoughts, in some greater or lesser measure, determine reality.
5. A belief that spiritual understanding is available without allegiance to a specific religion or doctrine.[24]

Those who knew the counsel of history, though, knew that what was touted as new in the 1970s was in fact decades, if not centuries, old. Already Americans had seen many of these ideas in the New Thought movements of the 1800s. A historian of the era explains that the novel theology of these new religions "taught that there was no material need or lack which could not be met by cultivating the proper frame of mind."[25] These beliefs became popular in the mid-1800s, much as they did in the wake of the 1960s, through an influx of Eastern ideas about reality and the rise of the occult following the American Civil War. Statements by leaders of these movements might easily have come from the gurus of the 1970s. Consider: Phineas Quimby, the guiding spirit behind the Christian Scientist theology, said, "All good things are found within."[26] The New Thought movement's Horatio Dresser wrote, "All development is from an inner center or seed . . . the only cure comes from self-help and the only freedom through self-knowledge."[27] The Unity movement's Emilie Cady argued that "the source of all knowledge" is "latent within ourselves."[28] And positive thinker Ralph Waldo Trine insisted, "Within yourself lies the cause of whatever enters your life."[29] This was what Oprah Winfrey had absorbed in Jesse Jackson's inspiring words, "If you can conceive it and believe it, you can achieve it," words he borrowed from the New Age/Human Potential movement of the 1970s. As she would later express this confidence, "The boundaries and limitations that prevent us from living our Utopia are those we have created in our own mind and have made a part of our own reality."[30]

By the 1980s, this insistence that all religion and all spiritual forces were to be focused on the enhancement of the individual had taken on messianic meaning. Marilyn Ferguson made this clear in her *The Aquarian Conspiracy: Personal and Social Transformation in the 1980s*, a book widely regarded as the Bible of the New Age movement. Ferguson insisted that the searching and experimenting of the 1960s counterculture had overthrown the dominant religions of the West—Christianity and Judaism in particular— and now a bold new moment in man's evolution could occur: "The goal of the New Age seeker would not be the heightened awareness or 'peak experiences' pursued by the counterculture, but rather a sense of unity with some cosmic power, be it the earth goddess Gaia, Hindu *Karma*, Sioux deity Wakan Tanka, or even Jesus Christ."[31] It would mean a new and transforming stage in the spirituality of humankind.

It is important to recall that the 1980s were a time when American society was focused on economic issues, particularly the methods of achievement, prosperity, and corporate success. It was the Reagan era, often recalled as a decade of greed, when the baby boomers in particular were amassing wealth and harnessing their awe-inspiring creativity to the American entrepreneurial dream. Instead of the pet rocks, streaking, and discos that had captured their attention in the 1970s, the boomers now focused on the potential of personal computers and how to reinvent corporate America.

In the innovative manner of that generation, New Age spirituality was wedded to corporate culture. Executives attended seminars on meditation as a pathway to greater creativity and marketing genius. Managers were told that their success in influencing others was determined by how they radiated healthy vibrations from an awakened core. Prosperity came, workers were told, to those who mastered the magnetism of their thoughts and who kept negative energy at bay. The message was that man makes himself and does so by cooperating with spiritual forces meant for his good.

The archetypical spiritual training experience of the era was the now notorious Erhard Seminars Training. Founded by Werner Erhard in 1971, these confrontational, tearful, boisterous seminars reached their peak of influence in the early 1980s. They were intended to be intense sixty-hour retreats in which participants were taught how to stop blaming and making excuses in order to take control of the power that defined their lives. Erhard, a handsome, intelligent, engaging personality, conducted the seminars himself and did so in a loud, finger-pointing, bombastic manner. His methods drew criticism but he got results. Corporate America in particular loved him because he spoke their language and did not encourage the kind of wispy, ethereal spirituality so common at the time. Erhard's seminars, or "est" as the movement became known, drew support from the nation's largest corporations.

Yet Erhard himself later admitted that his own inspiration was Zen Buddhism. This came as a surprise to followers who had long heard him rail against religion as a psychological crutch. As William Bartley recorded in his *Werner Erhard: The Transformation of a Man, the Founding of est*, Erhard believed that his techniques were rooted in the truths of Zen:

> Of all the disciplines that I studied, practiced, learned, Zen was the essential one. It was not so much an influence on me, rather it created space. It allowed those things that were there to be there. It gave some form to my experience. And it built up in me the critical mass from which was kindled the experience that produced est.[32]

This was simply consistent with the vision of the times: to remake America and all its institutions through the power of Eastern mysticism, spiritual therapies, and the ways of the occult.

This was all during the 1980s, when Oprah Winfrey moved to Chicago, achieved television talk show success, entered syndication, became wealthy, founded Harpo, Inc., and was nominated for an Academy Award for her performance in *The Color Purple*. Her career seemed a confirmation of her spirituality, the spirituality of the age; her confidence and unwavering sense of destiny before the press were a fruit of her divine empowering. She was nearly the perfect embodiment of her generation's religious vision, ambitions, values, flaws, and material success.

The Clintons: Exemplars of the Age

By the early 1990s, though, when Winfrey was turning forty and reconsidering the meaning of her career, she was joined as exemplar of her age by Bill and Hillary Clinton. This is to offer no political commentary nor to distract from their stellar achievements. Still, there is no question that the Clinton presidency marked both a generational and a spiritual shift, and it helps us in understanding the cultural forces that produced Oprah Winfrey to understand those who best captured the values and the vision of her times.

On the eve of Bill Clinton's inauguration as president in 1993, *Newsweek*'s esteemed political observer Howard Fineman declared, "America gets a New Age president this week."[33] He meant this less in the spiritual sense and more with an eye to the therapeutic culture of which Bill Clinton had become master. He "can speak in the rhythms and rhetoric of pop psychology and self-actualization," Fineman wrote.[34] Typically, Maureen Dowd and Frank Rich of the *New York Times* had said it less kindly. They compared Clinton to "a psychiatric social worker" who "sprinkles his interviews with the trendy language of codependency." He would be, they wrote, "the first post-therapy president ever to inhabit the White House."[35] Even the sympathetic *Mother Jones* complained. That publication's Richard Levine wrote that in an interview with Phil Donahue, Clinton had "struck a number of therapeutic chords . . . in exactly the right confessional tone" and "reached out to the rest of us in what I've come to think of . . . as Oprahland, a place populated by victims of one darn thing or another."[36] The more staid *Washington*

Post commented several months into Clinton's administration that the president was "the first chief executive whose values were shaped by the therapeutic movement that has come to dominate the way Americans think about themselves, not to mention the daytime talk shows."[37]

This leaning to themes of wounding, confession, recovery, and healing—what the press called Clinton playing "therapist in chief"—was a precursor of more aggressive spiritual forces soon to be welcomed in the Clinton White House. Yet this embrace of counterculture religion was certainly not betrayed in Bill Clinton's early years. He was raised a faithful Baptist, the only child of a single mother. He was a bright, eager, personable youth with a fiery devotion to his faith. In his teen years, friends called him Bible Bill because he regularly walked to church alone carrying a large family Bible. Later, when Clinton began wondering about how faith should inform public policy, he asked his pastor, the revered W. O. Vaught of Little Rock's Immanuel Baptist Church, what the Bible had to say about abortion. Vaught told him that a fetus is not a human being until it draws breath on its own. It was the church, then, that taught Bill Clinton his view of abortion. Clinton clung to his version of Jesus, wept at the singing of hymns, and, while he was president, attended church more regularly and publicly than most men who have held the office.

His wife was also raised in Christianity and yet with perhaps a stronger sense of social obligation. Hillary Clinton grew up in a Chicago home with a father who was often compared to General George Patton and a loving mother who was the nurturing center of the family's spiritual life. "We walked with God, ate, studied and argued with God. Each night we knelt by our beds to pray," she later recalled.[38] Yet it was the social vision of her Methodist church that most inspired her. John Wesley, the founder of the Methodist movement, had famously proclaimed, "Do all the good you can, by all the means you can, in all the ways you can, at all the times you can, to all the people you can, as long as you ever can." These values were urged upon her by her Methodist youth pastor, Don Jones, a profound influence upon her life. He was a young, energetic Christian leader with a faith-based vision for social change befitting the times. He took Hillary and her youth group into poor neighborhoods, led them in discussions of Bob Dylan lyrics, and even drove them to Chicago's Orchestra Hall in April 1962 to listen to a young black preacher named Martin Luther King Jr.

When Hillary entered her teen years and showed promise of a keen mind and a keener social conscience, Jones urged her to read Tillich, Niebuhr, Kierkegaard, and Bonhoeffer. He assigned J. D. Salinger's *Catcher in the Rye* and the Methodist devotional, Beat author Jack Kerouac and the Bible. Hillary carried the social gospel of this brand of Methodism with her through Wellesley, Yale Law School, and into marriage to the Baptist Bill Clinton.

The Clinton administration was the merging of Bill Clinton's brilliance and people skills with Hillary Clinton's social vision and spiritual hunger. Both had deeply absorbed the values of the 1960s counterculture. Both clung to their Christian faith but did not think this kept them from experimentation. Both understood from the eclectic spirituality of recent decades that invisible forces were available to help the willing rise above their flaws, heal from their wounds, and live the empowered life of their dreams.

This bled into their politics. Like the religious counterculture that had shaped them, they were mystical, messianic, and aware that they were bringing a millennium to a close. In an April 6,

1993, speech at the University of Texas, Hillary called for a greater sense of community in America by "redefining what it means to be a human being in the 20th century, moving into the new millennium." This would come, she assured, through this new kind of human being engaging in a new kind of politics: "We need a politics of meaning."[39] Phrases like this and the near-frantic pace of a White House determined to make massive changes quickly moved *Time* magazine to compare the last week of Clinton's first one hundred days to "a special edition of the Oprah Winfrey show titled 'Presidents Who Try to Do Too Much and the People Who Love Them.'"[40]

Phrases like "a politics of meaning" wrung peals of laughter from the press but were not original. That particular phrase was from a book by Michael Lerner, a psychotherapist, activist, and founder/editor of the liberal Jewish journal *Tikkun*. For Lerner, a politics of meaning was a "religious perspective on politics," one that responds to "the hunger that most Americans have for a society that supports rather than undermines loving relationships, ethical life and communities." He complained of "a crisis in values, the decline of family life, the instability in relationships and friendships" and a "deep sense of alienation and loneliness that leads people to hunger for communities of meaning that will transcend me-firstism."[41]

Though there were more than a few who questioned whether these were legitimate issues for government to address, Hillary Clinton took the words as her mandate. She invited Lerner to the White House and told him he had helped her "clarify my own thinking." "It's amazing how we seem to be on the same wavelength," she said, obviously delighted. "Am I your mouthpiece or what?"[42]

This was the faith-based politics of a new generation, yet it would lead to much more. The next year, in 1994, just as Oprah

Winfrey was trying to rise above her "slime queen" reputation, the Clintons were attempting to root their politics in the motivational spirituality that had nearly become the American religion. In the same month that Marianne Williamson appeared on *The Oprah Winfrey Show* to help its host shift focus from "victims to victors," Williamson also answered an invitation to meet with the Clintons at Camp David. Self-help gurus like Stephen Covey, author of *Seven Habits of Highly Effective People*, and "peak performance coach" Anthony Robbins were there as well. Though the discussions were kept confidential, the *New York Times* suggested that the Clintons were embracing a long-standing American faith:

> From the 1800's treatise "Self-Help" by Samuel Smiles to "The Power of Positive Thinking" by the Reverend Norman Vincent Peale, politicians, business executives, and millions of other Americans have gravitated to the message and messenger who tells them that the proper state of mind can produce physical, material and spiritual treasure.[43]

In fact, the Clintons were attempting to build their legacy on three spiritual values of the counterculture: that what was true of the human soul was true of other human pursuits like politics; that all human crises are essentially matters of thought, of attitude, of spiritual alignment, and of wholeness; and, finally, that enlightened masters could lead the way.

It was this matrix of beliefs that led Hillary Clinton into the most troubling and humiliating season of her White House years. She had long felt a kinship with Eleanor Roosevelt. Both were gifted women. Both yearned to lead social change. Both were betrayed by their husbands. Hillary often mentioned Mrs. Roosevelt in her speeches and even described imaginary conversations that left her feeling strong and inspired. After one of these speeches, New Age author Jean Houston, a frequent White House guest, suggested that she should "search further and deeper" into her connection with FDR's departed wife. According to Bob Woodward's account in *The Choice*, Houston arranged a session in the White House solarium in which she encouraged Hillary to conjure an image of Eleanor Roosevelt and then open her heart.

> Hillary addressed Eleanor, focusing on her predecessor's fierceness and determination, her advocacy on behalf of people in need. Hillary continued to address Eleanor, discussing the obstacles, the criticism, the loneliness the former First Lady felt. Her identification with Mrs. Roosevelt was intense and personal. They were members of an exclusive club of women who could comprehend the complexity, the ambiguity of their position. It's hard, Hillary said. Why was there such a need in people to put other people down? . . . I was misunderstood, Hillary replied, her eyes still shut, speaking as Mrs. Roosevelt. You have to do what you think is right, she continued. It was crucial to set a course and hold it.[44]

Once contact with Mrs. Roosevelt was made, Houston urged Clinton to conduct conversations with Mahatma Gandhi and even Jesus Christ, according to Woodward. Realizing that attempting conversations through channeling with the Son of God was going too far, the First Lady brought the session to an end.

When Woodward's book reached the public, Clinton became the focus of widespread outrage and disgust. Trying to clean up the mess, she explained, "The bottom line is, I have no spiritual advisors or any other alternatives to my deeply held Methodist faith and traditions on which I have relied since childhood."[45] It could not have been true, but it was a statement of the kind of woman Hillary hoped to be, of the way she envisioned herself despite the influences she had welcomed into her life and into the White House. To her credit, she was self-deprecating in the wake of this embarrassment. At a White House gathering, she told the audience, "I have just had an imaginary talk with First Lady Roosevelt, and she thinks this is a terrific idea."[46]

However inadvertently, the Clintons had come to symbolize the spirituality of their generation. They were Christian by background. They were experimental and open to the intriguing ideas of non-Christian religions through the influence of their searching, eclectic generation. They were willing to involve themselves in the occult to acquire spiritual power and insight their Christianity did not seem to offer them. Always, they understood religion as a source of betterment, of healing, of therapy for the soul.

By the end of the Clinton administration and with the advent of the new millennium, it became obvious that a spiritual revolution had occurred in American society. The Christian consensus was fractured and in question. The spirituality of the East was the *de facto* faith of millions of Americans, whatever their formal religious affiliation. The longstanding taboos against occult practices were gone. The New Age had dawned and then become subject to a uniquely American reinvention. As Horowitz concludes in his *Occult America*,

> Whether the occult changed America, or the other way around, this much is clear: The encounter between America and

occultism resulted in a vast reworking of arcane practices and beliefs from the Old World and the creation of a new spiritual culture. This new culture extolled religious egalitarianism and responded, perhaps more than any other movement in history, to the inner needs and search of the individual. At work and at church, on television and in bookstores, there was no avoiding it: occult America had prevailed.[47]

The Age and Oprah

By the end of the first decade of the third millennium, then, as Oprah Winfrey was bringing her successful talk show to an end and preparing to launch the OWN network on cable television, she could look back upon her spiritual life and see that it had conformed to the mystical flow of her generation. She had turned from the Christianity of her youth when much of her generation had. She had entered that other spiritual world through the portal of self-help, via the same hunger for uplift and self-improvement, for healing and recovery, that had moved millions like her in the same direction. She had blended Christian forms, Eastern mysticism, and sanitized occult practices into an intensely personal, customized religion. This was simply the way of her age.

She wove practices and beliefs once thought disparate into a religion that was, quite literally, the "Religion of Oprah." She encouraged others to do the same. She found no tension in blending a Hindu version of reality with ancestor worship with chanting Hindu mantras with the *The Secret*'s Law of Attraction with yoga with an animistic honoring of the spirits in nature with a belief in self-divinity with channeling with astrology with *karma* with the Bible with the certainty that right spirituality is rewarded with wealth and well-being with prayer to whatever force is god with the confidence we create the evil we experience with the unswerving assurance that a supernatural destiny rules human affairs. This was the buffet of beliefs she had chosen for herself and that she urged others to embrace as well. In retrospect, she had accumulated her beliefs as a fellow traveler with her generation, picking up doctrines and practices like so many souvenirs from the foreign travels of her times.

Yet, always and without doubt, she understood each doctrine and act of faith in terms of the self, in terms of creating blessing and wholeness and enchantment for the individual. This is a strange conclusion, given that each of the religions the New Age built upon stresses the loss of self as the path to fulfillment, but it is nevertheless the heart of the new American faith drawn from the New Age revolution that occurred during the decades of Oprah Winfrey's life.

This understanding of Oprah Winfrey as a product of her times changes how we see her. We are tender at the thought that she is one with her tribe, that she is a wounded, hopeful seeker like so many of her generation. In this we feel she is part of us. We are also inspired that she, like so many of her age, refused the atheism and the anti-supernatural, mechanistic view of the world she might have chosen and went in search of a supernatural life. Again, we feel kinship with her in this. Yet we should also feel caution, for given how much she has been influenced by her times, it is possible she has accumulated her beliefs uncritically, unwisely, unintentionally—as though these beliefs were so many barnacles attaching to a ship at sea. This is what makes us reconsider the faith she urges upon us and what makes us suspect that it is her fame that actually draws people to her brand of faith and not the virtues of that faith itself.

O

I conclude this chapter with sadness, for I see that what the baby boomer generation sought—what the beatniks praised and the hippies dropped out to find—was what the Christian church ought to have been. The young in the 1950s and 1960s sought some way to escape the materialistic machine, to connect to a life beyond the seen, to enjoy meaningful community and to band together to do good in the world. It was not too much to ask. This was what Jesus had long ago urged his followers to become.

Unfortunately, the American church was too much about externals to answer. It was offended at the long hair and concerned about the lack of bathing. It could not endure the beards and the beads and the odd ways of speaking. And so it lost a generation.

True, some of that searching tribe found their way back to the church, though it would be years later and at great cost. What might have happened, though, had Christians lovingly said to the Beats, "We understand. We even agree. The materialism and the greed are killing us all. Come with us and learn about another world. Come find rest for your searching souls."

Because they did not, that hungry young generation went in search of answers of their own. They discarded the time-tested and the ways of the elders and they began to create their own smorgasbord of faith. They took a little bit of Hinduism and a smattering of Buddhism and more than a touch of the way of the Tao and they blended it with Western self-centeredness and American entitlement and put it all in the service of their newfound hunger to achieve. They heard the whisper of the universe and always it was assuring them that they were chosen, they were graced, and there was nothing required of them in return. So they lived by the light of yoga and what their astrological sign revealed, and they heard the gurus of their generation telling them that all they dreamed was within reach. They had evolved, had moved beyond the faiths of the past, had become transformed beings their ancestors would have regarded as gods. Daily they made themselves; daily they fashioned their unswerving fate.

But something was wrong. A New Age wasn't dawning. A new epoch hadn't occurred. And as to spiritual power, there did not seem to be enough in all their blend of religions to even keep a marriage together or make the kids return love or even guarantee an evening of peace. And so an entire enchanted generation changed spouses, changed jobs, changed religions, changed homes, and changed social visions more than any other people on earth. Still they were searching but had not come to the end. Finally, they lived ravaged by recessions, disillusioned with their times, and staring at their cell phones in hope of community and belonging.

There had been a promise made to a generation, but it had not been fulfilled. Still, though, the Oprah Winfreys reworked old claims in new mediums and offered repackaged what had once been the spiritual hope of a generation. It felt to some like mockery, but to others it was the Oracle of The Matrix *or the God of* The Shack *calling us all to truth. And so they listened and did what they were urged and tried to awaken the fire within. And some grieved the heritage discarded and wondered if ancient paths might be reclaimed again.*

The universe felt colder, life lonelier and with less purpose. Gone was faith in a personal God, one who had created all things to reveal himself and who offered himself as a Father. Instead, there was "ultimate consciousness" and "oneness with the energy of the earth" and "man, erect, going alone to possess the universe," in Emerson's telling phrase. Impersonal. Distant. Solitary in experience. Like waiting on the phone with a pressing problem only to find a computerized voice answering back.

Always there was the promise of divinity. But deep inside, in the chapel of the soul where a man hears truth in the still of the night, we knew this was a lie. We knew we were not gods. We knew that daily we did not create our own reality. We knew we were creatures and not creators in any sense that governed the movement of planets or the fate of mankind. We clung to illusion because, having discarded God, we had nowhere to turn but to the hope that we might eventually prove to be gods ourselves. Secretly we doubted.

Still, we listened to Oprah Winfrey because she was fun and charming and because she seemed to believe so deeply. We wanted to be convinced. Always there was the lingering sense that she was but a troubled soul grasping at fantasy, like a lonely child lost in imagining that she is a princess. We wanted her to take us with her if she could. We knew there had to be something more and were willing for her to be our guide.

Now, at the end of our weary generation's journey, we begin to sense we have heard all this before. There is nothing new here, just new excitement about old ideas. We feel our age and the distance from when we once believed. And we wonder if we've been tricked, if what we sought was ours already, before we ever ventured forth.

4

Oprah's Spiritual Family

You done went and found you a guru,
In an effort to find you a new you.

—TOWER OF POWER, "WHAT IS HIP?"

In her encyclopedic biography of Oprah Winfrey, Kitty Kelley suggests that Oprah has created a new family to replace the embarrassing and troubled one life first handed her. In place of the demanding and lazy Vernita, for example, Oprah has chosen the poetess Maya Angelou. "I think that Maya Angelou was my mother in another life," Oprah has said. "I love her deeply. Something is there between us. So fallopian tubes and ovaries do not a mother make."[1] It is telling that Oprah keeps Angelou's monthly itinerary in her purse so she can reach her alternate mother any time of the day or night.

In the role of beloved uncle, Oprah has chosen Quincy Jones. "I truly learned how to love as a result of this man," Oprah insists. "It's not the first time I came to terms with, 'Yes, I love this man, and it has nothing to do with wanting to go to bed with him or be romantically involved. I unconditionally love him and . . . I would slap the living shit out of somebody who said anything bad about Quincy.'"[2]

Rather than the drug-addicted and betraying Patricia Lee, Oprah has chosen Gayle King, her constant companion, to be the sister of her dreams. Rather than Jeffrey Lee, the gay brother who died of AIDS, Oprah chose John Travolta, Kelley insists. And as a New Age father to replace the severe and Bible-spouting Vernon, Oprah chose famed actor Sidney Poitier: "I call Sidney every Sunday and . . . we talk about life, we talk about reincarnation, we talk about the cosmos, we talk about the stars, we talk about the planets, we talk about energy. We talk about everything."[3]

This is the nature of Oprah Winfrey. She is a social being who lives life in relational terms, whose soul ever reaches for vital connection. She draws her inspiration and creativity from others. She siphons from them, drinks from their lives so as to strengthen her own. She is not unlike a race car that drafts from faster cars on the racetrack, using them to propel her forward faster than she could ever achieve on her own. She is the classic extrovert, whose inner battery charges through social contact. This is what makes her an intriguing interviewer: she is genuinely eager to feed from the lives of others while making her audience want to do so too.

Yet there is danger in this. It is possible for someone of this personality to find there is nothing inside them except what has come from others. It is possible there is no authentic self, nothing original, nothing that has not been borrowed. In Oprah's case, this is very much a concern. Her most significant experiences, her most defining turning points, and her most life-changing realizations have all been generated through contact with other people. One wonders if Oprah in a room alone finds an authentic Oprah or merely the lingering reflections of other people, as though her soul is made of a thousand mirrors, each beaming the images of those she has known but nothing of Oprah herself.

This particularly seems to be the case with Oprah's spirituality. Though she has always been a spiritually sensitive being, she has seldom articulated original insights of her own. Time and again on her talk show, she thrills to the supernatural experiences and revelations of others and then just as quickly claims them as hers. Whatever the topic, she often jumps up and says, "This is what I meant all along! It is who I really am! This is what my show has been about for twenty-five years! This is what I've been trying to say!" Yet she has not said it. Instead, it has usually taken a series of guests or a successful book or a dramatic video to help her crystallize the principles that she says give meaning to her life.

This means that in order to understand who Oprah is spiritually, it is important to peer into the ideas of those she has gathered around her. It is not going too far to say that spiritually she is the composite of all that her gurus have taught her and that to know her one must first know them. She is not unique in this, though. She is actually much like those of her generation—ever piecing together a spirituality taken from other lives, ever making the stories of others a part of their own. It is the way of her age, and though it may well produce an inauthentic, hybrid, sometimes secondhand spirituality, this process does make it possible to peel back the layers and understand what has made her and those of her times the spiritual beings they are.

Marianne Williamson

Certainly no one in Oprah's spiritual family has been as influential as Marianne Williamson. She was a friend long before Oprah's public turning to spirituality. She was there at the decisive fortieth birthday celebration and it was to her that Oprah turned when she decided to refocus her show upon loftier themes. Oprah has long leaned to Williamson's insights and has told her audiences repeatedly that she looks to Williamson as a trusted spiritual guide.

Williamson is also influential among Oprah's band of New Age teachers because she has achieved a level of fame and visibility that few have. She was a spiritual advisor to First Lady Hillary Clinton and was there at the famous Camp David gathering of New Age leaders in 1994. She conducted a wedding ceremony for Elizabeth Taylor and has become a "guru to the stars"—respected by figures like Anthony Perkins, Lesley Ann Warren, Tommy Tune, Cher, Roy Scheider, David Geffen, Barbra Streisand, Dawn Steel, Rosanna Arquette, and Raquel Welch. Her books have sold in the millions of copies and she has founded teaching and healing centers around the United States. In December 2006, *Newsweek* magazine named her one of the fifty most influential baby boomers.

It is not hard to understand why Oprah might reach to her. Williamson is cool, hard charging, and good-looking. Her trim physique does justice to her designer clothes. She has a confident, engaging manner reflected most in her attractive but commanding face. Her voice is rich and full, with a slight rasp that endears. In other words, she is the perfect teacher/companion for a largely female television audience today.

Williamson was born in 1952 into a middle-class Jewish family in which, as a friend later told *Vanity Fair*, she was "always trying to get her family's approval. She had a remote father and a disapproving mother . . . a double whammy."[4] As unengaged as her father is remembered as being, he was nevertheless the kind of man who took thirteen-year-old Marianne to Vietnam in 1965 so she could learn to be suspicious of "military-industrial complex" propaganda. This fed a questioning, skeptical nature in Williamson that came into its own during a high school philosophy class in which she determined "God was a crutch" she didn't need.[5]

She attended Pomona College in Claremont, California, but dropped out after two years to join a commune. Dissatisfied with life as she knew it, she was pushing the boundaries to see what might answer her hunger for more. "Whatever sounded outrageous, I wanted to do. And usually, I did."[6] Her search took her from work as a cocktail waitress to owning a New Age bookstore to attempting a career as a cabaret singer. She also married, briefly, and soon after found herself a troubled single mother.

I went from relationship to relationship, job to job, city to city, looking for some sense of identity or purpose, some feeling that my life had finally kicked in. . . . I went into therapy several times, but it rarely made an impact. I sank deeper and deeper into my own neurotic patterns, seeking relief in food, drugs, people, or whatever else I could find to distract me from myself. There was some huge rock of self-loathing sitting in the middle of my stomach during those years, and it got worse with every phase I went through. As my pain deepened, so did my interest in philosophy: Eastern, Western, academic, esoteric, Kierkegaard, the I Ching, existentialism, radical death-of-God theology, Buddhism, and more. I always sensed there was some mysterious cosmic order to things, but I could never figure out how it applied to my own life. . . . By my mid-twenties, I was a total mess.[7]

In 1977, hurting and desperate, she noticed on a friend's coffee table a study guide called *A Course in Miracles*. Though she did not know it, she had stumbled upon one of the great religious oddities of the age. *A Course in Miracles* had been produced years before by Helen Schucman, an atheist psychology professor at Columbia University. According to Schucman, from 1965 to 1972, the entire *A Course in Miracles* manuscript was "scribed" under the direction of an inner voice Schucman knew to be Jesus Christ. The dictation began with the words, "This is a course in miracles, please take notes." The result would be 1,200 pages of spiritual-psychological revelation that would range over a 622-page textbook, a 478-page workbook, and a short explanatory manual, all presented as, in Marianne Williamson's words, a "correction to Christianity— beginning from a premise of original innocence rather than one of original sin . . . and focusing on the metaphysics of identity and ego formation."[8]

Strangely, *A Course in Miracles* countered nearly every accepted Christian doctrine as well as the picture of Jesus Christ presented in the New Testament. Most cardinal Christian beliefs were treated as inventions of the ill intentioned throughout church history. Original sin certainly takes a beating, as do the incarnation, the divinity of Jesus Christ, and the inspiration and authority of the Bible. What remains in the course after this doctrinal deck clearing is a simple belief: human beings must replace fear with love. This has been revelation enough to inspire sales of nearly two million copies of *A Course in Miracles* since 1976.

It was also enough to inspire Marianne Williamson. She read

the study guide "like a menu," her mother later reported, and found the message her soul had been waiting for. "So I went through this grandiose, dramatic moment where I invited God into my life. When it came to spiritual surrender, I didn't get serious until I was down on my knees completely," she writes. "The hysterical woman inside me was in a maniacal rage, and the innocent child was pinned to the wall. I fell apart. I crossed the line between in-pain-but-still-able-to-function-normally, and the realm of the total basket case. I had what is commonly called a nervous breakdown."[9]

By 1983, Williamson had healed and mastered the course so well that she moved to Los Angeles and took a job with the Philosophical Research Society. This is when she began to ascend. "Before long, she had begun to speak on *A Course in Miracles*. At first fifteen people would turn out, then forty: soon it was a hundred. She began renting spaces in churches, and her audience grew . . . [then in 1987] she started speaking in New York once a month as well."[10] Realizing the appeal of what she was teaching and eager for a larger audience, Williamson wrote *A Return to Love: Reflections on the Principles of A Course in Miracles* in 1992, essentially the CliffsNotes for *A Course in Miracles*.

The book was already popular when the Oprah Effect kicked in. On February 4, 1992, Winfrey invited Williamson to join her for a show entitled "My Life Is Driving Me Crazy." Oprah told her viewers that she had "never been as moved by a book" and that she had bought a thousand copies to give to her friends. It was the Oprah-sized plug of an author's dreams. The first print run of seventy thousand copies sold out the same day. *A Return to Love* then soared to the top of the *New York Times* best-seller list, where it remained for thirty-five weeks. It became the fifth best-selling nonfiction book of 1992. Williamson's life was never the same.

All of this arose on what appeared to be a simple idea: Release fear. Embrace love. As Williamson explained,

> When we were born, we were programmed perfectly. We had a natural tendency to focus on love. Our imaginations were creative and flourishing, and we knew how to use them. We were connected to a world much richer than the one we connect to now, a world full of enchantment and sense of the miraculous. So what happened? Why is it that we reached a certain age, looked around, and the enchantment was gone? Because we were taught to focus elsewhere. We were taught to focus unnaturally. We were taught a very bad philosophy, a way of looking at the world that contradicts who we are. We were taught to think thoughts like competition, struggle, sickness, finite resources, limitation, guilt, bad, death, scarcity, and loss. We began to think these things, and so we began to know them. . . . The thinking of the world, which is not based on love, began pounding in our ears the moment we hit shore.[11]

What that "thinking world" impresses on the soul, Williamson claims, is fear: "Love is what we were born with. Fear is what we have learned here. The spiritual journey is the relinquishment— or unlearning—of fear and the acceptance of love back into our hearts."[12] The goal, then, is to transform the "earth plane" by reconnecting with the "intuitive knowledge of our hearts" and choosing the "inner peace" that is "still buried within our minds."[13]

This simplistic formula is the bait of Williamson's teaching, but behind this pleasant face is a matrix of Eastern mysticism, redefined Christianity, and mind science, which comes as a surprise to those who follow Williamson for her emphasis on love alone. For example, Williamson does not simply believe in love; she believes that love is all that is real. This love, which is actually a form of god, is all that truly exists: "There's only one of us here . . . like spokes on a wheel, all radiating out from the same center . . . [we're] 'sunbeams' thinking we're separate from the sun, or waves thinking we're separate from the ocean . . . [when, instead, we are] one indivisible divine mind . . . holy beings, individual cells in the body of Christ."[14]

Indeed, Williamson believes that much of our present reality is an illusion. If we could see clearly, we would understand that all things are one and that there is no separateness. "We only think we're separated because we have bodies," she teaches, "when in truth, we have bodies because we think we are separated."[15] Our minds project the illusions we take as reality. This is why we experience death, lack, pain, and limitation, for example.

What is required is the *holy spirit*, but by this term Williamson does not mean the biblical Holy Spirit. She means, instead, the Hindu Third Eye or *urna*, what amounts to a "higher self." With the higher vision and enlightenment that this higher self allows, we can accept Christ. But, again, by *accepting Christ* Williamson does not mean the traditional, biblical act of repenting and becoming a follower of Jesus Christ. Instead she means a shift in perception, the miracle that is the goal of her spirituality. Accepting Christ, then, is an awakening from "the dream that we are finite, isolated creatures . . . [and acceptance of] the beauty within me as who I really am."[16] The word *salvation* is also reworked. It is made to mean the perception that you are one with love. *Crucifixion* is transformed, as well. It now represents "the energy pattern of fear. It represents the limited, negative thinking of the ego, and how it always seeks to limit, contradict or invalidate love."[17] *Resurrection*, of course, means embracing the energy pattern of love. Indeed,

Williamson asserts, "The message of the resurrection is that the crucifixion never occurred, except in our minds."[18] She takes this same approach to the concepts of *heaven* and *hell*: "Love in your mind produces love in your life. This is the meaning of Heaven. Fear in your mind produces fear in your life. This is the meaning of Hell."[19]

This reworking of Christian terms extends even to the definition of God and reveals how unclear and contradictory Williamson's teaching can sometimes be. She has said that God is an "it," "a force" that loves, cares, and protects.[20] Then she has said that God is "an impersonal love for all life."[21] She has also said that God is a "he" who "is the energy; the thought of unconditional love."[22] Yet Williamson is also sure that all human beings are "part of God" and that they are creations and extensions in the "mind" of an impersonal force or energy: "We were created in His image, or mind, which means that we are extensions of His love, or Sons of God."[23]

If Williamson is uncertain about God, she is absolutely certain about sin. One of the central tenets of *A Course in Miracles* and thus of *A Return to Love* is that there is no sin. The course celebrates that "sin is the grand illusion" and that human beings should "joyously [release] one another from the belief in sin." Guilt is then dissolved: "See no one, then, as guilty . . . [within all men] there is perfect innocence." As Williamson explains, "If a person behaves unlovingly . . . their behavior was derived from fear and doesn't actually exist. They're hallucinating. You forgive them, then, because there's nothing to forgive."[24] Oddly, though Williamson denies the reality of sin and the need for forgiveness—indeed, denies that wrongful deeds are more than hallucinations—she has often urged the United States to make amends for the Vietnam War and for mistreatment of blacks.

This rejection of sin leads Williamson into some interesting ethical territory. Asked "when do you know when you're supposed to have sex with a person?" Williamson answers, "When you hear a voice in your head say, 'Disrobe.'" She is also convinced that marriages that end in divorce may be more successful than marriages that last for decades but that are actually "two emotional invalids joined at the hip."[25]

One of the most unique elements of Williamson's already unique spirituality is healing. Remember that she believes the mind creates all ills. Accordingly, "disease is loveless thinking materialized." Clearly, a sick person is only sick because he believes he is. It is "okay to take medicine," though, "because the Holy Spirit enters our lives at our present level of consciousness." The ultimate solution is to strive to be like Jesus, who healed through the power of the mind. Leprosy, for example, departed at his presence because "Jesus did not believe in leprosy. Since all minds are connected, in his presence the leper no longer believed in it either. And so the leper was healed."[26]

This belief in sickness as simply a result of faulty thinking and healing as a return to right thinking gives Williamson the confidence to give advice to AIDS patients. She suggests that they should employ "enlightened visualizations" to bring about healing. "Imagine the AIDS virus as Darth Vader, and then unzip his suit and allow an angel to emerge." She also suggests that people with AIDS write letters to their disease, expressing their feelings about the illness and seeing sickness as "our own love that needs to be reclaimed." She insists that this is "a more positive approach to healing than is seeing the sickness as something hideous we must get rid of."[27]

She is also not shy in applying the power of positive thinking to economic problems. When she appeared on *The Oprah Winfrey Show* in 1994 and Oprah introduced her as "one of the wisest people I know," Williamson arrived fully armed with the phrases that her audiences had come to expect: "internal power is greater than the power of the external"; "a little bit of violence in the mind . . . is contributing to the violence of our times"; through prayer "the mind is lifted up to a new kind of thinking."[28] Yet some in the audience that day may not have been prepared for the advice she gave a troubled welfare mother. The problem lay in the mother's thinking, Williamson insisted. The woman was seeing welfare as "more powerful than God." Rather than thinking "I am the victim," the woman needed to think, "I have within me the power to break through these constrictions."[29] This shift in thinking would bring the salvation the woman needed, for her circumstances were merely inventions of her mind to begin with.

In the years following that 1994 program, Williamson wrote other books applying her beliefs to the challenges of losing weight, the sufferings of women, and even the crises of the United States government. She also penned a beautifully illustrated book for children, *Emma and Mommy Talk to God*, which was inspired by Williamson's talks with her daughter, Emma. "Who is God?" Emma asks at one point in the book. "God is all the love in the world. He is in you and in me and in everybody everywhere," the mother answers.[30]

We should summarize, then, what Marianne Williamson believes. She believes that the only thing that actually exists is love. All else—our physical separation from one another, evil in the world, even sickness—is an illusion of the mind. This love is as much god as anything is and we are all part of that love, extensions of it in the same way that sunbeams extend from the sun or that waves are part of the sea. There is no sin. There is no need for forgiveness. In fact, when we even make moral judgments we are denying love. We should have sex whenever we hear a voice in our heads say "disrobe." The sufferings of life are all illusions and those who endure poverty, for example, do so because they think they are victims, because they think poverty is more powerful than God, and because they have not learned to change their thinking in order to change their reality. The sick should see their disease as loveless ideas materialized; in other words, they are sick because of their unloving thoughts.

I must step in here in my other voice and point out in Marianne Williamson's teaching what we will encounter time and again in the ideas of the teachers we are about to consider. To wait would be to get lost in an avalanche of detail and to lose vital perspective.

The first matter I have to raise is the matter of evidence, of facts, of any real-world source for what Marianne Williamson believes. It seems to me that once our culture shifted eastward and embraced a mysticism apart from Judeo-Christianity and apart from the scientific influences of the West, that we ceased asking epistemological questions—epistemology being that big-boy word for the study of how we know what we know. Gurus merely proclaimed entire systems of thought on the strength of their personalities, their appearance, and the finely woven tapestries of their mystical visions. No one seemed interested in objective evidence once enlightenment became the goal rather than historical truth.

Were it not so, we might well ask where Marianne Williamson got her beliefs. Her critics only hope she says from Helen Schucman and A Course in Miracles. *The insistence that a Jewish atheist received a twelve-hundred-page verbal download from Jesus Christ—completely reversing everything the historical Jesus Christ taught—is too easy a target. So we return to the question: What is the basis for the teaching with which Marianne Williamson leads millions, rebukes welfare recipients, and urges AIDS patients to see their disease as a loving angel?*

I'll give you an example of what I am asking for. I am a Christian who believes that my faith is based in verified events of history. I believe that Jesus Christ was crucified, rose from the dead, and is alive today. Sounds weird, doesn't it? I am quick to say that I cannot prove this to be a scientific certainty. And yet I have good historical basis for what I believe. That Jesus Christ existed is without question. Even Roman historians who dismissed him confirm this—Tacitus, Suetonius, Lucian of Samosata, Flavius Josephus, Pliny the Younger. As to his resurrection from the dead, there were witnesses. Some of these wrote memoirs, which are found in the New Testament of the Bible. That Bible enjoys massive historical confirmation. Indeed, the Bible was used as a textbook of ancient history until relatively recently. Entire civilizations described in the pages of Scripture were doubted by scholars until, in time, they were discovered exactly as Scripture portrayed them. The ancient city of Nineveh is a storied example of this. And as for documentary evidence, no one would be thought educated in the Western world who had not read Homer, Plato, or Aristotle, and yet the documentary evidence for the New Testament vastly surpasses the documentary supports for these pillars of the Western canon. [31]

You see, then, that what I believe has at least some broad factual support. I cannot prove that Jesus rose from the dead. I can prove, though, that even Christianity's critics stated that belief in Jesus' resurrection was widespread in the first century. I can confirm that entire civilizations were changed by this belief. I can provide a body of doctrine that has survived largely unchanged for two millennia. I can also prove practical benefits, cultural improvements, blessings to mankind—indeed, entire civilizations—that have come from what I believe.

Now, let us hold this up against support for what Ms. Williamson believes, and urges upon millions. She believes that only love exists, all else is illusion, and that new thoughts are the key to changing what passes for reality. Is there any historical basis for what she teaches? Is there any documentation other than a questionably "channeled" manuscript? Is there a legacy from people of old who believed as she does? Is there any evidence that people have benefitted in large numbers and in measurable ways from what she has taught?

Sadly, I draw the conclusion that New Age teachers need only devise an appealing package of ideas and find the right endorsements in order to be taken seriously in our day. But how do we know that what they tell us is true? How can we even be sure that they have experienced for themselves what they urge upon us? What is the basis for their beliefs, particularly the beliefs they encourage the sick and the dying to accept?

There is none, and this will be increasingly obvious as we examine the views of the spiritual teachers Oprah Winfrey has gathered around her.

A second issue I must raise briefly is the issue of language. New Age teachers have a tendency to use language that barely makes sense, and yet millions sit nodding their heads know-ingly in response as though pearls of wisdom have fallen from heaven. What does it mean when Marianne Williamson tells us "we forgive because there is nothing to forgive"? What does it mean that God is the energy or thought of unconditional love? And what does it mean that if a person behaves unlovingly, that person's behavior derives from fear and doesn't actually exist? What? How did I know they behaved a certain way if their behavior doesn't actually exist?

Keep your eye on this. Watch how nonsensical is the language of some of Oprah's gurus, particularly Eckhart Tolle, whom we'll consider next.

Two more matters. It is interesting that Eastern and New Age theology doesn't like us very much. The East wants us to erase ourselves, to blank ourselves, to let go of what makes us really us and become one with the impersonal force behind the universe. We are illusions. We are projections of misguided minds. Or we are inauthentic because we perceive ourselves as physically separate from each other. Actually, there is only one of us here, we are told: all us who think we are individuals need to dissolve in the new reality.

I'm intrigued by this. In my faith, a God sees us as we are and loves us. In Eastern and New Age theology, a nondivine, impersonal force doesn't see us at all and wants us erased to become one with it. Hmmm.

Finally, there is this, and I say it to all New Age, hybrid, just-thought-up-yesterday, pulled-out-of-your-ear religions now on the scene: go get your own language! It really doesn't help the case of a Marianne Williamson or any other enlightened one when their entire scheme is a reworking of Christian terms. It seems inauthentic. If you really believe you have found the mystical keys to the universe, the true God of the True Order, it seems that there ought to at least be some new language to go along with it. Surely you can be that creative!

But I understand the underlying meaning. I understand that by reworking our language you are saying that we never got it right—that our version of Christianity was never true. Consider the words of one scholar, though, before we continue finding these same patterns in the teachings of still other enlightened masters of the New Age.

Clearly, if A Course in Miracles *is right, Jesus is the most misunderstood figure in history. History for two thousand years has had it wrong, the church never even got off on the right foot. And the long promised Paraclete, the Holy Spirit, which was to guide the church through history, has not even managed to get through to Christians about their misguided understandings. They have uniformly, all of them, believed a counterfeit gospel for two thousand years. And Christ's messianic act of sacrifice on the cross, that central historical fact of Christianity, was wasted blood and pain. . . . For there was no real sin to atone for, and our separation from God was just an illusion all along—that is, if you believe Helen Schucman.[32]*

Eckhart Tolle

Aside from Marianne Williamson, the figure who has had the greatest spiritual impact upon Oprah Winfrey is Eckhart Tolle. Winfrey first heard of Tolle's work from actress Meg Ryan, who had in turn been introduced to the author by her yoga instructor. Now, Winfrey keeps Tolle's books with her at all times. She quotes his words to her staff. She has called Tolle's *A New Earth* one of the most important books of our generation, "a wake-up call for the entire planet."[33] She considers her ten-part podcast series with Tolle to be one of the most groundbreaking acts of her groundbreaking career. Undoubtedly, Eckhart Tolle is at the least an elder brother in Oprah Winfrey's beloved spiritual family.

Tolle's international following and success as an author are certainly not betrayed by his presence. He is a slight figure who moves gently, almost unsteadily. His face is just odd enough to hold fascination. He has drooping eyes, a not unattractive upturned nose, and a small, unexpressive mouth. His voice summons images of the kindly German professor who is a bit absentminded and yet pedantically enthralled with every facet of his work. His laugh is more convulsion than sound and makes one think of what the Yoda of *Star Wars* would look like if he allowed himself a good belly laugh.

Tolle was born in 1948 in Lunen, Germany, to parents who stained his early life with their fighting and their rage. His life at school was as lonely and filled with fear as his life at home. To escape, he played among the bombed-out buildings near his house and later recalled that he felt the "pain in the energy field of the country."[34] As an adult, he lived first in Spain and then in England where he taught German and Spanish in a London school. He was troubled, though: haunted by depression, fear, and self-doubt, which ultimately drove him to the study of psychology, philosophy, and literature at the University of London. Despite the darkness that pervaded his life, he excelled academically and was granted an opportunity to study at Cambridge. He matriculated in 1977 and lived for some years in Glastonbury, England, before settling finally in Vancouver, Canada.

For much of this time, though, he was a man spiraling downward emotionally and spiritually. He contemplated suicide when he could not escape the besetting gloom. Finally, one night he had the epiphany that would define his life and teaching.

> I was deeply identified with a very unhappy, egoic entity I believed was "me." For years I lived in depression and continuous anxiety. One night I couldn't stand it anymore. The thought came into my mind, "I cannot live with myself any longer." Then I saw that my thought contained a subject and an object: I and myself. I stood back from the thought and asked, "Who is the self that I cannot live with? There must be two here. Who am I and who is the self that is impossible to live with?" In that moment, that mind-based sense of self collapsed. What remained was I—not the form "I," not the story-based "I," the mental story of me—but a deeper sense of being, of presence. I died that night psychologically. The mind-made entity died. I knew myself as pure consciousness, prior to form before it becomes something, before it becomes a thought, before it becomes a life-form: the One Life, the One Consciousness that is prior to egoic identity. Then came enormous peace.[35]

Tolle took years aside for "understanding, integrating and deepening that transformation," and this in turn led to the career as a spiritual advisor that has, largely through his writings, lifted him to international fame.

The core idea in Tolle's scheme of understanding is the certainty that all of reality is one—the belief scholars call *monism*. In this, he and Marianne Williamson agree. Tolle believes that when humans perceive themselves apart from the oneness of the universe they belong to, it is then that dysfunction and confusion set in.

> When forms that you identified with, that gave you your sense of self, collapse or are taken away, it can lead to a collapse of the ego, since ego is identification with form. When there is nothing to identify with anymore, who are you? When forms around you die or death approaches, your sense of Beingness, of I Am, is freed from its entanglement with form; Spirit is released from its imprisonment in matter. You realize your essential identity as formless, as an all-pervasive Presence, of Being prior to all forms, all identifications. You realize your true identity as consciousness itself, rather than what consciousness had identified with. That's the peace of God. The ultimate truth of who you are is not I am this or I am that, but I AM.[36]

Yet, typical of New Age teaching, not only is everything one, but everything is divine, including human beings. After quoting from the Hindu Upanishads, Tolle writes, "God, the scripture is saying, is formless consciousness and the essence of who you are."[37] He further explains,

> Being is the eternal, ever-present One Life beyond the myriad forms of life that are subject to birth and death. However, Being is not only beyond but also deep within every form as its innermost invisible and indestructible essence. This means that it is accessible to you now as your own deepest self, your true nature.[38]

It is intriguing to note that Tolle's core ideas are virtually indistinguishable from Hinduism: Man must escape his concept of himself, find his true soul, and become one with the ultimate reality beyond this present world. All is divine. Man is divine. But man does not know he is divine and thus cannot achieve union with ultimate consciousness. In short, there is little new here aside from Tolle's personality and the squishy language that seems to plague New Age teachers.

Still, Tolle insists that his beliefs are what all religions intended before they were corrupted. "All religions are equally false and equally true, depending on how you use them. You can use them in the service of the ego, or you can use them in the service of the Truth."[39] This is an important pillar of Tolle's worldview and one that is common in New Age thinking. Religions start with the truth but then become corrupted. Their "transformative truths" are lost. Mankind awaits Tolle and his fellow New Age devotees to bring restoration.

> If you go deep enough in your religion, then you all get to the same place. It's a question of going deeper, so there's no conflict here. The important thing is that religion doesn't become an ideology—so, "I believe this." And the moment you say "only my belief" or "our belief" is true, and you deny other people's beliefs, then you've adopted an ideology. And then religion becomes a closed door. But, potentially religion can also be an open door.[40]

Like most New Age teachers, Tolle borrows Christian terms but infuses them with meaning quite at odds with Christianity. *Sin* is redefined as "to miss the point of human existence."[41] The biblical concept of a *new earth* is redefined as "the outer forms created by awakened doing."[42] Even the biblical idea of *salvation* is refashioned: "In Hindu teachings, this transformation is called enlightenment. In the teachings of Jesus, it is *salvation*, and in Buddhism, it is the end of suffering. *Liberation* and *awakening* are other terms used to describe this transformation."[43]

Tolle's view of physical healing is particularly revealing. In an appearance on *The Oprah Winfrey Show*, Tolle spoke to a woman who suffered from systemic lupus and rheumatoid arthritis. He assured her that she was moving in the right direction by realizing she had identified herself with her illness. "The illness had become thought forms in your head," he told her, "and you had identified with these thought forms and took them to be who you are . . . There's a space now between yourself and your thought processes and the image of yourself as a sick person." Tolle then instructed the woman not to discuss her sickness with anyone but her doctors, for in doing so she would only reinforce the false notion that her identity was in being sick. She should focus her attention on well-being by dwelling on the beauty of nature or, perhaps, on the healthy parts of her body. By doing this she would be "sensing the inner body," which would lead to wholeness. The important thing for her was to "direct attention to well-being rather than dwelling on the idea of illness."[44] In other words, if the woman would change her thoughts, she would change the physical reality of her illness.

This idea of directing the soul's attention away from reality is an important part of Tolle's spirituality. He believes, as most New Age teachers do, there is intuitive knowledge in the heart that has been silenced. Yet he does not believe this knowledge is accessed through rational thought. Instead, the true self, "Being," is already in the deepest self: "Don't try to understand it," he counsels. "You can know it only when the mind is still. When you are present, when your attention is fully and intensely in the Now, Being can be felt, but it can never be understood mentally."[45]

One of the most unique aspects of Tolle's teaching concerns the "pain-body." He believes that this is a "semi-autonomous psychic entity" formed by "negative emotions that were not faced, accepted, and then let go in the moment they arose" and are now "stored in the cells of the body." He believes that there is also a "collective human pain-body containing the pain suffered by countless human beings throughout history."[46] This pain-body is the cause of all our negative experiences.

> When you realize that pain-bodies unconsciously seek more pain, that is to say, that they want something bad to happen, you will understand that many traffic accidents are caused by drivers whose pain-bodies are active at the time. When two drivers with active pain-bodies arrive at an intersection at the same time, the likelihood of an accident is many times greater than under normal circumstances. Unconsciously they both want the accident to happen.[47]

Equally troubling is Tolle's belief that these pain-bodies have an energy that can be transferred from one person to another. As an example, Tolle recounts a counseling session he once had with a female client who struggled with deep emotional issues. When the session concluded and the woman left his office, one of Tolle's friends entered the room and noted, "The energy feels heavy and murky—it almost makes me feel sick. You need to open the windows, burn some incense."[48] Tolle then went to dinner at a restaurant and took note when a nearby patron started a heated argument with the restaurant staff.

> I suspected that the universal human pain-body had come back to tell me, "You thought you defeated me. Look, I'm still here." I also considered the possibility that the released energy field left behind after our session followed me to the restaurant and attached itself to the one person in whom it found a compatible vibrational frequency, that is to say, a heavy pain-body.[49]

Tolle's concept of the pain-body sounds very much like the Christian belief in demons, particularly when he discusses whether victims of these pain-bodies are responsible for their actions. In answering the question, "Does this mean that people are not responsible for what they do when possessed by the pain-body?" Tolle says,

> How can they be? How can you be responsible when you are unconscious, when you don't know what you are doing? However, in the greater scheme of things, human beings are meant to evolve into conscious beings, and those who don't will suffer the consequences of their unconsciousness. They are out of alignment with the evolutionary impulse of the universe.[50]

Yet, as fearful as these pain-bodies are, they nevertheless play a valuable role in the process of enlightenment, Tolle believes. "When you can't stand the endless cycle of suffering anymore, you begin to awaken. So the pain-body too has its necessary place in the larger picture."[51]

Tolle's spirituality, then, is yet another murky reworking of

Eastern mysticism. He believes man achieves liberation and even divinity when he embraces his "Beingness," which is distinct from man as a personality, the product of an earthly story, man as connected to the physical world. Beingness is a spiritual thing, prior to man, transcendent to man, and after man. Once this Beingness is accepted, man can shape his reality by his thoughts and this can even be a key to physical healing. Still, man must be cautious not to believe that his Beingness can be understood through thought. This is very much the same with the pain-body, the imprint of past pain and unresolved trauma that has taken up residence in the cells. These pain-bodies can dominate a human being, create destructive acts, and even transfer themselves to other human beings who are by nature susceptible. The pain-body can be personal, but it can also be universal, the combination of unresolved pain and violence throughout history.

Remember now, this is the teacher whose book Oprah Winfrey referred to as a "wake-up call for the entire planet."

Gary Zukav

It would be hard to exaggerate Gary Zukav's impact on Oprah Winfrey. When he appeared on *The Oprah Winfrey Show* in April 1999 to discuss his best-selling book, *The Seat of the Soul*, Winfrey told her audience that the book was "one of the most powerful books I've ever read, except for the Bible, of course." When on that same program Zukav sagely announced that "intention is the single most powerful energy in our lives," Winfrey exulted, "I mean, I got it so big . . . this was bing, bing, bing, light bulbs, Indy 500 flags went off in my head."[52] She has urged his books on her website, has extolled his ideas on her programs, and has intentionally catapulted his *The Seat of the Soul* into stratospheric sales. Zukav is undoubtedly a beloved member of Oprah's spiritual family.

In appearance, Zukav is a surprise among Oprah's clan of spiritual experts. Physically, he is nearly the polar opposite of Eckhart Tolle—a handsome, athletic figure who still gives evidence of his years as a Green Beret in the Vietnam War. He is also a Harvard graduate, and this is what seems to give the imprimatur of academia to the principles Zukav impresses upon his followers.

The truth, though, is that Zukav embraces the visions of Eastern mysticism as uncritically as any spiritual teacher on the American scene today. His concept of the human soul, which is central to his spiritual scheme, is very much the same as the Hindu concept of *atma* or "higher self." That soul undergoes a constant cycle of reincarnation. According to Zukav, each soul learns from the varieties of its incarnations as well as its present lifetime:

> The lifetime of your personality is one of a myriad of experiences of your soul. The soul exists outside of time. The perspective of the soul is immense, and the perception of the soul is without the limitations of the personality. . . . For each incarnation, the soul creates a different personality and body.[53]

In between each incarnation the soul experiences, it undergoes a type of assessment session with spiritual beings: "When the soul returns to its home, what has been accumulated in that lifetime is assessed with the loving assistance of its Teachers and guides." This allows the "new lessons that have emerged to be learned, the new karmic obligations that must be paid, are seen. The experiences of the incarnation just completed are reviewed in the fullness of understanding."[54] This process continues for each succeeding incarnation. No incarnation can be successfully lived out without the insights gained from previous incarnations.

> If your soul was a Roman centurion, an Indian beggar, a Mexican mother, a nomad boy, and a medieval nun, among other incarnations, for example, and if the karmic patterns that were set into motion within those lifetimes are in motion within you, you will not be able to understand your proclivities, or interests or ways of responding to different situations without an awareness of the experiences of those lifetimes.[55]

A process of past-life recall, of "remembering" all previous incarnations, will be essential to fulfilling "karmic obligations" in the present lifetime.

Like most who lean spiritually to the East, Zukav replaces the Christian concept of sin with the Hindu understanding of *karma*. Actions cannot be judged by a firm standard of right or wrong, sin or righteousness, but rather by how they create good or bad karmic effect. This is particularly the case with how humans respond to temptation: "Temptation is the Universe's compassionate way of allowing you to run through what would be a harmful negative karmic dynamic if you were to allow it to become physically manifest."[56] Yet Zukav is always careful to merge the concept of the East with the language of recovery and self-help. He knows his audiences well. "If you decide that you cannot beat temptation, what you are really doing is giving yourself permission to be irresponsible. The desires and impulses that you feel that you cannot resist, that you lack the power to overcome, are your addiction."[57]

Deeply revealing of much that Zukav believes is his reworking of the biblical idea of Lucifer. History has been unkind, Zukav insists, and has made Lucifer into an image of evil and vileness. But Lucifer has been misunderstood. He is "the enlightener," the one who brings the knowledge necessary to free man to become God: "Lucifer means 'Light bringer.' Temptation, the *Luciferic principle*, is that dynamic through which each soul is graciously offered the opportunity to challenge those parts of itself that resist Light."[58] In other words, the process of temptation is a process by which Lucifer, the Light bringer, shines a light on weakness so that the human soul can gain self-knowledge and evolve. This is important, for all living things are actually expressions of Light: "Every physical form as well as every nonphysical form is Light that has been shaped by consciousness. No form exists apart from consciousness. . . . Physical reality and the organisms and forms within physical reality are systems of Light within systems of Light, and this Light is the same Light as the Light of your soul."[59] This is Zukav's convoluted way of saying that physical entities are part of the same ultimate soul as the human soul. And Lucifer points the way to that ultimate soul.

It is intriguing that Zukav does not shrink from the horrible implications of what he believes. Those who teach that human reality is created through the power of thought inevitably arrive at the conclusion that man creates the evils he endures. This means that teachers like Zukav end up looking into the eyes of rape victims or AIDS patients or soldiers wounded in war and telling them that they created their own dark experience through their misguided thought life. Aware of this dilemma, most New Age teachers find some fanciful way to explain away this unintended implication of their beliefs. Zukav, however, does not flinch: "Hold on to the thought that you create your experiences. Your fear comes from the realization that a part of you is creating a reality that it wants."[60] It is a mystifying assertion. Zukav obviously believes that while one part of a human being may be shocked at what he has to endure in life, another part is actually creating the painful experience—indeed, Zukav believes that it actually wants negative experiences to occur. This not only paints a schizophrenic portrait of the human soul, but also puts the responsibility for every evil endured in this life squarely upon the shoulders of the suffering. Their own thoughts have created their hardship and their pain.

Nor does Zukav shrink from the dark side of Hinduism. It has long been a criticism of the belief in reincarnation and *karma* that they destroy compassion and generosity, that they make it an offense to help the hurting for fear of somehow interfering with the law of *karma*. Remember that those who wish to help the untouchables of India are often violently opposed by orthodox Hindus who believe that the suffering must endure unaided in order to fulfill *karma*. Again, most New Age teachers find creative paths around this hard assumption of what they proclaim. Not Zukav: "When we see a person sleeping in the gutter in the winter, we do not know what is being completed for that soul. We do not know whether that soul engaged in a cruelty in another lifetime."[61] Thus, Zukav joins those orthodox Hindus who oppose benevolence for the hurting out of deference to *karma*, out of respect for the possibility that some wrong in another life is being atoned for by the present suffering and pain. Zukav, we can assume, would have opposed Mother Teresa and her Sisters of Charity as they worked to care for the untouchables of Calcutta. *Karma*, he would have said, must not be interfered with.

Yet as legalistic as Zukav is regarding wrongs committed in other incarnations, he is amazingly judgment-free about this lifetime. In fact, he is certain that morality itself is nothing more than a human invention: "*Karma* is not a moral dynamic. Morality is a human creation. The Universe does not judge. The law of *karma* governs the balancing of energy within our system of morality and within those of our neighbors. It serves humanity as an impersonal and Universal teacher of responsibility."[62] Indeed, Zukav insists that "when we judge, we create negative *karma*. Judgment is a function of the personality. . . . When we say of an action, 'This is right' or 'that is wrong,' we create negative *karma*."[63]

It is hard to imagine that Zukav cannot see his own inconsistencies. He is so certain about the possibility that a beggar has committed a wrong in a previous life that he would urge us not to offer aid. Yet he is also certain that in our present lifetime, there is no morality, no right or wrong. In fact, he would chastise us for creating negative *karma* if we even dare to pass judgment about the rightness of another's actions. This is typical of many modern spiritual gurus. They are selectively legalistic and libertine, selectively big-hearted and overbearingly harsh.

Zukav's libertinism is brightly present in his plan for "spiritual partnerships" as a replacement for modern marriage. He believes that traditional marriage has run its course, that it is no longer a workable relationship in modern society: "Just as external power is no longer appropriate to our evolution, the archetype of marriage is no longer appropriate," Zukav insists.[64] Instead, Zukav calls for spiritual partnerships as a new step in the evolution of human relationships. No longer will a man and a woman become "one flesh" and live their whole lives together sharing intimacy and shaping the next generation. Instead, people will enter alliances for mutual evolution. "Spirit partnership is a much freer and more spiritually accurate dynamic than marriage because spiritual partners come together from a position of spirit and consciousness," Zukav explains.[65] "The bond between spiritual partners exists as real as it does in marriage," he explains,

> but for significantly different reasons. Spiritual partners are not together in order to quell each other's financial fears or because they can produce a house in the suburbs and that entire conceptual framework. . . . The commitment of spiritual partners is to each other's spiritual growth, recognizing that that is what each of them is doing on Earth, and that everything serves that.[66]

Zukav envisions life as a series of spiritual partnerships, each coming to an end when the desired evolution is no longer occurring. There will be commitment, of course ("Without commitment you cannot learn to see others as your soul sees them—as beautiful and powerful spirits of Light"),[67] but these commitments will begin and end as needed. Though "this does not mean that the institution of marriage will disappear overnight," it does mean that spiritual partnerships are the next step in man's spiritual evolution: "The archetype of spiritual partnership—partnership between equals for the purpose of spiritual growth—is emerging within our species."[68] Zukav summarizes his views in a sentence typical of the grandiose but murky terms he uses to explain most of his ideas: "The archetype of spiritual partnership reflects the conscious journey of multisensory humans to authentic power."[69]

But this grandiosity is no accident. Zukav, misty-eyed as he is, fully believes that his reworked Hinduism is nothing less than the long-awaited transformation of humankind. Consider the sentiments he once proclaimed on his website:

My life is dedicated to the birth of a new humanity. That birth is now in progress. We are all involved in it. The new humanity is being born inside us. We are awakening to new perceptions and new values. These are leading us to new goals. . . . Our new values are the values of the soul—harmony, cooperation, sharing, and reverence for Life. Our new goals are authentic power—the alignment of the personality with the soul—and a planet without conflict.[70]

What Zukav is certain of—aside from his messianic mission—is that mankind is stepping into its divine destiny, which is nothing less than stepping into divinity itself:

You have always been, because what it is that you are is God or Divine intelligence, but God takes on individual forms, droplets, reducing its power to small particles of individual consciousness. . . . As the little form grows in power, in selfhood, in its own consciousness of self, it becomes larger and more Godlike. Then it becomes God.[71]

Confident that all is one, that all is divine, and that man is gaining the wisdom he needs for his liberation from each phase of his process of reincarnation, Zukav urges his followers to turn over control of their lives to the spirits that rule destinies: "Let Go. Trust. Create. Be who you are. The rest is up to your nonphysical Teachers and the Universe. Take your hands off the steering wheel. Be able to say to the Universe, 'Thy will be done,' and know it within your intentions."[72]

Zukav is a conundrum. We know that he can speak intelligently. The book he wrote prior to *The Seat of the Soul* was entitled *The*

Dancing Wu Li Masters, a book about spirituality and quantum physics that won the American Book Award for Science. This is what we would expect of a Harvard graduate and a former military man. Yet his spirituality as expressed in *The Seat of the Soul* is such a gushy and contradictory rehashing of Hinduism that it has made some reviewers wonder if Zukav is serious, if he isn't laughing all the way to the bank as he thinks about the gullibility of the American spiritual seeker. In the minds of some observers he has made himself into the caricature of the mystical motivational guru: ethereal, over-reaching, apocalyptic, and unbelievably abstruse. Clearly, Oprah Winfrey does not think so. After she promoted his books with all the force at her command, *The Seat of the Soul* required a further seven printings to keep up with demand.

Deepak Chopra

If there is an archetype of the highly successful New Age guru, it is Deepak Chopra. There are few who have achieved his visibility, his influence, or his wealth. His videoed lectures are so popular that PBS television stations routinely air them during their annual tele-thons. In an age in which celebrity nears divinity on the public stage, Chopra has numbered stars like Demi Moore, Naomi Judd, Elizabeth Taylor, Joan Lunden, Michael Milken, Steven Seagal, Diane von Furstenberg, Olivia Newton-John, George Harrison, and Michael Jackson among his followers. His books have sold in the tens of millions, he is a regular at high-profile celebrity events, and his healing centers draw the famous and the troubled from around the world. Deepak Chopra clearly gives Oprah Winfrey and Rick Warren competition for the most influential spiritual leader in America.

As with many of the major teachers of alternative spirituality,

Oprah Winfrey was critical to Chopra's success. As *Time* magazine reported, "Oprah Winfrey had [Chopra] on her TV show in 1993 for an uninterrupted hour. The next day the book *Ageless Body, Timeless Mind* sold 137,000 copies."[73] Winfrey gets Chopra's message. In response to his teaching, Oprah told *Newsweek* magazine that gurus are here "not to teach us about their divinity but to teach us about our own."[74] Chopra is unquestionably an Indian father in Oprah's mesmerizing spiritual family.

Deepak Chopra's rise to enlightenment is at the heart of his message to the Western world. He began life in India as the son of a British-trained cardiologist. He was a man of science, accepted at the All India School of Medical Sciences at the age of seventeen. He rose quickly in Indian medicine and this brought him to the United States in 1970 to serve an internship at a small hospital in New Jersey. His skills were desperately needed by a nation enduring a Vietnam-era doctor shortage. He received further training at the Lahey Clinic and at the University of Virginia Hospital. By 1980, when he was thirty-eight, he had become chief of staff at New England Memorial Hospital. "My ambition," he has said often, "was to equal or surpass my American colleagues."[75]

He found the lifestyle of the American medical doctor destructive. There were too many pots of coffee, too many packs of cigarettes, and always the Scotch each night to calm the mind and the heart rate. Though he had once seen medicine as heroic, now "all I was doing was seeing patients one after another, prescribing medication like a legalized drug pusher."[76] He had become the typical Western physician, whom he later described as "fostering a diseased system and beyond that, a diseased world, with himself at its center. Like a spider in its web, he gave off something sticky that entrapped his patients."[77]

Two experiences led to a turning point in his life. First, during a visit to New Delhi in 1981, he met Dr. Brihaspati Dev Triguna, a master of Indian ayurvedic medicine, in which health is understood as a harmony between mind and body. Triguna did nothing more than take Chopra's pulse at the wrist. He then said that Chopra was "thinking too many thoughts," should meditate, and chew his food more slowly.[78] Chopra was impressed but made no changes when he returned to the United States. Not long after, he picked up a copy of a Transcendental Meditation manual at a Boston bookstore. He began meditating, and this enabled him to quit smoking and drinking. By 1983, he was spending time with Maharishi Mahesh Yogi and rediscovering his discarded Hinduism. He had come to the West only to discover the East. It was a gift from the Beatles.

Chopra was smitten with the guru. "The Maharishi is a great sage," Chopra wrote at the time, "his philosophy, the classic Indian view, rubbed free of encrustations . . . is wisdom made bright and simple."[79] The yogi was riding a crest of fame spawned by the success of his Transcendental Meditation movement during the 1970s. He was eager for more, though, and had a plan to market Indian ayurvedic herbs and cures in the West. He added a hyphen to the word for the ancient practice and created Ayur-Veda Products International. Deepak Chopra became his chief salesman.

Like the Hindu theology that had to be sanitized to become Transcendental Meditation, ayurvedic medicine also had to receive the Westernizing treatment that the Maharishi Mahesh Yogi specialized in. In 1996, the *Weekly Standard* explained why:

However ancient, the Ayurveda of yesteryear is basically different from today's sanitized Maharishi-Chopra version. Most diseases were originally attributed to demons; often they were

cured with the wearing of gems and the use of fragrances . . .
Poor digestion was treated with goat feces prepared by washing
with urine. Got constipation? Drink milk—with urine. Male
potency was supposedly enhanced by 216 different kinds of ene-
mas, including the testicles of peacocks, swans, and turtles. If
that didn't work, one was supposed to follow up with an enema
of urine. Hemorrhaging was a nice break from the regimen,
since it was treated with an enema of the fresh blood of a rabbit,
deer, cock, or any one of numerous other beasts. Epilepsy was
treated with ass urine.[80]

These prescriptions have extended into modern times and have
even been the practice of leading Indian politicians, much to the
surprise and disgust of the international community. Mohandas
Gandhi was devoted to ayurvedic ways and regularly urged the
members of his ashram to use cow dung for medical conditions.
This followed naturally from the cow being a sacred figure in
Hindu spirituality. Gandhi even offered dried cow-dung powder
to Westerners with their tea, a gesture of kindness intended to
improve their health. A Gandhi disciple, Morarji Desai, rose to
such prominence in Indian politics that he very nearly defeated
Indira Gandhi for the role of prime minister in the late 1960s. His
ayurvedic health regime included drinking a daily glassful of his
own urine.[81]

The maharishi and Chopra cut away the superstitions and
began marketing the esoteric herbs and concoctions familiar on
the streets of Indian cities to the health-crazed wealthy in America.
Chopra excelled at this. He headed up the Maharishi Ayurveda
Health Center for Stress Management and Behavioral Medicine in
Lancaster, Massachusetts, and, until 1987, was the sole stockholder

of Maharishi Ayur-Veda Products International. He became wealthy and influential. In 1989, the maharishi awarded Chopra a title best translated as "Lord of Immortality."

A description of ayurvedic medicine from the pages of *New Age Journal* at the time is helpful:

> At times arcane, even by the standards of alternative medicine, Ayurveda is a multifaceted approach to health that relies on meditation, herbal remedies, pulse diagnosis, pancha*karma* purification techniques (which use massage, healing oils, and enemas), and special diets keyed to body type and personality. Treatments may include aromatherapy, stimulation of marmas, or sensitive points of the skin, even music therapy. . . . In Ayurvedic medicine, health comes when the forces of the body and mind are in balance, and restoring balance begins with a knowledge of the patient's mind-body type. . . . Different courses of diet, exercise, herbs and other treatments are prescribed to patients depending on their body type and which of the *doshas* [life forces] is perceived to be out of balance. Notes Chopra: "The first question an ayurvedic doctor asks is not, 'What disease does my patient have?' but, 'Who is my patient?'"[82]

Chopra's good looks, easy manner, and learning made him a convincing one-man sales force, particularly when the product was a more caring, whole-person, natural kind of medical care. His personality won baby boomer audiences eager for the ways of the East and this led to sales. The *Los Angeles Times Sunday Magazine* captured him well when it reported, "He is the lecturer par excellence, speaking effortlessly, without notes, his warm eyes covering the room, his sense of humor cloaking the seriousness of the subject, all done in the lilting tones of his native land."[83]

In 1993, Chopra split with the maharishi. The stated reason was disagreement between the two over control of Chopra's writing and speaking. The truth is the suave, Westernized doctor of Eastern methods had simply outgrown the guru. The next year proved this when Chopra's *Ageless Body, Timeless Mind* became a massive best seller, largely on the power of Chopra's personal appearances, the Oprah Effect, and crafty marketing to aging, wealthy baby boomers.

Time magazine summarized the core ideas behind *Ageless Body, Timeless Mind* in a 1996 article on Chopra:

> Our bodies, which seem so solid and finite, are not. For one thing, we replace most of our component cells regularly; thus, rather than collections of aging organs, we are works in constant progress. On the subatomic level, moreover, we are no denser than the air around us and indistinguishable from our surroundings. Finally, since quantum physics asserts that matter and energy are interchangeable, we are not individual beings at all but merely local expressions of an infinite, universal field of energy. A smart field of energy: "All of us are connected to patterns of intelligence that govern the whole cosmos. Our bodies are part of a universal body, our minds an aspect of a universal mind."[84]

It is good that these are *Time*'s words. The disease that troubles many preachers of alternative spirituality affects Chopra: he routinely strings words together in nearly unintelligible ways. In his book, *The Seven Spiritual Laws of Success*, he wrote that "the universe is nothing other than the Self curving back within Itself to experience Itself as spirit, mind and physical matter." On the matter of pain, Chopra is equally headache inducing. For the enlightened, he insists, "a rotten tooth, a tumor or a detached retina" can be seen as "a cluster of photons, a warped image made of light. . . . My identity floats in a quantum fog as photons wink in and out of existence. Observing these shifting patterns, I feel no attachment to any of them. They come and go. I am not even troubled by having no permanent home. It is enough to be bathed in the light."[85]

Not all of Chopra's followers have found being "bathed in the light" sufficient. In 1987, Chopra appeared on the *Phil Donahue Show* to argue his case for ayurvedic health: "If you are happy, then you are going to be healthy. The perfect chemistry of health is happiness." To prove his point, Chopra pointed to a woman who claimed to have been healed after ayurvedic treatment. As the woman, Marian Thompson, told Donahue's audience,

> I received psycho physiological techniques from Dr. Chopra . . . It's very, very simple. It's a mental technique. I sit and I close my eyes, and I just go within . . . and the body experiences an inner bliss, an inner happiness. And that gets translated into body— into the body feeling better and the body getting stronger and able to throw off the disease. My doctor was very, very amazed.

Thompson added, "I'm in complete remission. There's no sign of the disease now."[86]

Three years later, though, Thompson died. The cause of death according to the death certificate was breast cancer.

Traditional medical doctors shake their heads at such occurrences and complain that the laws in the United States do not hold Chopra and his fellow Eastern mystics accountable. This is fortunate for Chopra. His solutions to medical conditions sometimes border on the absurd. One prescription in particular prompts laughter as it makes the rounds in hospitals and doctors' offices. According to Chopra, to prevent and reverse cataracts, "each day one is to brush one's teeth, scrape the tongue, spit into a cup of water and wash the eyes with the mixture."[87]

Perhaps because he feels constricted by the material world of fact and consequence, Chopra has begun writing fiction. His first novel, *Merlin*, was a best seller. He prefers this genre, he told *Publishers Weekly*, because nonfiction leaves people saying, "'Where is the evidence?' And it's so boring to try and address that. But if you write fiction . . . with intensity and passion, you reveal yourself— and you write the truth."[88]

It may well be that Chopra wishes to avoid matters of evidence because the entire system of thought upon which he has achieved success is nothing more than Hinduism and a made-over version of its ayurvedic medical practices. There is no evidence for what Chopra teaches, nor is there even an attempt to hide the religious underpinnings of his science. On recordings of some of his teachings, he reads at length from the Bhagavad Gita, the Hindu scriptures. His books, fiction and nonfiction, lead us to the Hindu worldview: humans are divine minds seeking liberation from an artificial world to become one with *Brahma*, the divine energy of the universe. As a character in one of Chopra's recent novels, *The Daughters of Joy*, is told when he questions the reality of a visionary landscape of miracles, marvels, and fulfilled hearts he has just discovered, "Dear me, the places you came from, the things you've trusted all your life, the people you've invested in—those are the illusions."

And so Deepak Chopra would have us believe.

○

There are questions that come to mind and they press so deeply that I must raise them before we move on. I'm envisioning the process by which Oprah determines who will be on her program. It is essentially a matter of a staffer giving her a book. She reads it, feels or doesn't feel the supernatural vibration she needs to feel, and if she is pleased puts the author on a stage before millions. But does she know the history? Does she know the author's story? Does anyone do the due diligence necessary to find out what this next guest might represent?

I'm intrigued. When author James Frey admitted that he fabricated much of the narrative of his best-selling book A Million Little Pieces, *an Oprah book club selection, there was a huge scandal and a special mea culpa edition of* The Oprah Winfrey Show. *Yet Oprah and her team could not have known that the author faked his own autobiographical book. They cannot be blamed.*

When it comes to guests like Deepak Chopra, though, Oprah could know the backstory . . . and she should. It is not hard to learn what Chopra teaches. It is not hard to learn about the lawsuits and the embarrassments. It is easy to find out that Chopra has urged tongue-scrapings as a preventative for cataracts. Is this what she intended to put on the air?

This leads to another question. Is Oprah well educated enough in matters of religion to evaluate what her guru guests teach? She is a gifted interviewer, a wise businesswoman, and a brilliant media figure, but does she know religion? Does she realize that what Deepak Chopra teaches is an edited, Westernized version of the religion that has devastated India, leaving it, in V. S. Naipaul's memorable phrase, a "wounded civilization"?[89]

I picture Jenny in Abilene, Texas, who watches Oprah's show before her evening shift at the rendering plant on the edge of town. Jenny is a single mother one paycheck from poverty, her mother is dying of liver ailments, and her daughter has a glandular problem that makes her huge for her age, much to the laughter of the kids at school. And so for a change, for a break from the monotony and perhaps for something like time with a friend, Jenny watches Oprah. Some days she finds a "You go, girl!" kind of encouragement that helps her get through. Some days she learns to love her child better or what smart things she can do to make her $400-a-month apartment into a more nurturing home. She even likes knowing how a full-figured chick like her can wear the right clothes and still get her groove on. Oprah is almost always a help.

But then she listens to Deepak Chopra or Marianne Williamson or Eckhart Tolle and she finds herself in tears. "Is life really an illusion?" she wonders. "Did my thoughts create this miserable reality I'm in? I thought I was a pretty good person, but I can't seem to change my thinking the way they want me to. Maybe I've actually done these horrible things to my mom and my child. Maybe Marianne Williamson is right: their sickness is my loveless thoughts materialized. Forgive me! Oh, God or . . . er . . . whatever, forgive me! And, man, does it feel lonely to realize that there is no God, that I'm actually as much god as there is in this world. Makes life feel like that howling desert scene at the beginning of The Exorcist. *I'm just not ever going to be any good at getting detached from my reality the way that Dr. Chopra wants me to. What's wrong with me?"*

And so it goes. Because Oprah says it's so. Because Deepak
Chopra is a star. Because a staffer chose a book. Because the
maharishi we have always with us.

The Reverend Ed Bacon

Rev. Ed Bacon looks like the kind of priest who would have been
cast in a John Wayne movie. He is handsome with kind eyes, an
endearing smile, and a short burr haircut that adds to a slightly
military bearing. He is compassion and command personified, the
wise, experienced priest who evokes Bing Crosby's Father O'Malley
and George C. Scott's Patton.

This may have been just what Oprah Winfrey had in mind
when she first called Bacon to ask him to be on her "Best Life"
series about spirituality. She had completed her groundbreaking series of interviews with Eckhart Tolle not long before.
Though the interviews were met with widespread praise, there
was opposition. E-mail poured into Harpo complaining that
Oprah had abandoned her Baptist faith, had spread the shad-
owy ideas of that German mystic without so much as a word
of caution or balance. The African Americans among Oprah's
audience seemed particularly enraged. They were proud of her
as perhaps the richest and most famous of their race, but they
also loved their Jesus and their Bible and they felt Winfrey had
abandoned both and expected them to like it. They didn't, and
they wanted her to know.

Oprah had never met Bacon but had seen him in a documentary produced by Guy Ritchie. Called *The Ego Has Landed*, the
film was about the human ego or the "conceptualized self." As
Ritchie explained to the *Los Angeles Times*,

The only sort of evil—for lack of a better word—that there is in the world is what psychiatrists now call the conceptualized self. . . . That's what they used to call the ego. It manifests itself individually and collectively . . . I don't wish to make this too intellectual or even pseudo-intellectual. It's what we understand as selfishness and greed.[90]

Bacon had been interviewed for the documentary and Winfrey had seen it when friends suggested it was something she would like.

What Winfrey needed was someone to make the sign of the cross over her new spiritual direction. She sensed that Bacon was her man. She was losing Christians from her audience and she needed a churchman to stand by her side, to tell her churchgoing fans that she had not left the fold. When the call came, Bacon was eager to help.[91]

It was on the third day of the "Best Life" series that Winfrey got more than she bargained for. While fielding questions from the series' online audience, Bacon made a statement that stunned her along with many of her viewers: "Being gay is a gift from God."

Other guests, New Age leaders all, nodded their heads knowingly. But the host could hardly contain herself. "Well, you are the first minister I've ever heard say, 'Being gay is a gift from God,' I can tell you that."[92] The discussion then moved on to other themes, but Bacon was invited back days later to explain. "Tell us," Winfrey said, "what did you mean by that comment?"

"I meant exactly what I said," Bacon replied with a smile. "It is so important for every human being to understand that he or she is a gift from God, and particularly people who are marginalized and victimized in our culture. Gay and lesbian people are clearly outcasts in many areas of our life, and it is so important for them to understand that when God made them, God said, 'You are good.'"[93]

This second interview did not quell the storm. Harpo was flooded once again with e-mail, as was Bacon's All Saints Episcopal Church in Pasadena, California, a church the *Pasadena Weekly* described as "one of the most socially progressive religious institutions in America."[94] Bacon reported that the e-mails were "30-to-1 appreciative" of his statement.

Still, a controversial comment on an Oprah Winfrey broadcast was sure to draw too much attention to pass quickly. Criticism swirled and the media kept calling. Soon, Bacon felt the need to address the matter with his congregation. Describing much of the e-mail he'd received as "the most vitriolic stuff I have ever read, calling for the rescission of my ordination, saying I didn't know what I was talking about," Bacon then recounted the question that seemed to be at the heart of the issue: "Show me where in the Bible it says that being gay is a gift from God."[95]

Bacon's reply settled the matter for his congregation: "Well, if those folks would read the Bible, they would see that in Genesis it says that when God created humankind, God said that we are good—all good, didn't mention any exceptions."[96]

In a later interview, Bacon explained the hermeneutic that led him to his conclusions:

I think it's very clear that the Bible has an arc that moves towards inclusiveness. Peter himself had a conversion experience about his fixed certainties and the things he felt repugnant toward, and the entire New Testament is about inclusion, about bringing more and more people in and understanding that there's nothing God created which is inherently evil, and so the Bible itself moves towards inclusion.[97]

It was a nontraditional opinion but it was an opinion not lightly regarded. Ed Bacon is among the most respected liberal clergymen in America, his 3,500-member Episcopal congregation one of the most visible in the nation. He is a graduate of Emory Divinity School and has been honored by that institution as both a distinguished preacher and as an honored alumnus. He also received the Religious Freedom Award from the ACLU of Southern California in 2006 and the Peace & Compassion Award in 2005 from the Islamic Center of Southern California. He regularly appears in national media and since his appearance on the "Best Life" broadcast is now celebrated for his Christianized approach to the kind of alternative spirituality Oprah Winfrey advocates.

Bacon, then, has played the role Winfrey hoped he would when she first called him: the liberal churchman blessing her journey toward a non-Christian faith, the Episcopal priest making holy a religion of Westernized Hinduism and fashionable occultism. It is an odd role indeed, for Winfrey and her teachers of alternative spirituality find Bacon's Christianity an outworn, even destructive faith, one that they hope to redefine into obsolescence.

Still, Bacon is ever the all-inclusive, all-embracing priest. In a description of the human soul, he revealed just how broad he can be: "All of us have deep within us something very sacred. Some call that our Spirit. Some call it our Soul. Some call it our True Self. Some refer to it as God Within or The One. It matters less what we name 'it' than the fact that 'it' is our interior source of creativity, compassion and courage."[98] Thus Bacon is willing to merge into his Christianity streams of thought very much at odds with his faith, for this, he believes, is what Scripture intends.

Bacon is very much a part of Oprah Winfrey's spiritual family: the elder brother priest who blesses all pursuits, all persuasions, all practices, and gives even anti-Christian faiths the imprimatur of the modern Christian church.

Iyanla Vanzant

She is likely the rowdy black sister Oprah never had. She is loud and fun and has a wide, bright smile that wrings laughter from the hardest heart. She is so adept at inspiring and entertaining audiences that when she appeared on Oprah's program a watching Barbara Walters was moved to become her producer. Indeed, some say Iyanla Vanzant is almost as good as Oprah herself.

She certainly has much that Oprah offers. She has the "girl-friend" factor, that relatable combination of interest and wit and naughty that pulls women in. She also has business savvy. She is a lawyer, after all, before she is a Yoruba priestess and preacher of alternative spirituality. Most of all, like Oprah, she has a story, the journey that makes others know that she has been in the same pit of shame and hurt and despair.

She was born Rhonda Harris in a taxi on the streets of 1950s Brooklyn. Her mother died when Rhonda was two and the child was sent to live with her paternal grandmother. This woman was deranged, though, and regularly beat Rhonda with an electrical cord. Raped by a family friend at the age of nine, Rhonda gave birth to a son at sixteen, and by twenty-one had brought two more children into the world. She spent eleven years on welfare and at age thirty suffered a broken jaw at the hands of her abusive husband.

Then came the second nervous breakdown and the thoughts of suicide. Finally, one morning she heard a female voice tell her to get her children and leave. She did, with a few belongings and three dollars in her pocket.

Understanding that if she had the strength to leave the abuse then she had the strength for greater things, she decided to enroll in Medgar Evers College in Brooklyn in 1978. She did well, graduated, and then reached for the stars and enrolled in law school. She conquered this, too, and after passing the bar exam she joined a law firm in Philadelphia. She had done it. She had conquered poverty and abuse to win a life for herself and her children.

In Philadelphia, she delved more deeply into the motivational spirituality that had helped her rise. She held meetings in her home on Sundays and was a frequent guest on radio talk shows. Then came the change. One morning in 1990, she walked into her law office and saw that it was dark. "I told my secretary, 'Look, the lights aren't working.' She said, 'What's wrong with you? The lights are working. You better get your eyes checked.' Then she heard a message from within: 'You're standing in darkness.' So I just walked out."[99]

She began writing and speaking. Invitations were few at first but then slowly increased. In 1994, her book *Acts of Faith: Daily Meditations for People of Color* was a huge seller in the African American market, earning her a Blackboard Book of the Year award. She followed this success with *In the Meantime: Finding the Love You Want*, *One Day My Soul Just Opened Up*, and *Yesterday I Cried*, which landed on the *New York Times* best-seller list. By 1998, her reputation had become such that a producer at Harpo took note. Her appearance on the Winfrey show was one of the most successful of the season. Viewers flooded phone lines and e-mail boxes wondering who was that charismatic black woman whom

Oprah had introduced as an "empowerment specialist." Vanzant was invited back on *The Oprah Winfrey Show* twelve times.

There is little surprise in this. Vanzant is nearly the poster child for both the Oprah Winfrey message of uplift and the Oprah Winfrey brand of faith. Raised by a Native American mother who attended a Christian church but practiced her Indian superstitions, Vanzant learned early to draw from any spiritual source that gave her power to live. Her rise from poverty was fueled by a belief system very much like that Winfrey urges upon her audiences: any practice from any religion that leads to personal power, prosperity, and peace.

Vanzant founded Inner Visions Spiritual Life Maintenance Center and Bookstore, based in Silver Springs, Maryland, which offered classes and items for sale drawn from Buddhism, Taoism, Hinduism, Christianity, Yoruba spirituality, goddess worship, Islam, and a variety of occult expressions. Her bookstore sold amulets, chimes, crystals, herbs, incense, pyramids, candles, and crucifixes. The inconsistencies do not bother her:

> I grew up in a very diverse and eclectic environment. My Native American grandmother went to the Church of God in Christ every Sunday, but she would not cut your hair on a full moon. It's about integration and about not having lines of division but of having lines where you can coexist cohesively. So, yeah, she was a Native American, and she burned incense, and she honored the moon, and she made her own soap and she had prayer cloths pinned to her underwear. So, how do you explain that? I don't know, but it works.[100]

The altars that adorned her home as she rose to fame symbolized both her personal spiritual journey and the eclecticism that grows organically from Oprah Winfrey–style "anything that works" religion. In her bedroom was an altar where she did her daily 5:30 a.m. meditation. An amethyst crystal sat next to ashes from the altar of the Dalai Lama and images of Vanzant's spiritual gurus: Baba Muktananda, Babaji, Gurumayi Chidvilasananda, Vishnu, and Buddha. A second altar in her book-filled office was lined with seven glasses of water and an image of the Black Madonna. This altar was where Vanzant consecrated her eyes, head, mouth, and ears before working at her desk. She visited a third altar in the basement of her home only once a week. It was adorned with old family photos and pictures of the twenty-one African American women Vanzant venerates, Harriet Tubman, Audre Lorde, Queen Mother Moore, and Ida B. Wells among them. "I'm standing on my ancestors," she explained. "They are powerful people who have done so much of the work."[101]

Vanzant is also an ordained Yoruba priestess. Originating in southern Nigeria, Yoruba spirituality is very much like the Hinduism behind most New Age teaching. Every human being is destined to become one with Olorun, the divine creator and source of all energy. Human thoughts and actions in the natural realm (*aye*) make spiritual contact with other beings, including the earth. There is a cycle of existence not unlike reincarnation and there is search for meaning and destiny in a spiritual realm called *orun rere*. The goal is transcendence. Prayer and meditation facilitate this, as does honor for the multiplicity of sacred beings Yoruba venerates. Those who stop growing spiritually are destined for *orun apadi*, the realm of the forsaken. The holy color of Yoruba is purple, which was the defining color of the house she bought after her appearance on the Winfrey show, just as an eclectic form of Yoruba religion was the defining theme of her life.

She also clung to petty superstitions. A visitor to Vanzant's home who happened to mention a hope was quickly handed a sticky note and a pen and told to write down the wish. The paper was then folded in a precise way and put in a special basket. This is what Vanzant called her "dream incubator."[102]

What emerges from this is Vanzant as the perfect picture of Oprah Winfrey's spiritual eclecticism. She might well have been one of the millions of housewives who, urged along by Winfrey, set out on a journey of spiritual self-discovery and ended up with a house filled with altars, those altars in turn filled with competing and contradictory gods. This is what comes of a search guided by what seems to work rather than what is true and a filter of belief that sifts all spirituality in terms of its ability to make the human self divine.

In much that she believes, Iyanla Vanzant is consistent with the spirituality of Oprah's spiritual family. Yet in one matter she is distinct. Her faith did not bring her the success and near effortless living of the others. In a special program during the 2010–2011 season, Vanzant returned to *The Oprah Winfrey Show* to explain how her life had collapsed after her original appearance on the program years before. Her popularity as an Oprah guest had meant more money. This she foolishly mismanaged, she said. Her marriage dissolved, her grandchildren grew cold, and her publisher sued her. She lost her house, her reputation and, to a ravaging disease, her daughter. As she sat before a mystified Oprah, Vanzant was humble and eager to rebuild, but clearly she was confused. What had happened? How could such good intentions have gone so awry? Why hadn't the gods saved her?

Indeed, in her transparency and guilelessness, it was easy to see the true Vanzant: a capable, valiant woman eager to touch lives with truth. It was also easy to see that her former truths had failed her, that she hoped for a greater revelation of some truth that could rescue her and transform her life forever.

○

This, then, is Oprah Winfrey's spiritual family. There are others, of course, but they are well represented by the six we have considered here. What astonishes me about them—beyond the lack of evidence for what they believe, the inexactitude of their language, and the almost obsessive need to reframe Christianity—is how these intelligent, gifted, sweet people can believe things that are—and I can say it no other way—silly.

Iyanla Vanzant is a brilliant attorney and author, and yet she once kept glasses of water on a shelf in her house to influence spirits. She folded paper in precise patterns and put it in a special basket, believing this helped her dreams come true.

Rev. Ed Bacon, for all of his graciousness, believes the New Testament encourages inclusiveness, tolerance, and openness to all expressions of faith and sexuality. This despite the fact that the words of Jesus and Paul as recorded in the New Testament contend exactly the opposite. Indeed, even the effeminate are said to be disqualified from the kingdom of God in Paul's letter to the Corinthians.[103] How then did the New Testament become a manual of inclusion? In fact, how did Bacon, a well-educated man, fail to remember that one of the oldest criticisms of the New Testament is its exclusive nature, its insistence that faith in Jesus Christ and his truth is the only way to God? Whatever the Bible is, it is no support for postmodern eclecticism.

And so it goes. Marianne Williamson thinks people are poor because they think they are. Eckhart Tolle believes that auto accidents are caused by "pain-bodies" that result from universal, unresolved wounds. Deepak Chopra believes that toothaches are best endured by floating "in a quantum fog as photons wink in and out of existence."

It occurs to me that my complaints about these views are not necessarily distinctly Christian. My complaints are those that any rationalistic atheist could also share. In short, is there any evidence for what these people believe, are their views consistent with the known facts of the universe, and would anyone want to live in the world their philosophies would create?

I should say before concluding what is true and part of the problem. The people I have reviewed here are, for the most part, nice people. I have interviewed most of them for this book. They were kind and helpful and even concerned about me. They surely knew I disagreed with them—a simple visit to my website by a staffer would have hinted at this—and yet they met with me or made themselves available by phone. How very gracious they were—and yet they hold to the ideas you see above. And this presses the problem of their spirituality and that of Oprah Winfrey. Are flawed ideas gaining sway in the world because their advocates are nice or attractive or humorous or kind or, in Oprah's case, rich and famous? There can seem to be little other explanation, given that the ideas that make up much of New Age thinking, much of the alternative spirituality industry, are so mystifyingly unsubstantiated, contradictory, and destructive.

5

Oprah's Favorite Things

Well, it may be the devil or it may be the Lord
But you're gonna have to serve somebody.

—Bob Dylan, "Gotta Serve Somebody"

Despite the fact that Oprah Winfrey is one of the most visible people in the world and despite the fact that her story and views are broadcast in some form nearly every day, the details of her religious life tend to come to us in bits and pieces. She is not a theologian and does not speak in systematic and connected ways. She is also not a teacher who expresses herself in fully formed thought. Instead, we learn what we can of her faith because of what she affirms in the thinking of others, because of the glimpses into her soul she occasionally grants to her audiences, and because of what an ever-attentive media has been able to divine.

We know, for example, that she keeps a Bible by her bed.[1] We know she calls her estate "The Promised Land" and that she has named its two roads "Glory" and "Hallelujah."[2] We know she is eclectic, that she lights candles to her ancestors, chants Hindu mantras, prays to the God of the Bible, but believes that her thoughts control her destiny. She has affirmed her belief in reincarnation, in *karma*, in *maya*, in the Law of Attraction, in the power of intention, in channeling spirits, and in spirituality as the key to prosperity.

Yet she angrily rejects labels. Remember that she has said, "I am not New Age anything and I resent being called that. I am just trying to open a door so that people can see themselves more clearly and perhaps be the light to get them to God, whatever they may call that. I don't see spirits in trees and I don't sit in the room with crystals."[3]

Still, she roots every aspect of her life in the spiritual. "I answer to the Spirit of God that lives in us all," she has said.[4] Each year, she makes a request of God: strength for one year, clarity for another.[5] She believes God speaks through her circumstances. Once when a former lover returned to his wife and the couple had a child who was born on Oprah's birthday (January 29), Oprah took it as a sign of God's forgiveness for the affair.[6] She relies on the guidance of "spirit" in business decisions as in all areas of life. "I have this inner spirit that directs and guides me," she has told reporters.[7] In fact, she understands her success itself to be a blessing from God: "I had the blessed assurance that I am God's child . . . and nobody else's. That is really the source of my strength, my power. It is the source of all my success."[8] She seeks guidance even for choosing what interviews to do.[9] Her political decisions are also sometimes determined by spiritual forces and by her understanding of the Bible. When she decided to support Barack Obama for the presidency, she was led by the words of Matthew 16:26: "What does it do for a man to gain the world and lose his soul?" "If I had not come out for Barack Obama when I did," she explained, "I know I would have lost a piece of my soul."[10]

And she knows that she is destined. Words like *chosen, mission, calling, ministry,* and *intended* flow freely from her lips. Maya Angelou believes she is a "moral mountain" for our age.[11] Her boyfriend, Stedman, believes she is "one of those chosen people. You know, hand-picked by the universe to do great things."[12] She is confident that some force has placed her on earth at this time for some reason.

And so it goes: the bits of Winfrey's spiritual life that fall upon an eager public, the puzzle taking form with each new revealing piece.

Yet from this scattered detail, broader ideas do emerge. They are important ideas and it is not going too far to say they may prove to be the more lasting part of her impact upon our times. To both describe them and to contend with them, it would be best to deal with them in a series of lists, thus providing some systematic approach to the foggy sea of beliefs she calls her own.

The Four Pillars of Oprah Winfrey's Brand of Faith

1. Religion and spirituality are two different things.

It is a principle that Oprah's audiences often hear, one that was particularly important in her pioneering "Best Life" series. Religion and spirituality are two different things. You can "do" the one without "doing" the other. You can belong to your church or your temple or your mosque and still join Oprah in adopting practices from other faiths. You can be Roman Catholic and still chant mantras. You can keep your Jewish faith and still invoke the spirits of your ancestors. You can be a Muslim and give yourself to a life governed by *karma*. In other words, you can keep your traditional religion but create a completely different kind of informal spirituality to help you live out each day. As the written introduction to the "Best Life" series assures, "The terms 'spirituality' and 'religion' are often confused, but . . . you can be one without being the other."[13]

Oprah's audiences love this distinction. It allows them to create a spiritual life based on what is meaningful to them, rather than what is mandated by traditional religion. For those who are unchurched or unaffiliated with a formal religion, it serves as an invitation to a spiritual life free of the formalities and judgments of traditional faith. For those already part of a traditional faith, it serves as an invitation to explore alternative spirituality without fear of the prohibitions against the occult that most mainline faiths insist upon. For most of Oprah's followers, it has been a liberation, allowing them to make meaningful spiritual practices part of their lives regardless of the source and regardless of the contradictions with their prior faiths.

This idea that religion and spirituality are two different things is one of the most innovative concepts to arise from Winfrey's programs. The esteemed *HarperCollins Dictionary of Religion*, published by the American Academy of Religion, did not even include an entry for *spirituality* when Winfrey began distinguishing the word from religion. Debates over this distinction quickly arose. Theological faculties at colleges and universities conducted conferences and sponsored seminars. Writers and practitioners grappled with the matter of definition. Finally, psychotherapist Karen Herrick offered a definition that seemed to take hold. In her article "Learning the Language of Spirituality" for the *Journal of Religion and Psychical Research*, she suggested that spirituality was best defined by characteristics such as a sense of profound inner peace, overwhelming love, unity with earth and living things, complete joy and ecstasy, meeting with or listening to a spiritual teacher or master, a sense of God's energy or presence, seeing a spiritual figure, witnessing or experiencing a healing of body or mind, a miracle, communicating with someone who has died, and near-death or life-after-death experience.[14]

These were terms Oprah Winfrey's audiences knew well.

It was all so appealing. It fit the American need for freedom from restraint. It answered the baby boomer need to innovate, to modify and blend opposing streams of thought. It answered the emotional needs of an increasingly secular age.

Tragically, Winfrey's distinction between religion and spirituality was artificial. She had made a distinction without a genuine difference in order to draw her followers into her novel brand of faith. The truth is, of course, that religion and spirituality are very much the same thing, that religion defines the very nature of spirituality, even makes it possible. To say otherwise is to try to escape the wisdom and guidance of religion in order to pursue spirituality unrestrained. It is risky. It is unwise. It is an insult to time-honored faiths. This is what Winfrey was doing, whether she was discerning enough to know it or not, and this is how she led millions of her followers into what their own faiths would have defined as dangerous territory.

In order to comprehend this, we should explain our terms better. Spirituality is probably best understood as belief in an invisible world and the mastery of practices designed to connect with that invisible world. It is the lifestyle and habits that allow our lives to merge with the unseen. But religion, on the other hand, is the broader understanding of truth that includes an explanation of the unseen. In other words, religion and its doctrines are the map for the invisible realm that spirituality navigates.

This is what makes it disingenuous of Winfrey to act as though spirituality can stand apart from religion. Spirituality depends upon religion, requires it for definition. Indeed, there is no meaningful spirituality apart from the worldview religion provides. To say otherwise is a trick. It is acting as though there is only one kind of spirituality when in fact there are as many types of spirituality as there are religions. It would be like a car salesman telling a customer that his kind of car is the only one that exists, that if you want a car you will have to buy his brand because his brand is all there is. Obviously, this would be silly in car sales, given all the brands known in the world. Apparently it is not silly in religion if Oprah Winfrey is any guide.

Consider for a moment the invisible world as Christians understand it. There is a God who created all things but who is separate from his creation. He created all things along with his Son, Jesus Christ, who is both fully God and fully man. Both reign from heaven, a place outside of this created universe. Both are tended by angels who do their bidding. Also part of this Godhead is the Holy Spirit, who is God in spiritual form and whose job it is to continue the work Jesus Christ began when he walked the earth. There are also demons, evil beings who were once angels but who rebelled against God prior to human history. These demons are led by an arch demon named Satan or Lucifer. The kingdom of God and the kingdom of Satan are in conflict with each other and the earth is where much of this ongoing war plays out.

This is the map of the spiritual world according to Christians. Their spirituality, then, is about knowing and worshipping God.

They pray. They read Scripture. They fast. They worship. They eat bread and drink wine in rituals designed to remember the life of Christ. They do works of service for other human beings. They are given spiritual gifts. Some are evangelists. Some are pastors. Some are good at administration. Some are gifted to govern. Some are empowered to care for the poor. And so it goes. They live their lives as part of a mystical body of Christ on earth, and they honor Jesus Christ by obeying his command to tell others about their faith.

Now, it is easy to see how this thumbnail description of Christian spirituality is at odds with the New Age, alternative spirituality of Oprah Winfrey. Oprah urges her followers to chant mantras, but there are no mantras in Christianity. In fact, repetitive praying of meaningless or insincere prayers is forbidden.[15] Oprah urges her followers to believe in reincarnation, but there is no reincarnation in Christianity. The Christian New Testament makes it clear that a man is supposed to live one lifetime and then face judgment by God.[16] Oprah summons the spirits of her ancestors and calls her followers to do the same. Yet while Christians honor their ancestors, most of them would regard invoking ancestral spirits or anything close to channeling as the same thing as invoking demons. And while Christians believe their thought life is important and should be conditioned by God's will and the Scriptures, they would never believe destiny is determined by thoughts alone as Oprah does.

For Christians, the universe is personal. It was created by God. It reveals God. It is governed by God. It is God whose hand they hope to move in prayer and fasting. It is God whose goodness they acknowledge in their worship services. Needless to say, the idea that human beings will become gods themselves is arrogant blasphemy to Christians. Christians live in a relationship with a God who rules in the affairs of men. Human beings are creatures. They are servants of God. They do not create themselves or their destinies by thoughts or mantras or anything else. They are subjects of the one God, creator of all things.

Consider the story of Tina. She is an attorney in Atlanta. She is single, fun loving, and adventurous. She faithfully watches Oprah Winfrey because she loves seeing the stars and getting ideas for her home. Besides, Tina is Asian and can't wait to catch the next Lisa Ling report from some troubled hot spot in the world. Tina is also devoted to her young, cool, Bible-preaching Methodist church.

Then one day she turns on the television and Oprah Winfrey is telling her that religion and spirituality are two different things. Oprah wants Tina to believe that she can still be part of her "happenin'" church but that she can also make up a spirituality of her own. Oprah says Tina should meditate. She should light candles and speak to her ancestors. She should chant and even try to sense who she might have been in a previous life. She should believe that what looks like reality is actually artificial and that there is an ultimate reality she should try to be part of. She should also forget about good and evil and start living in terms of *karma*.

So, since Tina trusts Oprah, she follows her. She comes home from work in the afternoons, lights candles, chants what she has heard others chanting—"*Hare Krishna, Hare Krishna*"—and she asks her Asian ancestors to indwell her soul. She also begins doing as Marianne Williamson has encouraged her to do: she tries to see the world as one thing, to believe "there is only one of us here" and to remove from her mind the idea that she is separate from others. She tries to merge with cosmic consciousness. She also starts reworking her thought life to obey the Law of Attraction—that thoughts become things. Tina visualizes the reality she wants. She creates a vision board adorned with pictures of the things she dreams of having and images of the kind of person she wants to be, all cut from magazines. She stares at it every day. She is trying to conceive it. She is working to believe it. She is intent on achieving it.

The transformation continues. Tina does as Oprah suggests. And it is not long before Tina's friends realize that she is no longer a member of her fired-up Methodist church. In fact, Tina is no longer even a Christian. Tina has become, for all practical purposes, a Hindu, perhaps with some occult overlay. She chants, she meditates, she does yoga, she believes in *maya*, she lives in terms of *karma*, and she believes in her divine self. She has become a Hindu and all under the encouragement of the Baptist Oprah Winfrey who said that Tina could practice an alternative form of spirituality without having to abandon her Methodist Christian faith.

But Tina did abandon her former faith and the reason is simple. Spirituality and religion are the same. In fact, to be spiritual is to affirm some religious vision, some map to the invisible world. Tina thought she could keep her Christian map but navigate as a Hindu. It doesn't work that way. She ended up throwing out her Christian map and giving in to the map demanded by her daily practices. She became Hindu because that was what Oprah Winfrey led her to be.

2. Opposing religions can be casually blended.

There is a wish, a hope really, that has long shaped the religious vision of the baby boomers. It is the belief that all religions are actually part of each other, that they ultimately lead to the same place and can be intertwined. It is what we hear in the words of Eckhart Tolle when he says if we drill down far enough into each religion we find the same common spiritual base. It is what we hear Oprah urging when she says all religions can be served by the same spiritual practices. It is even what we hear in the words of Barack Obama when he says, "I am rooted in the Christian tradition," but "I believe that there are many paths to the same place and that is a belief that there is a higher power, a belief that we are connected as a people."[17]

It is a hope that is rooted in the thinking of the East, of course, and it has helped to create the highly eclectic boomer spirituality. It is why one woman can describe herself as a "Christian Buddhist" and another can explain, straight faced, that she is "a Christian incarnation of Vishnu." It is why a Baptist boomer can read his horoscope, speak of how *karma* shapes his business, and even lean to the lessons of *The Secret*—though he would never want his family or his pastor to know. It is why a Jew can have his tarot cards read before he watches Joel Osteen. It is why one boomer speaks of Jesus as an "advanced guru" and another first encountered him through a peyote high and a third chants the name of Jesus while sitting in a lotus position accompanied by incense and sitar.

This hope certainly lives in the heart of Oprah Winfrey. She is rooted in her Baptist faith but she believes Jesus isn't the only way to God, as she famously said while arguing with an audience member. Instead, she holds to the dream of her generation: that all religions can somehow be blended into one. This is what allows her to treat religions as though they are each offerings on the same spiritual buffet. She can pick one practice from Religion A and another practice from Religion B in much the same manner that she might order from a Chinese restaurant menu. It is how she has fashioned the unique, eclectic religious life she portrays on her programs.

There is intellectual dishonesty in this, however. It is more mood than method, more about religious feeling than about religious possibility. It is only possible to blend competing religions when they aren't taken seriously, when their spiritual claims are ignored or refashioned. This can only be envisioned by those who think they know better, who believe they see the genuine truth behind the religions of others and who intend to merge that truth with the truths behind still other faiths. This requires a certain degree of disregard for what religions claim for themselves. It requires a sense of messianic purpose. It also requires an astonishing degree of arrogance.

Those who wish to fashion new faiths out of a blend of traditional faiths miss the fact that there is inherent in religion, as in all claims of truth, a certain exclusivity, a certain rejection of counterclaims. This is not necessarily bigotry. It is the nature of truth. If 1+1=2, then it does not equal anything else. It is an intolerant, exclusive fact that does not admit any other claim. It is not possible to merge 1+1=2 with some belief system that claims the opposite. Yet in the matters of religion, this is exactly what Oprah Winfrey and her fellow syncretists attempt to do. They want to borrow bits and pieces of Christianity or Islam or Buddhism or Hinduism or Wicca and blend them into a new faith, despite the fact that each of these religions makes claims that deny the claims of the other.

As much as advocates of New Age and alternative spirituality might want to deny it, the major religions of the world do not fundamentally align with each other. Instead, they strike out in nearly opposite directions. For example, Christianity maintains that Jesus Christ is a God/man, the only son of the only God. Islam maintains that Jesus Christ is but one in a series of human prophets. Hinduism maintains that Jesus Christ was at best an

181

especially enlightened guru. Judaism maintains that Jesus Christ was an errant rabbi. How can these claims be reconciled? They cannot be, unless what these religions say about themselves is not taken seriously.

Consider, too, that Christianity holds sin to be at the root of the troubled human condition. Buddhism teaches that suffering is man's greatest problem. Islam maintains that failure to fulfill the will of Allah is responsible for human tragedy. Hinduism teaches that the human condition is not even real.

Hinduism also teaches that evil is an illusion. Christianity teaches that evil is a result of a human fall from grace. Islam teaches that evil exists and is encouraged by Satan, who often takes the form of a black dog. Buddhism insists that the only true evil is human suffering.

Christians maintain that human beings must believe in the atoning work of Jesus Christ. Hindus believe that man must fulfill *karma* in order to be liberated from *maya* and become one with *Brahma*. Buddhists believe that man should seek nirvana through the Eightfold Path. Muslims believe that men must submit to Allah if they are to enter paradise.

These are completely different belief systems, offering completely different views of the world and insisting on completely contradictory solutions. It is dishonest to contend that they somehow point in the same direction and that with a little modification they can be fashioned into something unified and new.

Yet this is precisely what Oprah Winfrey believes she can do.

3. Religions can be redefined at will.

There is a third pillar of the Oprah Winfrey religious worldview and it is that the religions of the world can be remade for comfort and convenience. This is not only a characteristic of Winfrey's approach to religion, but it is one of the hallmarks of baby boomer spirituality. Religions that have existed for centuries, some for millennia, are redesigned according to the mores of the moment, according to the creative impulses of a people just decades old. Theologies are simplified. Terms are redefined. Religious mythologies are reworked, often according to Freud, Marx, Darwin, or Kant. Entire ancient belief systems are reinterpreted and popularized. It is a breathtaking conceit and it is an astonishing disregard for the traditions of the centuries, for the ancient ways granted to this generation as a gift.

The best example of this tendency is in the reworking of Hinduism by the baby boomers that we have already examined. The postwar generation wanted to lean to the mysticism of the East but they found pure Hinduism too difficult to accept. It required a belief in this world as a false reality, in a brand of reincarnation that meant any human being walking the earth might once have been an amoeba or a gnat or a chimp. It meant that rather than life being groovy, it might actually be a prison. It might be a constant cycle of existence and not necessarily upward to enlightenment and ultimate release. It also meant associating with the embarrassing varieties of Hinduism found in India. The knowing understood that in the Hinduism of India there were temples where rats were worshipped as incarnations of gods. There were penis cults and nudity cults and temples devoted to the ritual deflowering of teenaged girls.

Then there was the assault of Hinduism on the human personality. The boomers had asserted themselves against the stilted conformity of their parents' generation and had demanded freedom of expression for themselves. They wanted their individualism, their right to be as vibrantly unique as they wanted to be. This is part of what led to the "generation gap" and to the great flowering of art and creativity with which the boomers graced the world. But then that same generation turned eastward spiritually and found in Hinduism an insistence that they divest themselves of personhood, erase themselves for the sake of becoming one with *Brahma* or cosmic consciousness or the One of universal existence. Some youths took this call seriously, moved to India from the suburbs of America, learned the ways of the gurus and, often, descended into madness. Most remained in the West and joined their generation in removing the offending portions of Eastern thinking. This produced the faux Hinduism of the New Age movement we know today.

Maya, then, was transformed from the belief in an artificial reality that ought to be escaped to a malleable reality that could be shaped by thought and soul force. Reincarnation, or *samsara*, became not the hellish imprisonment of unending life cycles it was in the East but a trendy belief in previous existences as the famous and the glamorous. "I was Queen Elizabeth I in a previous life," was one expression of this popular belief. Mantras became syllables to chant for de-stressing rather than the names of Hindu deities to be summoned in meditation.[18] And yoga became merely exercise rather than the physical positions of worship designed to create "union"—the meaning of the word *yoga*—that it was understood to be in the East. And never would a Western youth who looked East for his spirituality have dreamed of endorsing the caste system of Hinduism, which left the poor and the broken languishing in their agony in honor of the law of *karma*. All was sanitized. All was rearranged. All was made conformable to the values of a generation eager to break from tradition in every form.

This became the manner of a generation and of the advocates of alternative spirituality for decades to come. None was more adept at this than Oprah Winfrey. She would chant mantras before her breathless audiences and never acknowledge that she was borrowing from a practice designed to summon deities. She would devote an entire one-hour program to the topic of *karma* and never come close to dealing with the original Hindu concept. She would do hours of interviews with the likes of Marianne Williamson, Gary Zukav, Deepak Chopra, or Eckhart Tolle and perhaps never realize that all of these teachers were advocating a modified Hinduism that would have been foreign to the orthodox Hindus on the streets of New Delhi. She moved effortlessly among the religions of the world, borrowing from them at will, redefining their meaning according to her need, untroubled by the ancient ways or respect for the cherished faiths of billions of the faithful.

The great concern was not just that she did violence to traditional religions but that she and her fellow spiritual innovators created new, untested, unsupported religions. They were religions without text, without history, without system, without creed, and without proof of benefit to human lives. These were spiritual faiths, true, but they were also secular, in the sense that the word *secular* means "of the age." These religions were fashioned for the moment, comprised of trendy ideas but then presented as ancient beliefs through stolen language and rituals. This gave the wispy, ethereal, religious mood of the moment an aura of depth and gravitas, when in fact it was simply another stage in the passing parade of *avant-garde* experimental spirituality that exhausted so many baby boomers and made no lasting contribution to religions of substance.

4. All true religion enhances self.

In the great religions of the world, there is nearly always a hero story. In Christianity, that hero is Jesus Christ, who sets aside the privileges of divinity to die a horrid death for all mankind. In Judaism, there are Abraham and Moses and David and, of course, the coming Messiah. In fact, in Judaism, the Torah itself is celebrated as heroic. In Islam there is Mohammad and the prophets who come before him: Adam, Noah, Abraham, Moses, and Jesus. In Buddhism there is Siddhartha Gautama, the Buddha himself, and in Hinduism there are thousands of hero tales and as many heroic gods.

In these religions, and in the other historic faiths there is not space to mention here, there is nearly always a call for man to focus on a venerated being or some force beyond him. There is a god or a divine consciousness or some wholly other entity to which the faithful are meant to sacrificially devote themselves. It might be the glory of God or the cause of the faith or the obedience to a creed, but there is at heart the understanding that man must put himself in the service or the pursuit of something beyond.

In the religion of Oprah Winfrey, and certainly in the religions of the teachers she gathers around her, the opposite is true. The hero of the story of faith is self. It is the individual that is the object, the beneficiary, the focus of adoration, and the ultimate purpose of the faith. The universe is understood to be ever bending to enchant the individual. All doctrines and creeds are measured in terms of the self. The final victory of the religion is a liberated, happy, self-possessed, prosperous, peaceful individual. The faithful do not seek God or the good of mankind but rather their "divine self," their "spiritual self," their "deified form," or their "transformed beingness."

This, in short, is the complete inversion of most traditional religions and it is not hard to imagine this as the spirituality that the "me generation" might naturally devise for themselves. The boomers are more about self-fulfillment, self-expression, self-enhancement, and the enchantment of the divine self than any other generation on earth. Some have seen this as the product of stunted development. In this view, the boomers are perpetual adolescents who will not pass out of what would otherwise be a natural, self-centered phase. Others have seen this as the by-product of rebellion. Having broken from the frozen spirituality and regimented culture of their parents' generation, the boomers in this view remained in perpetual rebellion, which meant that they remained in perpetual focus on themselves and their own prerogatives. They resisted the outer, the traditional, the expected, and anything that felt to them like conformity. Always the focus was upon themselves. Then, of course, there were the promises of the gurus. The boomer generation was told they could have it all and feel good about it, too, that this was more than the will of the divine; it was their birthright. Any generation that watches Deepak Chopra on PBS will conclude that the universe waits to grace them with belonging, with feelings of well-being, and riches of every kind. It is a hard message to resist and it found a welcome home in the souls of those who came of age in the 1960s.

We find, then, that the religion of Oprah Winfrey and her tribe is much about the kingdom of self. There is generosity, yes, and a touching hope to do good in the world. Boomers have been among the most socially conscious of nearly any in history. Still, the religions this generation have fashioned for themselves have been almost without exception religions that center upon the self and the self's well-being. This has even led the boomers to dramatically transform concepts borrowed from other religions and to transform them so as to make the self the center of all things. The classic example of this is *karma*—the duty owed by man trapped in a hellish incarnation according to Hinduism but made the measure of "how much good fortune can come to me" in a trendy New Age brand of spirituality.

The self-centeredness of the boomer brand of spirituality has created such a magnetic pull upon the culture that it has even affected religions that esteem unselfishness as a virtue. The core message of Christianity, for example, was well expressed by Dietrich Bonhoeffer in his masterful *The Cost of Discipleship* when he wrote, "When Christ bids a man, he bids him come and die." Bonheoffer lived out this ethic by laying down his life to oppose Nazism during World War II. Yet Christian pastors today often bemoan the "what have you done for me lately" demands of self-oriented boomers. This generation's self-serving insistences and the acquiescence of Christian churches have created a Christianity of therapeutic preaching, me-oriented worship, self-enchanting theology, and ministries desperate to meet every social need of their parishioners. This is a far cry from the kind of Christianity created by the Jesus Christ who commanded men to lay down their lives for God.

There is also the question of what evidence there is for believing the human self ought to be the center of the universe. Science does not confirm this. The major world religions do not confirm this. Even psychology does not confirm this. A human being too much enveloped in self is considered in some way mentally dysfunctional. And certainly the opposite would seem to be true, though the evidence for this may be anecdotal. Survey after survey confirms that individuals are happiest when giving to others, when immersed in a cause alongside others, or even when they "lose themselves" in a sport, an art, a hobby, or an experience.

We should ask, too, about the results. We have had decades of a self-interested, self-invested, self-preoccupied spirituality, and surely we should have seen culturewide benefits if it indeed is the answer to the human condition. Have we seen divorce rates drop? Crime rates? More contentment in the workplace? A greater sense of personal fulfillment? A reduction in the reliance on psychiatric drugs? An overall more enlightened, contented society? No, none of these. Instead, we live in a culture, if recent major magazine covers are any guide, of whining, offended, resentful citizens who feel betrayed by society and life and believe they are entitled to more.

It would seem, then, that the Oprah Winfrey brand of self-centered faith—one in which she insists that "gurus" are sent "not to teach us about their divinity but to teach us about our own"—is a setup for disillusionment.[19] If man is not intended to find contentment in pursuit of the divine self, then Oprah Winfrey's spirituality is not only a fairy tale but a dangerous lie that could lead millions into greater dissatisfaction with life, into greater retreat from society into the personal, and into the illusion of being gods rather than seeking a genuine God who answers the soul's cry.

○

These, then, are the mainstays of Oprah Winfrey's religion. She believes that spirituality and religion are two different things and that her audiences can follow her in her nontraditional spirituality without abandoning the religions of their youth. She also believes that the great religions of the world can be blended, though they often make completely competing claims. She believes it is her right to take portions of these faiths and rework them as she wills, as her culture and needs demand. And she believes inherently that true religion finds its object in the self, in the enhancement and enchantment of the human being. These are the pillars, the certainties of the Oprah Winfrey religious worldview, and they are the basis for what she believes.

The Seven Principles of Oprah Winfrey's Philosophy

Having understood her broader religious assumptions, we should try to understand Oprah Winfrey's core religious beliefs. These will have to be discerned from her pronouncements and what she endorses in the thoughts of others, but they are essential to understanding Winfrey's spiritual/religious vision.

1. Reality is "thin."

The term *thin* is often used to describe an ancient pagan Celtic belief about the physical world. The Celts believed the earth was the gateway to the spiritual world and that some places, like groves or springs, were particularly "thin," meaning they provided easier access to the invisible realm. The Celtic priesthood, the Druids, was adept at knowing where these thin places were and establishing altars and structures of worship there. When the Celts turned to Christianity, they carried this belief—that the divine intersects with nature—with them into their new faith and gave the Christian church a grand theology of "sacred space" or "sacramental geography."

To say that Oprah Winfrey believes that reality is thin is not to say that she believes what the ancient Celts believed. Still, thin is perhaps the best term to use in describing the central truth of Winfrey's view of reality. She believes—as her gurus have taught her—that the seen world is not as real as it appears. It is not a fantasy, but it is not ultimate reality either. Instead, it is thin. It is a mist over ultimate reality. It is infirm and malleable. It is, as the classic definition of *maya* suggests, real only as a dream is real: it actually exists, but it does not depict ultimate reality.

This concept is at the heart of what nearly all of Winfrey's favorite teachers believe. Each of them builds their spirituality around a concept of this present physical world being less real, less impermeable, than it might appear. In each case, this belief opens the door to the next logical step, which is a shift in understanding of the individual, both his mind and his body. As Deepak Chopra suggests in one of his leading books,

> Our bodies, which seem so solid and finite, are not . . . we are no denser than the air around us and indistinguishable from our surroundings. Finally, since quantum physics asserts that matter and energy are interchangeable, we are not individual beings at all but merely local expressions of an infinite, universal field of energy. A smart field of energy: "All of us are connected to patterns of intelligence that govern the whole cosmos. Our bodies are part of a universal body, our minds an aspect of a universal mind."[20]

This belief in a reality that is insubstantial and pliable is at the basis of much that Oprah Winfrey believes. Because reality is probably only a kind of energy field, we are all one with it. This leads to the monism of many of Oprah's favorite teachers. It is why Marianne Williamson can say that there is "only one of us here." It is why Gary Zukav believes that we should let go and let the universe and the lessons learned in reincarnation elevate above reality. It is why Deepak Chopra does not fear pain: he "floats in a quantum fog as photons wink in and out of existence. Observing these shifting patterns, I feel no attachment to any of them. They come and go. I am not even troubled by having no permanent home. It is enough to be bathed in the light."[21] In other words, pain does not trouble him because he believes that ultimately pain is unreal.

It is this unreality of the seen world that allows Oprah to believe that thoughts, intention, visual imaging, and believing enough can shape reality. And this, of course, is what leads to believing in the divine self. If the universe is all there is, and if the universe is all energy, and if human beings are nothing more than "local expressions" of that energy, then human beings are as much God as anything else is. Moreover, if human beings can shape the energy of the universe through thought or action, then they, as creators of the known world, are indeed gods: gods of a Godless reality.

2. If there is a God, he may be no more than energy.

In her early years, when Oprah Winfrey was a Baptist, she believed in a God who was a living being, all-powerful and all-knowing, who stood apart and above from his creation. He spoke the universe into being and he created man in his own image. He had a personality, a voice, a will, emotions, and he had presence, which was, if not quite a human body, then at least the ability to be in one place if he chose to be.

As Oprah moved through her reconsideration phase, after the "jealous God" sermon at Baltimore's Bethel A.M.E., she did not set out to rewrite her understanding of God but she did gravitate to ideas that brought a sovereign God into question. Her self-help books taught her about a universe made of energy. This energy is all there is, some of her favorite authors taught, and human thoughts or intention channel this energy in order to alter reality. This means that human thought is the most powerful thing in the universe. It also means that what passes for God is either that energy itself or it is the human beings who can control energy. But if this scheme is true, there is no God of the kind Oprah Winfrey worshipped in her youth.

The oddity here is that Oprah Winfrey claims to be a Christian and claims to believe in a God. Yet she affirms the philosophies of dozens of New Age teachers who believe that God is at best impersonal intelligence and that Jesus Christ was simply a man who mastered the art of controlling that intelligence or energy for his purposes. In other words, Oprah regularly affirms beliefs that completely undo her Christian faith, and nowhere is this clearer than in the conflict between the Christian view and New Age view of God.

This is likely why she frequently seems confused when referring to God. She often speaks of God but then adds explanatory phrases like "or whatever they may call that."[22] This is not the certainty of a Christian who believes in God and his son, Jesus Christ. It is instead the hesitation born of the New Age influence, born of the belief that what passes for God is thought or energy or universal consciousness but nothing approximating the all-powerful individual being that Christians call God.

This is not unique to Winfrey. We have already seen that Marianne Williamson speaks of God in half a dozen conflicting ways and some of them do not admit a God who is a person at all. Nor do the schemes of Deepak Chopra or Eckhart Tolle or Gary Zukav allow for a personal God, ruler of all things. Yet Oprah nods at their pronouncements and then is uncertain about her own beliefs, as her many murky explanations of God reveal.

This idea of God as consciousness or energy is, just like Winfrey's beliefs about reality, at the heart of much else that she believes. If God is energy, then we are all God. If God is universal mind, then thoughts rule reality. If God is consciousness, then human beings are not accountable to a personal God who makes his will known. If God is merely spiritual potential, then what passes for God is nothing more than a nameless, faceless spiritual force serving the wishes of mankind.

It should be said, too, that in much of alternative spirituality, uncertainty seems to be the point. It is possible to listen to a best-selling New Age motivational speaker and realize that he is uncertain about what God is, uncertain about what reality is, and uncertain about what human beings are. He is not uncertain, though, about the fact that the universe intends us only wealth and happiness and he is not uncertain about the fact that the old Judeo-Christian morality is hindering the evolution of mankind. Sleep with whomever you choose.

This explains Oprah Winfrey's hesitation about exactly who God is. It also explains why she is slow to identify herself as a Christian anymore. She is a smart woman and she knows that God cannot be the perfect Lord of all and a universal benevolent vibration of energy at the same time. And so she is unsure, which, sadly, may very well have been what her teachers intended from the beginning.

3. Thoughts shape reality.

In a universe in which there is no personal, all-powerful God and in which everything is an extension of energy or consciousness, human thought or intention rules. This is what Oprah Winfrey believes and it explains why she was so wildly drawn to *The Secret* and its irrefutable Law of Attraction: "thoughts become things." For *The Secret* to be true, there cannot be a divine will operating in the universe. In other words, there cannot be a being approximating the biblical God. Instead, the universe must be made up of eagerly available energy, sensitive to the influence of human thought. As Winfrey exulted when *The Secret* was presented on her program in 2007, "It means that everything that happens to you, good and bad, you are attracting to yourself. It's something that I really have believed for years, that the energy you put out into the world is always gonna be coming back to you. That's the basic principle."[23]

It is a belief as old as the Hindu concept of "cosmic conscious-ness" and as recent as cutting-edge experiments in "noetic science." The core principle is simple: thought is a substance outside the human body that takes the form of highly ordered energy capable of changing the physical universe. We likely think of parlor tricks like bending spoons, but experiments have been done purporting to prove that thought affects the rate of plant growth, the direc-tion fish swim, and even chemical reactions in the human body. As new science author Lynne McTaggart has written, "Living con-sciousness somehow is the influence that turns the possibility of something into something real. The most essential ingredient in creating our universe is the consciousness that observes it."[24]

This phenomenon played a prominent role in novelist Dan Brown's best-selling *The Lost Symbol*. One of Brown's charac-ters exults, "Human thought can literally transform the physical world. . . . We are the masters of our own universe. . . . This is the missing link between modern science and ancient mysticism."[25] It is a hope many harbor, not only in the scientific community but also in the arena of alternative spirituality. It is also a hope that has had profound impact on Oprah Winfrey. This possibil-ity of thought affecting matter is behind her belief in the Law of Attraction, her confidence in the power of intention, her certainty that meditating creates its own realities, and her belief in the con-nection between prosperity and inner vision.

Yet even if there is a connection between human thought and the physical universe—and there does seem to be evidence for this at lower levels of impact—there are nevertheless two troubling considerations. First, that thought can affect the human body or perhaps influence the swimming patterns of fish is a far cry from believing that a woman's entire existence is shaped by her thoughts. Yet this is the dynamic upon which Oprah Winfrey has based her life and by which she explains her success. It is also the dynamic she urges upon her audiences. A second and even greater concern is that this matter of thought impacting the physical world works for both positive and negative results. As Oprah herself said of the Law of Attraction, "everything that happens to you, good and bad, you are attracting to yourself." While this principle may make for an intriguing parlor game when it comes to good things like prosperity and a new love, it becomes a horrendous accusation against those who experience tragedy. Has the rape victim drawn a rapist through her thought life? Is the welfare mother really impoverished because she believes she is? Is a family who has lost a child to be charged with destructive thought patterns as the cause of their heartbreak? The Law of Attraction removes good and evil in the world and leaves only productive and destructive thoughts. It is a mysticism with far-reaching repercussions, on a scope more vast than is ever considered on *The Oprah Winfrey Show*.

4. The universe intends only good.

One of the central certainties of Oprah Winfrey's spirituality is that the universe in all its various forms only intends to grace human beings with good. It is benevolent, even loving. Uninhibited by destructive human thought and action, the universe would extend nothing but blessing and kindness to human beings. The best human response, then, is as Gary Zukav urges: "Let go. Trust. Create. Be who you are. The rest is up to your nonphysical Teachers and the Universe. Take your hands off the steering wheel. Be able to say to the Universe, 'Thy will be done,' and know it within your intentions."[26]

This belief in the essential goodness of reality is a result of the monism that Oprah and her spiritual teachers insist upon. If there is indeed only one being in the universe, if—as Marianne Williamson insists—there is only one of us here, then that oneness must be at least morally neutral if not inherently good. In fact, monism removes the whole question of good and evil. If there is only one living being and all human beings are an extension of that one being, then as the Beatles once sang on their *Magical Mystery Tour* album, "I am he as you are he and you are me and we are all together."[27] There are no opposites, no one part acting on the other, no varying categories. Good and evil do not exist. There is only existence and there is only the question of how each being integrates into that single existence.

For Oprah Winfrey, this means only good, only blessing, only enchantment. Humans create what is perceived as evil through their destructive thoughts and actions. The universe itself is either neutral or good and can be approached so that only good things come to human lives.

This insistence upon the inherent good intentions of the universe has made Winfrey both confused and frustrated with the existence of evil in the world. She has said, for example, that she chose to build her famous leadership academy for girls in South Africa because she was frustrated with the state of American schools. As she told *Newsweek*, "I became so frustrated with visiting inner-city schools that I just stopped going. The sense that you need to learn just isn't there. If you ask the kids what they want or need, they will say an iPod or some sneakers. In South Africa, they don't ask for money or toys. They ask for uniforms so they can go to school."[28] When a local broadcaster asked her if she would give money to help improve the schools of Baltimore, the city that was her home for many years, she angrily retorted, "What I've learned from my philanthropic giving is that unless you can create sustainable change, then it's a waste, you might as well pee on it."[29] Winfrey was equally confused by the events of September 11, 2001. As Jennifer Harris and Elwood Watson have written in their book *The Oprah Phenomenon*, following 9/11, Oprah found herself caught between "the problematic immanent world and the other-worldliness of eastern mysticism."[30] For a woman who believes that her spirituality carries with it the power to change reality for the better, her irritation with "the problematic immanent world" is odd indeed. Couldn't she change the experience of Baltimore schoolchildren through the Law of Attraction?

Obviously, what Oprah's religious worldview does not contain is a solution for the problem theologians call "theodicy," which deals with matters like God's just government of the world and the problem of good and evil. At the very least, a religious worldview that includes the reality of both good and evil is a realistic worldview. Those who hold to it will not be surprised by suffering and pain. They will grieve at the hardships of mankind, but they will not be confused or spiritually shattered by the existence of tragedy and loss. But the monistic universe that Oprah believes in has no answer for the presence of evil beyond blaming individual thoughts and intentions. If trusting the universe does not produce blessing and fortune, there is no further explanation.

The evidence seems to suggest that the universe is, in fact, a place of great beauty and peace but also a place of danger and horror. In space, collisions between astral bodies occur constantly. On earth, floods, earthquakes, tsunamis, fires, and volcanic eruptions occur quite apart from man's involvement. Animals kill, diseases ravage, and human beings give in to both the better and the lesser angels of their nature. No objective observer of life on earth would conclude that a universal energy is ever capable of granting goodness but that man is in the way. Instead, he would conclude that the universe is a powerful, thrashing place that is both glorious and terrifying, both creative and cruelly destructive.

Monism does not allow for this. Nor does the religious worldview of Oprah Winfrey.

5. Destiny rules.

If there is anything certain of Oprah Winfrey's beliefs, it is that she believes in the power of destiny. She speaks of it often and is confident that it explains much that is in the world, including her life and success. She began to believe she was destined to do great things from the time of that memorable conversation with her grandmother when she was four. Later, in high school, she thought nothing of introducing herself to a teacher by announcing she would be famous. She told her father she would be great one day and even felt that destiny was calling when she placed her hands on the famous names in front of Grauman's Chinese Theatre in Hollywood. Throughout her life, whether it was being on television or getting a part in *The Color Purple* or producing *Beloved* or turning her television show toward spiritual themes, she has never hesitated to acknowledge that destiny played a role.

It is not hard to understand the original source of this idea in her life. The idea of a God who rules the world as he wishes and determines a purpose for every human life is a cherished belief in Christian theology. Oprah would have absorbed this from the Christian teaching she received at her grandmother's knee and from the Baptist church she attended in Kosciusko. Later, in Nashville, Vernon would have emphasized this confidence, particularly as he was calling his wayward daughter to live a life honoring to the purposes of God. There is every indication that Oprah took these lessons to heart and made a belief in destiny part of her budding religious worldview.

Yet with both men and nations, there is a tendency to secularize the idea of destiny. The calling of a sovereign God becomes the certainty of a charmed life; a people once determined to be a "city upon a hill" descend spiritually and grasp instead an arrogant doctrine of manifest destiny. So it seems to have been with Oprah Winfrey. As she moved away from the faith of her youth and clung to other, more motivational beliefs, she nevertheless held on to the idea that she was destined, that somehow the universe had chosen her for a purpose.

It was easy to understand the Baptist Oprah believing this. It was even possible to understand the secularized Oprah believing it. It is difficult to understand, though, how New Age Oprah is able to believe in a personal destiny for her life. If she has made the teachings of Williamson, Tolle, Zukav, and Chopra her own, she has laid aside the idea of the personal God who determines destinies. She has even laid aside the idea of the personal at all. Instead, there is only energy or cosmic consciousness or universal mind. And what have these to do with destiny? How would universal energy determine one human life for a given purpose and another for yet a different purpose?

What Oprah has done is borrow a favorite idea from a religion she no longer holds and attach it to a religious pastiche that is foreign to it. The Hinduism to which she now leans does not teach personal destiny. It teaches that the individual person is imprisoned in his personhood. He must be liberated and become one with the impersonal cosmic consciousness of the universe. There is no destiny. In fact, no one is special or chosen or called. Instead, all is one: "I am he as you are he and you are me and we are all together." Still, the New Age movement, which was built upon Hinduism and filtered through Western culture, tries to hold on to the biblical concept of destiny or, more properly, predestination. We see this theme played out in dozens of movies, books, and television shows today. Modern man desperately wants to believe there is a purpose for life in general and for each man specifically, and yet the more he turns toward New Age spirituality the more he turns from the concept of God out of which comes the idea of destiny in the first place.

It is easy for a woman to believe herself special. It is easy for her to believe that she is chosen, magical, graced, or touched by the hand of fate. All that is required is a few fortunate events, a certain deferential treatment by others, and the right amount of arrogance and pride. Believing, though, does not alone make it so. Instead, if a woman believes herself destined, she should have a broader belief system consistent with her idea of destiny and she should live humbly as befits a recipient of undeserved grace. Both of these are in question in the life of Oprah Winfrey.

6. The only ethic is love.

There is a curious underlying theme to New Age spirituality and thus to the spirituality of Oprah Winfrey. It is that traditional morality has failed us. The moral constraints of the Judeo-Christian tradition are no longer a fit. We should fashion a new morality, then, free from the narrow restrictions of the past and built upon the power of universal love.

But what would this new morality look like? Would it be modeled on the teachings of Gary Zukav, who believes that temporary spiritual marriages should replace traditional marriage and families? Would it be modeled on the urgings of Marianne Williamson, who believes it is proper to have sex with someone the minute you hear a voice in your head saying, "Disrobe"? Or would it be modeled on the consensus of New Age teaching, which is that there is no good or evil, only bad *karma*, only actions that bring positive or negative energy in return?

There simply is no way to know. The problem with New Age ethics is they are built on positive feelings, on energy or vibrations that are affirming and tender and warm, but they provide no guidelines, no truths or commandments or principles or maxims that allow a person to live wisely and lovingly in the modern world. And they are inconsistent. Is it loving to a spouse to have sex with another person simply because the word *disrobe* forms itself in the mind? Is it loving to children to end a marriage simply because the relationship has "ceased to evolve"? Is it loving to take property from a rich man to give it to the poor? Is it loving to pay a man if he refuses to work, or pass a student if he refuses to study? Is it loving to have sex with a minor? With a child? With the mentally infirm? With an animal? In other words, what ethical content does the idea of love offer us if it is nothing more than a good feeling about one another?

It is easy to understand how this vision for a new morality arose from the moral revolution of the early baby boom years. They had grown up in their parents' traditional morality, which often amounted to a code of behavior without source, without consistency, and without noble purpose. Societal expectations usually reinforced a code of required behaviors violated at risk of punishment. It was the morality of the American Judeo-Christian heritage without benefit of Judeo-Christian convictions. And so the young chafed, then questioned, then resisted, and then openly rebelled. The cultural revolution of the 1960s was the result. In nearly every arena, from sexual ethics to language to religion to drugs to politics, boundaries were challenged and then destroyed if possible.

What began as a casting off of restraint evolved into a hope for a new order, a refashioned society. The counterculture spoke of the greening of America or the age of Aquarius or a new world a-coming. It was naïve but it was heartfelt, and it arose from the certainty that the ways of the past had failed mankind and that it fell to the young to experiment their way to something new and more human.

Sometimes this experimenting was horrifying. Parents of the World War II generation walking the streets of Berkeley, California, in the late 1960s were often stunned to read alternative newspapers celebrating syphilis as a disease of honor. Free love meant sex with anyone anywhere and all as a blow against marriage and the demands of family and anything that smacked of a traditional vision of holiness. To be physically unclean was to be free. To be broke was to be superior. To be anti and counter was to be wise and enlightened.

In time, this adolescent phase passed and a more serious moral purpose emerged. The mysticism of the East worked its way into an already experimenting, libertine culture to produce a society striving to convince itself that it could exist on a single-principle morality: love is all you need. Simply be kind and accepting. Nothing else matters. This became the moral vision of the baby boom generation. As the years passed, conscientious boomers strove to embrace every alternative lifestyle, every perverse preference.

The result was, well, *The Oprah Winfrey Show* of the early years, in which every freakish variation was paraded before cameras for its shock value, the underlying message being, "This is what we must allow if we are to be a free people." The typical episode would reveal Winfrey exploring some new alternative lifestyle, appetite, or subculture with intense fascination yet with a studied aversion to judgment or moral appeal. Once Winfrey entered her spiritual phase in the mid-1990s, this refusal to pass judgment shifted into full acceptance as long as a loving relationship was somewhere at the heart of the social deviation in view.

What seemed to work for an episode of *The Oprah Winfrey Show*, though, did not seem to work as well for society as a whole. What did the ethic of New Age love have to say about the treatment of child molesters? Or illegal immigrants? Or the perpetrators of 9/11? And could this ethic prevent new, petty legalisms from arising? Many boomers stood by mystified as those who smoked in public places were sometimes treated with a rage befitting rapists. The overweight became targets, as did those whose words violated the shifting tides of political correctness. It became increasingly obvious that a murky ethic of love did not provide the fully orbed vision of justice or a beefy enough concept of the noble society to inform manners and mores, much less a system of jurisprudence.

The ethics of New Age spirituality might have been thrilling to the ticket-buying audiences of Zukav, Williamson, or Chopra, but they provided little of value to society as a whole. This did not prevent the prophets of alternative spirituality from urging their experimental morality on the world. Nor did it prevent Oprah Winfrey from endorsing that morality from her lofty media perch.

7. Experience trumps truth.

It has been well said that when it comes to matters of religion and spirituality, this generation is more concerned with what works than what is true. The measure of every belief and practice is how effective it is in creating meaningful experience. There is little concern for whether that experience is based on anything lastingly true. In fact, modern spirituality is not always certain that there is anything true in the revealed or eternal sense. Instead, the word *truth* is replaced with the word *valid*, and always the focus is upon valid experiences that bring wealth and happiness to the ever-enchanted self.

Oprah Winfrey has been a champion in this cause. In fact, it is this refusal to speak in terms of what is true but rather in terms of what creates thrilling experience that allows her to distinguish her spirituality from her religion. She is not interested in debating weighty matters such as the existence of God or the resurrection of Jesus Christ or the reality of nirvana or the ascension of Mohammad. She sidesteps these, sometimes with statements as direct as "I'm not going to get into a religious debate with you," and this just after she has urged a religious concept upon her audience. She wants the experiences her stable of teachers have promised. She wants peace and well-being and focus. She wants to feel one with an otherwise lonely universe and she wants to be empowered to live out her life. She wants the ancestors to enable her to act and "Greater Spirit" to guide her in business and the Law of Attraction to grant her vast wealth. Never, though, is truth a concern. Never is the measure of an idea or a practice whether it derives from what is immutable and sure.

There is, of course, danger in this. It is theoretically possible that Oprah Winfrey can live stress free through her mantras and her yoga and her visualization and still offend a deity who requires something else of her. It is possible that she might live a fabulously wealthy life and attribute it all to the power of her thoughts and intentions when in fact it is all the gift of God for a purpose she has never fulfilled. It is also possible that she might genuinely make contact with the spirits of her ancestors or the genie of Islam or the *kami* of Japanese Shintoism or the spirit guides who give counsel between incarnations whom Gary Zukav extols, never imagining that those spirits might not be as loving and good as she assumes them to be.

The reality is that feelings and experience are no indicator of truth. We know this from daily experience. The pilot who flies his plane according to what his body tells him, according to how he feels rather than by his instruments, is heading for a crash. The doctor who relies on his feelings about the amount of medicine to give to a patient is likely to do great harm. We want bus drivers to drive by their instruments and the road signs and we want bankers to leave their feelings at home when managing our accounts. This is because feelings and experience often have little to do with truth. In fact, they can be highly unreliable, as every investigator of a traffic accident knows: eyewitnesses, those who experienced the crash, are usually the least reliable sources of fact.

What would seem to be the most satisfying to the human soul is experience based on truth rather than experience for its own sake. If there is a God, then it would seem that the hunger of the heart is to know him, to hear his voice or feel his love or know when he is near. If the message of Buddhism is true, then it would seem that the genuine experience comes after rising above suffering and divesting oneself of passion through the Eightfold Path. Experience alone will not achieve this goal. If the vision of Allah presented in Islam is true, then there is an obedient life to be lived, regardless of how the subjects of Allah feel about it and regardless of what they experience. "Valid experience"—joyous, pleasurable experience—is for paradise. And Judaism extols joy in the presence of God and celebration of the blessings of life, but only after the sacrifice of obedience is made.

Indeed, much of what traditional faiths require is purposefully counter to the sweet experience of alternative spirituality. A number of the major traditional religions call for fasting. Some require sacrificial giving. Most urge self-denial. Christianity even extols laying down one's life for others, and the word used for *life* in the original language of the New Testament does not refer to biological life but rather to the inner life, the realm of dreams and hopes and aspirations. None of these experiences are judged by whether or not they work, but rather by whether they are true—true in the sense that they are based on a system of truth beyond the individual.

The great fear, of course, is that by questioning and then reworking traditional religions and then making experience the arbiter of all spiritual value, Oprah Winfrey may very well be leading millions into a hodge-podge spirituality that will fail them in the time of trouble, that will not answer their soul's need and will ultimately prove false, both as a matter of genuine experience and as a matter of eternal truth.

O

And so we have examined four pillars of Oprah Winfrey's religious worldview and seven principles of her philosophy and

I have disagreed with all of them. I can do no other. I am, as I admitted in the introduction to this book, a Christian, and what Oprah Winfrey believes cuts across every major doctrine of the Christian faith. In fact, it cuts across nearly every major doctrine of nearly every major traditional faith except Hinduism and a few other Eastern religions. Beyond my own perspectives, though, what she believes is illogical, inconsistent, arrogant, destructive, and amazingly naïve.

Still, having said this, there are some matters about which I agree with Oprah and it would be disingenuous of me—and un-Christian—not to acknowledge these while I am expressing my disagreement with such vehemence.

I can applaud, for example, Winfrey's emphasis on man as a spiritual being. I believe with her that man is more than his body, more than what he does, and more than what is seen. She is right to say that we are a spiritually needy people and that we are incomplete without a supernatural filling of our souls.

Ask the average modern man what he desires in life and he will say that he wants food and shelter, he wants a place to belong, he wants people who care for him, and he wants enjoyment and fun. But this is a dog's life, the canine version of destiny. Man is made for more. As St. Augustine said, "Lord, you have formed us for yourself, and our hearts are restless until they find their rest in thee." Both Oprah and I agree on the restless heart, though we would disagree about how that heart finds the rest it seeks.

I can also affirm Oprah's emphasis that only spiritual wholeness leads to complete healing for the soul. Life wounds. Life scars. Life deforms us with its bludgeoning ways. We can be restored somewhat by physical treatment and psychological therapy, but Oprah is right that spiritual power is needed as well. As the most famous psalm of King David assures, "He restores my soul." Man is a spiritual being and requires spiritual restoration as well as natural. Again, Ms. Winfrey and I would disagree about how this happens, but I can stand with her for spiritual healing as a valid need of all men.

She is right, too, about the connection between the spiritual life and material prosperity. This is not merely the province of overheated television preachers and charlatans. Most all the great faiths promise blessings to those who bless, prosperity to those who prosper others, generosity upon those who are generous. Most religions build around the idea of sowing and reaping, call it whatever they may. Even agnostics can affirm that "what goes around comes around." It is a principle of the universe. I believe it is a principle, perhaps a law, devised by a loving God who is himself generous and delights when his children are likewise. Ms. Winfrey believes it is the financial side of karma. Regardless, we can see in the cultures of the world as we can in history that there is a connection between prosperity and the religious worldview of a people.

I can also celebrate her emphasis on spirituality leading to generosity and a desire to do social good. In fact, my Christianity leads me to believe I really only know if someone believes sincerely by the fruit he bears in his life, and generosity and care for the needy is one of the most important "fruits" of true religion among them all. This is not trying to buy off a deity with giving as some have contended. It is instead, for Christians, the right response to grace, part of the way one gives thanks for the goodness of God. To the extent that Oprah Winfrey has urged millions to evaluate what they believe by its social impact, I'm grateful.

She is also not wrong about rituals. Ceremony, liturgy, rituals—all of these are ways that we break into the routine and acknowledge the spiritual, that we express truth and remind ourselves of the unseen. A Christian crosses himself or kneels to receive Communion or raises his hands during worship or folds his hands in prayer. He lights a candle or bows his head or asks a blessing before a meal. The more liturgical Christians observe a church calendar, keep the offices of the day, or pray from the Book of Common Prayer. Every faith and every variation on every faith has its rituals and symbols.

This desire for liturgy is hardwired into our souls. It has always been a source of amusement to me that a young couple planning to get married will insist upon a vast array of liturgical expressions even if they are not particularly religious and have never darkened the door of a house of worship. They will want altars and candles and ministers in robes. They will ask for sacred songs and kneeling and a sacred space like a church in which to hold the ceremony. They will want time-honored words and rings—ancient symbols of eternity—and acolytes and blessings from the elders, all from a couple who live their lives as though there is nothing beyond what is seen. The reality is simply that they sense their union is holy and so their innate need for ritual surfaces. Oprah is right, yes, even when she talks about candles and chanting and the discipline of quietness. From my perspective she is wrong about its object, wrong about the kind of connection she is trying to make, but she is right that liturgy and rituals are meant to be part of the grace of life.

She is right, also, about the issue of attitude. We all know that attitude is as important to a person's success and happiness as the attitude of an airplane—its position in the face of the wind—is essential to flight. Now, this is not the same thing as saying that attitude or intention creates reality, but Ms. Winfrey's belief that you can "change your attitude to change your life" is one I can only support. I can even affirm that thoughts are important, but not because I believe they create reality. Instead, I believe what the ancient text says: "As a man thinks in his heart, so is he." Yes, we are at least in part the sum of our thoughts and though I would differ as to the reason, I can be grateful for the emphasis Oprah places upon them.

Finally, I can be glad of her attention to spiritual community. We are not meant to live our spiritual lives alone. In fact, lone-wolf spirituality is dangerous. How many extremes, how many cults, how many perversions have come from the man alone who thinks he has seen a truth no one else knows? We need others to even know ourselves with certainty—how much more then to know God and his ways? Though I cannot be further from what Oprah Winfrey believes and from the teachings of the people she has drawn around her, I can at the least charitably applaud the fact that she does not try to go it alone. One might expect this given her fame and her vaunted beliefs about herself. But she has leaned to others and this is as it should be in matters of religion. No woman is an island in any arena of life, matters of the supernatural in particular.

Despite my many agreements with Oprah, I end this chapter again saddened. I disagree with her about so much, and yet I see her as one who is indeed called as she believes but who has stepped off the certain path. She began well but faltered and chose a thin religious jumble instead of a bold, tested connection with God. She may recover herself, but there is already much damage done to the millions who have followed her into a vain and self-serving spiritual mix. I look back over the principles she has embraced and I fear for her—and not because I believe she will be judged by an angry God. The God I worship is merciful and time is in his hands. Instead, I fear that she will run to the end of her tether and find that what she has proclaimed is what I believe it to be—a mishmash of mystical folly and deception that will leave her empty and broken in the day of challenge.

Epilogue

And Wisdom is the principle thing for Kings and
Queens . . .

—KILLAH PRIEST, "BLESSED ARE THOSE"

There is a grand nobility to the Oprah Winfrey story. To capture it, we should picture in our minds her beginning. She
was the illegitimate daughter of a part-time maid. This was in the
Mississippi of the 1950s when a wrong word or a wayward glance
by a person with black skin could mean death. Still, she had the
safety of her extended family, who taught her to read, gave her a
sense of destiny, and planted in her a love of Jesus Christ.

Times were hard and so her mother went north. Oprah stayed
behind and this tainted her with the emotions of an abandoned
child. It wasn't true, but the heart feels what it feels. In time, she
would rejoin her mother, but it would only make her feel even
more out of place. There was no money. There was no place to
sleep. And her mother's attention was turned to men. So she was
sent to her father in Nashville.

213

This is where her foundations were laid. She read. She washed. She learned her manners. She went to church and saw what God meant her to be. Then her mother pulled her back to the North. And Oprah forgot who she was. She drank. She lied. In the manner of her mother, she gave herself to men. She nearly ended up in jail. Then, once again, her father intervened, this time for good. And the girl reclaimed herself.

She survived an early pregnancy and the death of her child and somehow allowed the pain to power her rise to stardom. She knew she was special and gave herself to performance. This served her well in high school and college and she gained a bit of the fame that she longed for.

But there was a deformity. It was a warp in her soul. It may have come from an innate insecurity, or it may have come from a distorted version of Christian destiny. Whatever the cause, she was ever on her own mind, ever certain that she was chosen and destined for good. This led to arrogance and then folly. People took this in stride as an endearing part of her personality, but they were also distanced by the self-centeredness and the pride. She simply saw this as the confidence that comes from being chosen.

It served her well when she failed dramatically early in her career and it helped her reclaim her footing. She knew she was made for greatness. And greatness came. With a move to Chicago and after less than two years, she became a famous talk show host, became rich, became a celebrated actress, and laid the business foundation for the historic wealth and influence that were about to be hers. There had simply never been anything like her before.

The story might have continued in an uninterrupted arc from there. There might have been even more great feats of generosity and even more noble foundations and even greater causes served in her name. Millions more might have been led into more gracious living, more learned thinking, and an expanded view of the world.

But there was that deformity, that warp in the makeup of her soul. She was chosen by the universe and could not put this from her mind, could not stand before the world without pushing this certainty forward.

Then, like all of us, she needed God. Or at least some supernatural connection by which to live her life. She had already pushed away the faith of her youth but she was still hungry and went searching with the seekers of her generation. She found just the bandages to tend her wounded soul. They wrapped so perfectly around that deformity and did not require a change. She could believe the universe bent to exalt her and could use its powers to make her more of what she hoped to be—at peace, fulfilled, empowered, directed, and prosperous in all her ways.

So she gathered the voices of this new faith around her and she took her followers along for the journey. They told her what her soul had longed to hear—that she was divine and could create reality with a focusing of her mind. She was a god. Perhaps *the* God. And now she had a spiritual life that did not challenge that deformity, but instead made all conform to its contours.

Millions followed her. Her teachers prospered. The world pondered her ways. The faith that first gave her rise was damaged but she did not take note. She had convinced herself that she could keep that faith and practice its opposite at the same time.

The grand nobility of her story remained but it was tarnished. She did not seem to know it. She did not seem to understand that while making herself divine she had struck at the God who made her. She did not seem to understand that believing your thoughts attract all that happens to you means you are responsible for the crimes and the abuse and the tragedies too. And she did not seem to realize that the unseen world is not a blank awaiting your thoughts. It is filled with beings, some of whom are not given to your good. And so when you think you are channeling your ancestors or when you summon the gods with your chants, you may well be creating a portal for an evil you no longer believe in to nevertheless invade your life.

Because of who she is, millions will do likewise.

They also followed as she ransacked the faiths of mankind, remaking into a self-help tonic doctrines that were timeless and weighty and loved. Her new television network would help her proclaim these, for she would give voice to the spirits beyond what any other had achieved.

And it may be that there will be a change. She may recover herself, humble herself, and find what she has so obviously lost. Always there is the nobility of her story and there is the honor she is due in this world. That cannot be taken away. But it is the honor of the next world for which we ought to live, and those who understand her error can only hope that all her magnificent gifts may one day be harnessed to the truth she has left behind. To a truth beyond her divine self. To a truth beyond enchantment for this world alone.

There is a grand nobility to the Oprah Winfrey story. And it may yet be nobler still.

Acknowledgments

The writer's life is a lonely life. True writing is not a group activity. The writer sits alone to digest his material. He sits alone with his thoughts to design his work. He sits alone to write. He also faces his critics alone. This means that those who help as they can—as they are allowed—are all the more dear, their wisdom and skills all the more treasured.

My chief counsel is always my wife, Beverly Darnall Mansfield. When a woman of such experience and achievement is introduced only as a wife, it somehow seems to lessen her. Beverly is more than a respected and award-winning songwriter and producer; she is also among the best-read people I know and has wisdom for books and publishing that surprises me nearly every day. I draw from no one as I do her. I argue with no one as I do her—about books and writing. I need no one as I do her. I am addicted to nothing as I am to her.

Stephen Mansfield as a writer would not exist without George Grant. Dr. Grant created the opportunity for me to write my first book on Winston Churchill. He has given advice on nearly every book since. The combination of barbeque, George, and heated talk of books is one of the great delights of my writing life.

Emily Mulloy Prather provided counsel and research for this book while she was—almost literally—giving birth to a beauty named Grace Mulloy Prather. Her wisdom, her business sense, her discipline, and the sacrifices of her family have enhanced this book as they have my work on many other projects.

Disagreements over theology need not create enemies, and I was touched to sense this desire in many of the alternative spirituality teachers I interviewed for this book. I could not disagree with them more, but they knew this and talked with me, laughed with me, thought with me nevertheless. I am grateful, then, to Iyanla Vanzant, Rev. Ed Bacon, Doris Lessing, Roger Kemenetz, Byron Katie, Maria Coffey, Larry Dossy, Elizabeth Lesser, and Jenny Phillips.

My gratitude as well to Josh McDowell. He has been arguing for historic Christianity and against New Age thinking for decades and it was an honor to know his imprint on this book.

Much of the early phase of the Oprah Winfrey story took place in Nashville, my hometown, and so it was a pleasure to meet with people who knew Oprah when she lived here and who understood her Tennessee roots. Harry Chapman has long been a prominent Nashville broadcaster and honored citizen. He coanchored with Oprah and knew her well. His love for her, and yet his concern, was tenderly evident in our time together. Also tender was my time with Vernon Winfrey, Oprah's father. He was surely weary of interviews, but he was gracious to allow us into his thoughts about his famous daughter. He is, truly, a hero of the Oprah Winfrey story and it was inspiring to hear from his lips what he tried to impart to her life.

There were others who poured their wisdom or their skill or their eagerness into this book. Some cannot be named. Others, like Father Thomas McKenzie, Barbie Doyle, Isaac Darnall, Dan Williamson, Darcy Anderson, Dimples Kellogg, and Flip Blaney, made contributions that cannot be measured.

It is always a joy to work with the team at Thomas Nelson. Joel Miller, publisher and friend, ever inspires me with his vision for great literature and the full-bodied Christianity of his Orthodox faith. Kristen Parrish, Heather Skelton, and a dozen of other stalwarts make my work better than I could make it alone and try not to mutter in my presence their favorite mantra: "The only good author is a dead author."

About the Author

S tephen Mansfield is the *New York Times* best-selling author of *The Faith of George W. Bush*, *The Faith of the American Soldier*, *Never Give In: The Extraordinary Character of Winston Churchill*, and *The Faith of Barack Obama* among other works of history and biography. Founder of both The Mansfield Group, a research and communications firm, and Chartwell Literary Group, which creates and manages literary projects, Stephen is also in wide demand as a lecturer and inspirational speaker. For more information, log onto www.MansfieldGroup.com.

Notes

Introduction

1. Tom Shales, "Talk Is Cheap," *Washington Post*, Nov. 18, 1988.
2. Leah Garchik, "The Oprah Backlash," *San Francisco Chronicle*, Oct. 29, 1998.
3. Frank Bruni, "A Sapphic Victory, but Pyrrhic," *New York Times*, Nov. 15, 2009.
4. Kitty Kelley, *Oprah: A Biography* (New York: Crown Publishers, 2010), p. 425.
5. LaTonya Taylor, "The Church of O," *Christianity Today*, April 1, 2002.
6. Janice Peck, *The Age of Oprah* (Boulder: Paradigm Publishers, 2008), p. 1.
7. Brian Stelter, "Endorsement From Winfrey Quantified: A Million Votes," *New York Times*, Aug. 11, 2008.
8. Sam Schechner, "Oprah: Give Me the Night," *Wall Street Journal*, April 8, 2010.
9. Patricia Sellers, "Oprah's Next Act: Full Version," *Fortune*, Sept. 30, 2010, money .cnn.com/2010/09/29/news/companies/oprah_most_powerful_full.fortune/ index.htm#oprah (accessed Feb. 16, 2011).
10. "Joel Osteen's Still the Name Leaders Know," *The Washington Times*, Sept. 5, 2008, www.washingtontimes.com/news/2008/sep/05/osteen-still-the-name-leaders-know/ (accessed Feb. 16, 2011).
11. All quotes from Queen Noor, *Leap of Faith: Memoirs of an Unexpected Life* (New York: Miramax Books, 2003), p. 96.

Chapter 1

1. "*A New Earth* Online Class, Chapter 1," transcript, images.oprah.com/images/obc_classic/book/2008/anewearth/ane_chapter1_transcript.pdf, November 14, 2010, pp. 11–12.
2. Kitty Kelley, *Oprah: A Biography* (New York: Crown Publishers, 2010), p. 87.
3. Ibid., p. 20.
4. LaTonya Taylor, "The Church of O," *Christianity Today*, April 1, 2002.
5. Kelley, *Oprah*, p. 22.
6. Ibid., p. 26.
7. Ibid.
8. Ibid., p. 30.
9. Ibid., pp. 33–34.
10. Ibid., p. 49.
11. Ibid., p. 38.
12. Laura B. Randolph, "Oprah Opens Up About Her Weight, Her Wedding, and Why She Withheld the Book," *Ebony*, October 1993.
13. Kelley, *Oprah*, p. 40.
14. Ibid.
15. Ibid., p. 43.
16. Ibid., p. 41.
17. Ibid., p. 49.
18. Pat Embry, "Oprah Winfrey's Father Says Her Success Is No Surprise," *Nashville Banner*, Jan. 20, 1986.
19. Kelley, *Oprah*, p. 45.
20. Ibid., p. 60.
21. Ibid., p. 68.
22. "Oprah Winfrey," interview, American Academy of Achievement, Feb. 21, 1991, www.achievement.org/autodoc/page/win0int-1 (accessed Feb. 17, 2011).
23. Ibid.
24. Ilene Cooper, *Up Close: Oprah Winfrey* (New York: Penguin, 2007), p. 75.
25. Author interview with Harry Chapman, July 28, 2010.
26. Kelley, *Oprah*, p. 70.
27. Ibid.
28. Ibid., p. 71.
29. Author interview with Harry Chapman, July 28, 2010.
30. Kelley, *Oprah*, p. 78.
31. Ibid., p. 80.
32. Ibid., p. 83.
33. Elizabeth Colt, "Oprah Winfrey Goes National," *Boston Globe*, Sept. 2, 1986.
34. Gerri Kobren, "Co-Hosts Love Their Work," *Baltimore Sun*, Sept. 17, 1978.
35. Kelley, *Oprah*, p. 84.
36. Ibid., p. 87.
37. Ibid.
38. Ibid., p. 29.

Chapter 2

1. Kitty Kelley, *Oprah: A Biography* (New York: Crown Publishers, 2010), p. 91.
2. Bill Carter, "'People Are Talking': A Breath of Hot, Stale Air," *Baltimore Sun*, Aug. 15, 1978.
3. Bill Carter, "Channel 13 Getting Over Its Morning Jitters," *Baltimore Sun*, Aug. 23, 1978.
4. Kelley, *Oprah*, p. 97.
5. "Stars Say Success Isn't Always Sweet," Associated Press, July 14, 1987; Stephanie Mansfield, "And Now, Heeeeeeere's Oprah," *Washington Post*, Oct. 21, 1986.
6. Judy Markey, "Brassy, Sassy Oprah Winfrey," *Cosmopolitan*, September 1986.
7. Norman King, "Learning to Talk: Oprah Winfrey Flopped at News, but Discovered a Gift for Gab," *Providence Journal*, Oct. 11, 1987.
8. Maralyn Lois Polak, "Oprah Winfrey: So Much to Reveal," *Philadelphia Inquirer Magazine*, Oct. 12, 1986.
9. R. C. Smith, "She Once Trashed Her Apartment to Make a Point," *TV Guide*, Aug. 30, 1986.
10. Mansfield, "Heeeeeeere's Oprah."
11. Bill Zehme, "It Came from Chicago," *Spy*, December 1986.
12. Kelley, *Oprah*, pp. 150–151.
13. Nan Robertson, "Donahue vs. Winfrey," *New York Times*, Feb. 1, 1988.
14. Dennis Kneale, "Titillating Channels," *Wall Street Journal* (Eastern edition), May 18, 1988.
15. Kelley, *Oprah*, p. 213.
16. Daniel Ruth, "Has the New Winfrey Diet Made Oprah Light-Headed?" *Chicago Sun-Times*, Sept. 1, 1988.
17. Kelley, *Oprah*, p. 223.
18. Dana Kennedy, "Oprah Act Two," *Entertainment Weekly*, September 1994, pp. 24–25.
19. Kelley, *Oprah*, p. 259.
20. Jonathan Van Meter, "Oprah's Moment," *Vogue*, October 1998, p. 393.
21. Kelley, *Oprah*, p. 260.
22. Bill Adler, ed., *The Uncommon Wisdom of Oprah Winfrey* (Secaucus: Birch Lane Press, 1997), p. 223.
23. Kennedy, "Act Two," p. 25.
24. K. Kest, "What Oprah Really Wants," *Redbook*, August 1995, pp. 74–77, 116.
25. George Mair, *Oprah Winfrey: The Real Story* (Secaucus: Carol Publishing, 1994/1998), p. 340.
26. Vicki Abt and Leonard Mustanzza, *Coming After Oprah: Cultural Fallout of the Age of the TV Talk Show* (Bowling Green, Ohio: Bowling Green State University Press, 1997), p. 8.
27. Tom Shales quoted in "Are Talk Shows Bad? Part II," *The Oprah Winfrey Show*, Sept. 13, 1994, from a BurrellesLuce transcript, p. 22.
28. Janice Peck, *The Age of Oprah* (Boulder: Paradigm Publishers, 2008), p. 130.
29. Oprah Winfrey, *Journey to Beloved* (New York: Hyperion, 1998), p. 18.
30. Ibid.
31. Jonathan Van Meter, "Oprah's Moment."

32. Amy Longsdorf, "Oprah Embraces Fearlessness While Filming 'Beloved'," *Morning Call*, Oct. 11, 1998.
33. Winfrey, *Journey to Beloved*, p. 27.
34. Ibid., p. 25.
35. Ibid., p. 54.
36. Ibid., p. 72.
37. Ibid., p. 56.
38. Ibid., p. 148.
39. Ibid., p. 62.
40. Ibid., p. 118.
41. Ibid., p. 120.
42. Kelley, *Oprah*, p. 326.
43. Ibid., p. 335.
44. Winfrey, *Journey to Beloved*, p. 135.
45. Kelley, *Oprah*, p. 135.
46. King World Productions, Inc., General Statement of Beneficial Ownership (SEC Schedule SC 13G), filed Oct. 13, 1998.
47. "Oprah's 'Splendiferous' but Too Obsessed with Herself," [Springfield, IL] *State Journal Register*, Oct. 16, 1998.
48. Ibid.
49. Libby Copeland, "Our Lady of Perpetual Self Help," *Washington Post*, June 26, 2000.
50. Ibid.; see also *The Oprah Winfrey Show*, season 12, episode 8.
51. Leah Garchik, "The Oprah Backlash," *San Francisco Chronicle*, Oct. 29, 1998, p. E10.
52. Steve Johnson, "Oh, No, Oprah! Enough!" *Chicago Tribune*, November 23, 1998.
53. Kelley, *Oprah*, p. 343.
54. Richard Roeper, "'Deepak Oprah's' Inner Journey Is an Ego Trip," *Chicago Sun-Times*, Oct. 12, 1998.
55. Johnson, "Oh, No, Oprah!"
56. Jeff MacGregor, "Inner Peace, Empowerment, and Host Worship," *New York Times*, Oct. 25, 1998.
57. "The Gospel According to Oprah," *Vantage Point*, July 1998, Watchman Fellowship, www.wfial.org/index.cfm?fuseaction=artNewAge.article_1 (accessed Mar. 21, 2011).
58. Janice Peck, *The Age of Oprah* (Boulder: Paradigm Publishers, 2008), p. 212.
59. Ibid.
60. Ibid.
61. Ibid.
62. Ibid., p. 213.
63. Ibid.
64. Kelley, *Oprah*, pp. 424–425.

Chapter 3

1. *Church of the Holy Trinity v. United States*, 143 US 457–458, 465–471 36 L. ed 226.
2. Quoted in John Clellon Holmes, "Nothing More to Declare," *Listener*, June 27, 1968, p. 841.

3. Jack Kerouac, "Beatific," *Encounter*, August 1959, p. 60.

4. David Halberstam, *The Fifties* (New York: Villard Books, 1993), p. 301.

5. Ibid.

6. Ibid.

7. Jeff Nuttall, *Bomb Culture* (New York: Dell Books, 1968), p. 104.

8. Kerouac, "Beatific," p. 57.

9. Ibid., p. 58.

10. Quoted in Robert Wuthnow, *After Heaven: Spirituality in America Since the 1950s* (Berkeley: University of California Press, 1998), p. 49.

11. January 20, 1961.

12. Stefanie Syman, *The Subtle Body: The Story of Yoga in America* (New York: Macmillan, 2010), p. 202.

13. "Lennon & McCartney Interview, *The Tonight Show* 5/14/1968," The Beatles Interview Database, The Beatles Ultimate Experience, www.beatlesinterviews. org/db1968.05ts.beatles.html (accessed Mar. 21, 2011).

14. United States District Court, District of New Jersey, Docket No. 76-341 (H.C.M.) Civil Action, in the case of Alan B. Malnak, et al., Plaintiffs, v. Maharishi Mahesh Yogi, et al., Defendants, in a summary judgment issued Oct. 19, 1977, followed by an order and judgment, filed Dec. 12, 1977.

15. This was the experience of the author at Valley High School in West Des Moines, Iowa, in August 1975.

16. Burton H. Wolfe, *The Devil's Avenger: A Biography of Anton Szandor LaVey*, 1974; quoted in Larry Kahaner, *Cults That Kill* (New York: Warner Books, 1988), p. 65.

17. Anton Szandor LaVey, *The Satanic Bible* (New York: Avon Books, 1969), p. 25.

18. Kahaner, *Cults*, p. 70.

19. Philip Norman, *Symphony for the Devil: The Rolling Stones Story* (New York: Linden Press/Simon & Schuster, 1984), p. 333.

20. Ibid., p. 338.

21. Gary North, *Unholy Spirits: Occultism and New Age Humanism* (Fort Worth: Dominion Press, 1986), p. 8.

22. Mitch Horowitz, *Occult America: The Secret History of How Mysticism Shaped Our Nation* (New York: Bantam Books, 2009), p. 255.

23. Ibid, p. 257.

24. Ibid.

25. R. C. Fuller, *Mesmerism and the American Cure of Souls* (Philadelphia: University of Pennsylvania Press, 1982), p. 156.

26. P. Cushman, *Constructing the Self, Constructing America: A Cultural History of Psychotherapy* (Boston, Addison-Wesley, 1995), p. 125.

27. Ibid., p. 128.

28. H. E. Cady, *Lesson in Truth* (Lee's Summit: Unity Press, 1894), p. 8.

29. Ralph Waldo Trine, *In Tune With the Infinite* (New York: Crowell, 1980), p. 16.

30. M. Long, "Paradise Tossed," *Omni* (April 1988), pp. 36–39.

31. Jennifer Harris and Elwood Watson, eds., *The Oprah Phenomenon* (Lexington: University of Kentucky Press, 2007), p. 129.

32. William Warren Bartley III, *Werner Erhard: The Transformation of a Man: The Founding of est* (New York: Clarkson N. Potter, Inc., 1978), p. 121.

33. Howard Fineman, "The New Age President," *Newsweek*, Jan. 23, 1993, p. 22.

34. Ibid.
35. Maureen Dowd and Frank Rich, "Democrats in New York—Garden Diary: I'm in Therapy, You're in Therapy," *New York Times*, July 15, 1992, p. A7.
36. Richard M. Levine, "I Feel Your Pain," *Mother Jones*, July/August 1993, np.
37. T. McNichol, "The New Co-dependent Covenant: Sure, He'll Lead—but Can Clinton Heal your Inner Democrat?" *Washington Post*, Feb. 28, 1993, p. C1.
38. Hillary Rodham Clinton, *It Takes a Village* (New York: Simon & Schuster, 1996), p. 171.
39. D. Schorr, "Behind the 'Politics of Meaning,'" *Christian Science Monitor*, June 21, 1993, p. 18.
40. M. Duffy, "Urging the Boss to Lighten Up," *Time*, May 10, 1993, pp. 32–33.
41. Michael Lerner, "Hillary's Politics, My Meaning: What are these ideas everyone seems afraid of?" *Washington Post*, June 13, 1993, p. C1.
42. Schorr, "Politics of Meaning."
43. K. De Witt, "Dial 1-800-MY-GURU," *New York Times*, Dec. 5, 1995, Sec. 4, 2.
44. Bob Woodward, *The Choice* (New York: Simon and Schuster, 1996), pp. 130–32.
45. Paul Kengor, *God and Hillary Clinton: A Spiritual Life* (New York: HarperCollins, 2007), p. 155.
46. Ibid.
47. Horowitz, *Occult America*, p. 258.

Chapter 4

1. Kitty Kelley, *Oprah: A Biography* (New York: Crown Publishers, 2010), p. 142.
2. Ibid, p. 143.
3. Ibid.
4. Leslie Bennetts, "Marianne's Faithful," *Vanity Fair*, June 1991, p. 172.
5. Marianne Williamson, *A Return to Love: Reflections on the Principles of a Course in Miracles* (New York: HarperCollins, 1992), p. xi.
6. Ibid., p. xii.
7. Ibid., pp. xii–xiii.
8. LyInda Gorov, "Faith: Marianne Williamson Is Full of It," *Mother Jones*, Nov. 21, 1997, p. 31.
9. Williamson, *Return to Love*, p. xv.
10. Bennetts, "Marianne's Faithful," p. 174.
11. Williamson, *Return to Love*, pp. xix–xx.
12. Ibid., p. xx.
13. Ibid., p. xxii.
14. Ibid., pp. xii–xiii.
15. Ibid., p. 195.
16. Ibid., p. 68.
17. Ibid.
18. Ibid., p. 257.
19. Ibid., p. 21.
20. Ibid., p. 45.
21. Ibid., p. 51.
22. Ibid., p. 17.

23. Ibid.

24. Ibid., p. 84.

25. Steve Rabey, "Prophet of Love: Popular Author Preaches a New Understanding of How to Tap into God," *Colorado Springs Gazette*, Mar. 21, 1992.

26. Williamson, *Return to Love*, pp. 162–164.

27. Ibid., pp. 197–216.

28. Janice Peck, *The Age of Oprah* (Boulder: Paradigm Publishers, 2008), p. 130.

29. Ibid.

30. Marianne Williamson, *Emma and Mommy Talk to God* (New York: HarperCollins, 1996), np.

31. As an introduction to the evidences for the historical Jesus and the claims of the New Testament, I would recommend Josh McDowell's *Evidence That Demands a Verdict: Historical Evidences for the Christian Faith* (Nashville: Thomas Nelson, 1999). For an examination of the historicity of the New Testament, I would recommend F. F. Bruce's *The New Testament Documents: Are They Reliable?* (Grand Rapids: William B. Eerdmanns Publishing Company, 1985). The brief apologetic claims in this paragraph are supported by these two foundational works.

32. Tal Brooke, "The Cosmic Christ of Channeled Revelation," in *The Conspiracy to Silence the Son of God* (Eugene: Harvest House Publishers, 1998), pp. 97–112.

33. Bob Minzesheimer, "World Is Oprah's Classroom: Weekly Webcasts about 'A New Earth Break' New Ground," *USA Today*, Mar. 3, 2008, p. D1.

34. Douglas Todd, "Profile: Eckhart Tolle – Of the present, future and mother," originally published in the *Vancouver Sun* on Oct. 5, 2002, communities.canada. com/vancouversun/blogs/thesearch/pages/profile-eckhart-tolle-of-the-present-future-and-mother.aspx (accessed on Feb. 22, 2011).

35. Kathy Juline, "The Presence of Now," interview with Eckhart Tolle, from Eckhart Teachings, copyright 2002, blog.eckharttolle.com/blog/2008/10/08/the-presence-of-now/ (accessed Mar. 21, 2011).

36. Eckhart Tolle, *A New Earth* (New York: Plume, 2005), pp. 56–57.

37. Ibid., p. 219.

38. Eckhart Tolle, "You Are Not Your Mind," blog, Oct. 7, 2008, blog.eckharttolle. com/blog/2008/10/07/you-are-not-your-mind/ (accessed Mar. 21, 2011).

39. Tolle, *A New Earth*, p. 70.

40. "A New Earth Online Class: Chapter 1 Transcript," images.oprah.com/images/ obc_classic/book/2008/anewearth/ane_chapter1_transcript.pdf, Nov. 14, 2010 (accessed Mar. 21, 2011).

41. Tolle, *A New Earth*, p. 9.

42. Kathy Juline, "Awakening to Your Life's Purpose," interview with Eckhart Tolle, from Eckhart Teachings, copyright 2006, blog.eckharttolle.com/ blog/2008/10/07/awakening-to-your-life's-purpose/ (accessed Mar. 21, 2011).

43. Tolle, *A New Earth*, p. 13.

44. Oprah.com, "A New Earth Online Class: Chapter 2 Transcript," http://images. oprah.com/images/obc_classic/book/2008/anewearth/ane_chapter2_transcript. pdf, Nov. 14, 2010 (accessed Mar. 21, 2011).

45. Tolle, *A New Earth*, p. 55.

46. Juline, "Awakening To Your Life's Purpose."

47. Tolle, *A New Earth*, pp. 162–163.

48. Ibid, pp. 164–168; see also Warren Nozaki, "Paradise Still Lost in Eckhart Tolle's 'A New Earth,'" *Christian Research Journal*, vol. 31, no. 5, 2008, www .equip.org/articles/paradise-still-lost-in-eckhart-tolle-s-a-new-earth- (accessed Mar. 22, 2011).

49. Ibid.

50. Ibid., p. 163.

51. Ibid.

52. Janice Peck, *The Age of Oprah* (Boulder: Paradigm Publishers, 2008), p. 193, quoting from a transcript of the Apr. 23, 1999, *The Oprah Winfrey Show*.

53. Gary Zukav, *The Seat of the Soul* (New York, Simon and Schuster, 1990), p. 34.

54. Ibid., p. 122.

55. Ibid., p. 198.

56. Ibid., p. 143.

57. Ibid., p. 146.

58. Ibid., p. 144.

59. Ibid., p. 111.

60. Ibid., p. 153.

61. Ibid., p. 43.

62. Ibid., p. 41.

63. Ibid., p. 43.

64. Ibid., p. 126.

65. Ibid.

66. Ibid., p. 125.

67. Ibid., p. 162.

68. Ibid.

69. Ibid.

70. Gary Zukav, "Academy Fellow Gary Zukav," World Business Academy, www.worldbusiness.org/about/academy-fellows/gary-zukav/ (accessed Mar. 21, 2011).

71. Zukav, *Seat of the Soul*, p. 186.

72. Ibid., p. 239.

73. David Van Biema, "Emperor of the Soul," *Time*, June 24, 1996.

74. Wendy Kaminer, "Why We Love Gurus," *Newsweek*, Oct. 20, 1997, p. 60.

75. Van Biema, "Emperor."

76. Ibid.

77. Ibid.

78. Tony Perry, "So Rich, So Restless," *Los Angeles Times*, Sept. 7, 1997.

79. Van Biema, "Emperor."

80. Matt Labash, "The End of History and the Last Guru," *Weekly Standard*, July 1, 1996, pp. 18–24.

81. Richard Grenier, *The Gandhi Nobody Knows* (Nashville: Thomas Nelson Publishers, 1983), p. 46.

82. Gregory Dennis, "What's Deepak's Secret," *New Age Journal*, January/February 1994.

83. Perry, "So Rich, So Restless."

84. Van Biema, "Emperor."

85. Ptolemy Tompkins, "New Age Supersage," *Time*, Nov. 14, 2008.

86. Labash, "The End of History."
87. Kurt Butler, *A Consumer's Guide to "Alternative Medicine"* (Buffalo: Prometheus Press, 1992), pp. 110–117. Text quoted is from Tal Brooke, "The Temptations of Deepak Chopra," *SCP Journal*, volume 21:3, p. 18.
88. Van Biema, "Emperor."
89. See V. S. Naipaul, *India: A Wounded Civilization* (New York: Vintage, 2003).
90. Gina Piccalo, "Guy Ritchie's Years-Long Head Trip," *Los Angeles Times*, Dec. 8, 2007.
91. Author interview with Ed Bacon, July 6, 2010.
92. Drew Zahn, "Oprah tackles new issue: 'Gay is a gift from God,'" *WorldNetDaily*, Jan. 19, 2009, www.wnd.com/?pageId=86534 (accessed Mar. 21, 2011).
93. Ibid.
94. Ibid.
95. Ibid.
96. Ibid.
97. Kim Lawton, "Interview, Reverend Ed Bacon, July 18, 2008, episode 1146," Religion & Ethics Newsweekly, PBS, www.pbs.org/wnet/religionandethics/week1146/interview_bacon.html (accessed Mar. 22, 2011).
98. Rev. Ed Bacon, "The Real Message Behind *The Lost Symbol*," Oprah.com, www.oprah.com/spirit/The-Real-Message-Behind-the-New-Dan-Brown-Book/print/1 (accessed Mar. 22, 2011).
99. Diane Weathers, "At Home with Iyanla Vanzant," *Essence*, July 1996.
100. Brenda L. Webber, Gina Henderson, "Iyanla Vanzant," *Emerge*, April 2000, vol. 11, no. 6, p. 34.
101. Weathers, "At Home."
102. Ibid.
103. 1 Corinthians 6:9.

Chapter 5

1. Kitty Kelley, *Oprah: A Biography* (New York: Crown Publishers, 2010), p. 177.
2. "Oprah Talks About 'Legends Ball'," *Good Morning America*, ABCNews.com, abcnews.go.com/GMA/Entertainment/story?id=1989964&page=3 (accessed Feb. 23, 2011).
3. "The Gospel According to Oprah," *Vantage Point*, July 1998, Watchman Fellowship, www.wfial.org/index.cfm?fuseaction=artNewAge.article_1 (accessed Mar. 21, 2011).
4. Skip Hollandsworth and Pamela Colloff, "How the West Was Won Over," *Texas Monthly*, March 1998, vol. 26, no. 3; p. 100.
5. Oprah Winfrey, "What I Know for Sure," *O, The Oprah Magazine*, Apr. 15, 2002; LaTonya Taylor, "The Church of O," *Christianity Today*, Apr. 1, 2002.
6. Kelley, *Oprah*, p. 107.
7. Maralyn Lois Polak, "Oprah Winfrey: So Much to Reveal," *Philadelphia Inquirer Magazine*, Oct. 12, 1986.
8. Kelley, *Oprah*, p. 207.
9. Ibid., p. 137.

Notes

10. Interview with Oprah Winfrey, Nov. 4, 2008, *The Ed Lover Morning Show*, Power 105 (New York, NY). Note: this interview, transcribed by the author's editorial assistant in February 2010, and has since been removed from the website.

11. Jonathan Van Meter, "Oprah's Moment," *Vogue*, October 1998, p. 393.

12. Kelley, *Oprah*, p. 234.

13. Elizabeth Lesser, "Your Spiritual Journey," *The Oprah Winfrey Show*, June 10, 2009, www.oprah.com/oprahshow/Your-Spiritual-Journey/4 (accessed Mar. 22, 2011).

14. Karen Herrick, "Learning the Language of Spirituality," *Journal of Religion and Psychical Research* 28 (2005), pp. 25–34.

15. Matthew 6:7.

16. Hebrews 9:27–28.

17. Cathleen Falsani, "I Have a Deep Faith," *Chicago Sun-Times*, Apr. 5, 2005.

18. In *Malnak v. Yogi*, 592 F.2d 197 (3d Cir. 1979), part of the court's ruling concerned the fact that the mantras prescribed in Transcendental Meditation were actually the names of Hindu deities or the names of deified gurus like "Guru Dev."

19. Wendy Kaminer, "Why We Love Gurus," *Newsweek*, Oct. 20, 1997, p. 60.

20. David Van Biema, "Emperor of the Soul," *Time*, June 24, 1996, quoting Deepak Chopra's 1994 book *Ageless Body, Timeless Mind*.

21. Deepak Chopra, *How to Know God* (New York: Three Rivers Press, 2000), p. 142.

22. "The Gospel According to Oprah," *Vantage Point*, July 1998, Watchman Fellowship, www.wfial.org/index.cfm?fuseaction=artNewAge.article_1 (accessed Mar. 21, 2011).

23. *The Oprah Winfrey Show*, Feb. 7, 2007, from a BurrellesLuce transcript.

24. Lynne McTaggart, "The Key to the Lost Symbol: the Power of Intention," Sept. 22, 2009, The Intention Experiment, www.theintentionexperiment.com/the-key-to-the-lost-symbol-the-power-of-intention.htm (accessed Mar. 22, 2011).

25. Dan Brown, *The Lost Symbol* (New York: Doubleday, 2009), pp. 55–57.

26. Gary Zukav, *The Seat of the Soul* (New York: Simon & Schuster, 1990), p. 239.

27. The Beatles, "I Am the Walrus," *Magical Mystery Tour*, Apple Records, 1967.

28. Allison Samuels, "Oprah Winfrey's Lavish South African School," *Newsweek*, Jan. 8, 2007.

29. D. Rodricks, "Listen up Oprah: there are other ways to help city kids," *Baltimore Sun*, Apr. 13, 2006.

30. Jennifer Harris and Elwood Watson, *The Oprah Phenomenon* (Lexington: The University of Kentucky Press, 2007), p. 141.

Index

A

abortion, B. Clinton's view on, 106
Abrams, Eugene H., 10–11
Abt, Vicki, xi, 55
accepting Christ, Williamson on, 125
achievement, 29, 30, 48
ACLU of Southern California, Religious Freedom Award, 162
Acts of Faith (Vanzant), 67, 164
adolescence of Oprah, 11
affair with married man, 40–41
affirmative action, 21

African Americans
in media, 43
response to Oprah's lifestyle, 47–48, 159
age of Oprah
Beats movement, 79–80
Eastern views, 80–83
events impacting, 76
generation of seekers, 77–78
"age of Satan," 94
AIDS patients, Williamson advice to, 127
Ali, Muhammad, 39
All Saints Episcopal

Church (Pasadena, California), 161
altars, 166, 167
A.M. Chicago, 42, 44
ambition, 16–23, 36
American Book Award for Science, 149
American dream, 78
American religion, OWN network role in change, xv–xvi
ancestors, 63, 72, 206
altars for, 166
as bridge, 64
Christianity and, 177
prayer to, 61
Winfrey views on, 50
worship of, 92

Angelou, Maya, 39, 53, 117, 173
Even the Stars Look Lonesome, 63
angels, Winfrey on, xii
Apponaug Cotton Mill, 8
The Aquarian Conspiracy (Ferguson), 102
atma ("higher self"), 142
attitude, 210–211
Augustine (saint), 208
authority, for Winfrey, 33
awakening, Tolle on, 138
awards for Winfrey, 23, 49
Ayur Veda Products International, 151
ayurvedic medicine, 151–153

B
baby boomers, 114, 179, 186–187
    as seekers, 77–78
    spirituality and religion, 183
    wealth accumulation in 1980s, 103
Bacon, Ed, 70, 159–163, 168
Bailey, Pearl, 39
Baker, William F., 36–37
    on Turner, 26–27
Baltimore station WJZ-TV, 1, 25–29, 42
Baltimore Sun, 37
Bartley, William, *Werner Erhard*, 104

"Beat Zen," 81
Beatles, 83, 86, 93, 100, 197
Beats movement, 79–80, 114
beauty, evil side of, 93–99
Being, 136, 138–139
Beingness, and liberation, 141
Beloved, 57–65
    as box office failure, 63–64
    director search for movie, 58–59
    Oprah's preparation as lead, 59–61
    Oprah's reaction to, 58
    story, 57–58
Bennett, William, 53
Bethel African Methodist Episcopal Church, 1, 30, 31
Bhagavad Gita, 156
bias, xxi–xxii
Bible
    Genesis, 161
    Exodus 20:5, 2
    Matthew 16:26, 172
    Romans, 6
    historical confirmation, 130
    and inclusiveness to all faith expressions, 168
    Oprah and, 171
    Orpah and Ruth, 5
    questions truths of, 32
Birkenhead, Peter, on *The Secret*, 71

birth certificate, 5
birthday celebration at age 40, 52–54
black arts, 94
Black Elks Club, competition, 18
Black Mass, 95
Blackboard Book of the Year award, 164
Bonhoeffer, Dietrich, *The Cost of Discipleship*, 188
books, childhood interest in, 10
Brahma, 156
broadcasting, Oprah's talents and, 19–20
Brown, Dan, *The Lost Symbol*, 195
Bryant, John Richard, 1, 31
Buddhism, 80, 81, 206–207
    heroes, 186
    on sin, 182
Buffalo Baptist Church, 6–7
Byrne, Rhonda, *The Secret*, 70–71, 91, 194

C
Cady, Emilie, 102
Campion, Jane, 58
Carlyle, Thomas, 75
Carter, Bill, on Oprah as talk show host, 38–39
cataracts, Chopra's treatment, 156
Catcher in the Rye (Salinger), 107
Cavett, Dick, 39

Index

CBS, takeover of King World, 65

Celtic belief about physical world, 190

"Change Your Life" television, vision of, 66–68

channeling, 61, 110

chanting of mantras, xii, 177, 184

Chapman, Harry, 24–25

charity donations, xiv

Chicago
  Oprah's move to, 42–43
  Winfrey in, 43–46

Chicago Sun-Times, 50

The Children (Halberstam), 22

The Choice (Woodward), 110

Chopra, Deepak, xi, 70, 149–159, 169, 191–192
  Ageless Body, Timeless Mind, 150, 154
  Daughters of Joy, 156
  and lifestyle of American medical doctor, 150
  and the maharishi, 154
  Merlin, 156
  on *Oprah Winfrey Show*, 150
  on *Phil Donahue Show*, 155
  The Seven Spiritual Laws of Success, 154
  solutions to medical conditions, 156

Christian Scientists, 91, 102

Christianity, 93, 207
  basis for beliefs, 130–131
  challenge to, 100
  Clintons and, 111
  complaints of Oprah's abandonment of, 159
  conflicts in Oprah's claims to, 193
  core message, 188
  vs. Eastern religion, 82
  hypocrisy and, 94
  invisible world as understood by, 176
  Oprah and, 16, 41, 75–76, 208
  Oprah's doubts about, 39
  spirituality and, 176–177
  teaching on spiritual development, 73
  view of Jesus, 181
  in Western society, 77

church attendance, by Oprah, 25

Church of Satan, 94–97

churches in U.S., 81, 114

Churchill, Winston, 77

Civil War in U.S., rise of occult after, 102

Clark, Chris, 20–21, 23

Clinton, Bill, 105–112
  and counterculture spiritual values, 109
  inauguration as president, 105
  religious background, 106

Clinton, Hillary, 105–112
  and counterculture spiritual values, 109
  religious background, 106–107
  Williamson and, 120

coanchor for WJZ-TV, Oprah as, 26–28

cocaine, at WLAC, 24

Colasante, Peter A., Oprah's interest in paintings, 68–69

Cole, Corny, xvi

The Color Purple, 44, 46

compassion, 23
  Hinduism and, 145

"conceptualized self," 159–160

conformity, 77

consciousness
  God as, 193–194
  Light shaped by, 144
  pure, 135

corporate culture, 103

corrupted religions, Tolle on, 137

Cosby, Bill, 43

"cosmic consciousness," 83, 195

Cosmopolitan, 41

The Cost of Discipleship (Bonhoeffer), 188

countercultural movement, 203
  and Clintons, 107–108
  Manson and, 99

courage, 22

A Course in Miracles (Schucman), 122–123, 130
  and understanding of Jesus, 133

Court, John Kirthian,
68–69
Covey, Stephen, *Seven
Habits of Highly
Effective People*, 109
cow-dung, for health
improvement, 152
Cowley, Malcolm, 79
Cox, W.D., 19
Creative Visualization,
48
crucifixion, Williamson
on, 125
cultural revolution of
1960s, 203
curiosity, 20

D
*The Dancing Wu Li
Masters* (Zukav),
148–149
Davis, Sammy Jr., 96
daytime talk show
in Baltimore,
beginnings, 36–39
Demme, Jonathan, 59
demons, 142, 176
depression, 40–41, 64
Desai, Morarji, 152
destiny, 36, 44–45, 51,
173, 199–201, 214
detachment, Oprah's
weakness in
attempting, 23
"dialing for dollars"
segment in TV show,
37, 38
DiMaio, Debra, 42, 55
discipline, 13
diversity, television
stations' need for, 20
divine appointment, 51

divine self, 192
divinity, 148
promise of, 116
Domingo, Plácido, x
Donahue, Phil, x, 44,
49, 96
doubt, 2
Dowd, Maureen, on
Clinton, 105
dramatic presentation
by Winfrey, 30
dream incubator, 167
Dresser, Horatio, 102
drugs, at WLAC, 24
Druids, 190
due diligence, on *Oprah
Winfrey Show* guests,
157
Dyer, Wayne, 70
Dylan, Bob, 171

E
East Nashville high
school, Oprah's
graduation, 18
Eastern mysticism,
Zukav and, 142
Eastern views. *See also*
Buddhism; Hinduism
in U.S., 89–90
views of self, 132
education, 7
Egan, Edward
(cardinal), ix
ego, 136
of Winfrey, Ruth on,
50–51
The Ego Has Landed
(Ritchie), 159–160
Eisenhower, Dwight,
77–78
Elise, Kimberly, 59

*Emma and Mommy Talk
to God* (Williamson),
128
energy, 195
coming back, 71
God as no more
than, 192–194
and money, 68
Engel v. Vitale, 85
enlightener, Lucifer as,
144
enlightenment, 138
pain-body and, 142
Entertainment Weekly, 54
epistemology, 34, 129
Erhard, Werner,
103–104
"est," 103–104
Esters, Katharine Carr, 4
evangelical Christian,
xxi
*Even the Stars Look
Lonesome* (Angelou), 63
evil, 160, 182
efforts to explain, 74
Zukav on, 144–145
exclusivity in religion,
181
experience
and spiritual
formation, 33
vs. truth, 205–207

F
faith
of Beat generation,
114–115
challenges to, xvi
devotion in high
school, 16
of Oprah, 25, 73,
171–172

faith-based politics,
108–109
faith pillars for Oprah,
173–189
  flexibility to redefine
    religions, 182–185
  religion vs.
    spirituality,
    173–179
  religious blending
    of conflicting
    perspectives,
    179–182
  self enhanced by
    religion, 185–189
fame
  price of, 48–52
  vs. truth in religion,
    xvii
family
  created by Oprah,
    117–118
  father. See Winfrey,
    Vernon
  mother. See Lee,
    Vernita
  spiritual, of Oprah,
    168–169
Farrow, Mia, 87
fear vs. love, 122
  Williamson on,
    124–125
Feder, Robert, 50
feelings, reliance on, 206
Ferguson, Marilyn, *The
  Aquarian Conspiracy*,
  102
Ferguson, Sarah, xv
The Fifties
  (Halberstam), 79
Fineman, Howard, 105
Fisk University, 19

Foster, Jodie, 58
Freemasons,
  competition, 18
Frey, James, *Million
  Little Pieces*, 157
Fryowski, Voytek,
  murder, 98

G
Gandhi, Mohandas, 152
Garner, Margaret, 57
generosity, 47, 90, 209
  Hinduism and, 145
Gimme Shelter, 98
Ginsberg, Allen, 79
  "Howl," 80
Giuliani, Rudy, xii
Glover, Danny, 59
God
  Christian view, 176
  as jealous God,
    31–34
  knowledge to free
    man to become,
    144
  and love, 132
  multiple paths to,
    xii, 82
  as no more than
    energy, 192–194
  Oprah's belief in, 172
  Williamson on, 126
God-centeredness,
  Oprah's certainty of,
  51
*God's Trombones; Eight
  Negro Sermons in Verse*
  (Johnson), 17
Goldberg, Whoopi, 46
good and evil, 197. *See
  also* evil
Graham, Billy, xiii

Graham, Stedman, 47,
  48, 173
Gray, John, xi
  *Men Are from Mars,
    Women Are from
    Venus*, 67
greatness, Winfrey's
  faith in, 73
greed, 160
Greenwood, Lee, x
guilt
  for TV show
    direction, 51–52
  Williamson on, 126
Gumbel, Bryant, 43

H
Halberstam, David
  The Children, 22
  on Donahue, 49
  The Fifties, 79
happiness, and health,
  155
*HarperCollins Dictionary
  of Religion*, 174
Harpo Productions,
  xvi, 44
Harris, Jennifer, *The
  Oprah Phenomenon*,
  198
Harris, Rhonda, 163
Harrison, George, 75, 87
Haynes, Andrea, 17
healing, 127, 208–209
health, and happiness,
  155
Hearst, Patty, 22
Heaven, Williamson
  on, 126
Heidelberg, John, 18
Hell, Williamson on,
  126

Hell's Angels motorcycle gang, 97
Hendrix, Jimi, 100
hero stories, 185–186
Herrick, Karen, 174
Hesse, Hermann, *Siddhartha*, 99
"higher self" (*atma*), 125, 142
Hindu Third Eye (*urna*), 125
Hindu Upanishads, 136
Hinduism, 82, 179. *See also karma*; reincarnation
  heroes, 186
  and personal destiny, 201
  reworking by baby boomers, 183–184
  Tolle's core ideas and, 137
  view of Jesus, 181
  Zukav and dark side, 145
historical Jesus, 130. *See also* Jesus Christ
Hollywood Walk of Fame, 17
Holy Spirit, Christian view, 176
holy spirit, Williamson on, 125
homosexuality, 39, 160–161
Horowitz, Mitch, *Occult America*, 100–101, 111–112
Houston, Jean, 110
Hubbard Hospital (Nashville), 15
human condition, 182

humility, 73
hypocrisy, Christianity and, 94

I
ideas, consequences of, xviii
illness
  faulty thinking as cause, 127
  Tolle on, 138
illusion, reality as, 125
imagination, 20
Immanuel Baptist Church (Little Rock), 106
In the Meantime (Vanzant), 164
inclusion, Bible and, 161–162
Indian ayurvedic medicine, 151–153
Indian gurus, 82
individual, enhancement of, 102
infant son of Oprah, death of, 15
Inner Visions Spiritual Life Maintenance Center and Bookstore, 165
intention, 141
interviews, 38
Irving, Julius, 52
Islam, 207
  heroes, 186
  Queen Noor views vs. current conditions, xvii–xviii
  teaching on spiritual development, 73

  view of Jesus, 181
Islamic Center of Southern California, Peace & Compassion Award, 162
Izak-El Pasha, Imam, ix

J
Jackson, Jesse, 29, 39, 90, 102
Jacobs, Jeffrey D., 44
Jagger, Mick, 98
Jakes, T.D., xv
Jesus Christ
  Christian view, 176
  differing religious views of, 181–182
  as healer, 127
  historical, 130
  Oprah's changing beliefs, 32
  Schucman manuscript and, 122
  verified existence, 130
Johnson, James Weldon, *God's Trombones; Eight Negro Sermons in Verse*, 17
Jones, Don, 107
Jones, James Earl, x
Jones, Quincy, 52, 117–118
Joplin, Janis, 100
Josephus, 5
Journal of Popular Culture, xi, 55
Journal of Religion and Psychical Research, 174
Jubilee (Walker), 18, 30
Judaism, 207
  heroes, 186

teaching on spiritual
development, 73
view of Jesus, 182
Judeo-Christian
heritage, morality of,
203
judgment, 146
juvenile detention
center, Vernita's
efforts to commit
Oprah, 12

K
Kamenetz, Roger, 70
karma, xi, 67, 88, 89,
182, 187–188
East vs. West views,
89, 92
negative, 146
Oprah's view vs.
original Hindu
concept, 185
and reincarnation,
145–146
vs. sin, 143
Katie, Byron, 70
Kelley, Kitty, 72
on family created by
Oprah, 117–118
on Oprah, xii, 16,
27–28
on Oprah and
Stedman, 48
on those at birthday
celebration, 53
Kennedy, John F., 83–86
Kerouac, Jack, 81–82
On the Road, 79, 80
Killah priest, 213
King, Gayle, 118
King World, 47, 65
Kinski, Nastassja, 52

knowledge, study of, 33
Kosciusko, Mississippi, 3
Ku Klux Klan, 22

L
labels, Oprah's rejection
of, 172
LaBianca, Leno and
Rosemary, murder,
98–99
language
issue for New Age
teachers, 131–132
stolen, 185
LaVey, Anton Szandor,
93–96
The Satanic Bible,
94–95
Law of Attraction, 71,
194, 196
Leap of Faith (Queen
Noor of Jordan), xvii
learning
devotion to, 7
and success, 11
Lee, Hattie Mae, 4
Lee, Vernita, 3, 8
Lee, Vincent Miquell, 15
Lennon, John, 87, 93
Leonard family, 6
Lerner, Michael, 108
Lesser, Elizabeth, 70
Levine, Richard, 105
liberation, Tolle on, 138
lies, 14
Life, 78
Light, Lucifer and, 144
liturgy, 210
loneliness, 42
*Los Angeles Times
Sunday Magazine*,
153–154

The Lost Symbol
(Brown), 195
love, 201–205
vs. fear, 122, 124–125
God and, 31, 132
Williamson on,
124–125, 128
LSD, at WLAC, 24
Lucifer
Christian view, 176
Zukav reworking of
idea, 143–144
Luciferic principle, 144

M
MacGregor, Jeff, 69
MacLaine, Shirley, 51
Mae, Earlist, 3
Mae, Hattie, 3
devotion to learning,
7
impact on Oprah, 6
magick, 96
Maharishi Ayurveda
Health Center for
Stress Management
and Behavioral
Medicine, 152
Maharishi Ayur-
Veda Products
International, 153
Maher, Bill, on *The
Secret*, 71
Mahesh Yogi,
Maharishi, 83, 151
Beatles and, 86–87
man, as spiritual being,
208
man-made religion,
73–74
Mansfield, Jayne, 96
Manson, Charles, 99

mantras, xii, 45, 184
 Christianity and, 177
March of Dimes, 18
marijuana, at WLAC, 24
marriage
 Oprah's views on, 47
 rituals for, 210
 spiritual
 partnerships to
 replace, 146–147
 Williamson view of, 127
materialism, 47, 78
materialistic reality, call to create, 92
The Matrix, 115
maya (Hinduism), 81, 91, 184, 191
McCartney, Paul, 87, 100
McTaggart, Lynne, 195
"me generation," 186–187. *See also* self
media, African Americans in, 43
meditation, 67, 83, 103
 in Yoruba spirituality, 166
Meharry Medical College (Nashville), 15
Men Are from Mars, Women Are from Venus (Gray), 67
men, in Nashville, 24
Meredith, James, 3
Merlin (Chopra), 156
messianic mission, of Zukav, 148
Methodist Church, H. Clinton and, 106–107

Midler, Bette, x
Milwaukee, Oprah's childhood move to, 8–9
Miss Black Tennessee contest, 19
Miss Fire Prevention contest, 18
Mississippi in 1950s, 3–4
money, 46–47
 and energy, 68
monism, 136, 191, 197
moral code, 41
moral revolt, 23–25
morality, 145–146
Morrison, Jim, 100
Morrison, Toni, 57
Mother Jones, 105
movie career, Oprah's interest in, 45–46
Myers, Zelma, 9
Myss, Carolyn, 70
mysticism, xii, 81, 129

N
Nader, Ralph, xi
Nashville
 civil rights struggle, 22
 Oprah as child in, 9–10
 Winfrey and men, 24
National Forensic League, 17
National Honor Society, 18
The Nature of Personal Reality, 48
negative energy, 103
negative experiences,

pain-body as cause, 141
negative *karma*, 146
New Age Journal, 153
New Age movement, 70, 91–93
 Christian spirituality vs., 177, 193
 and destiny, 201
 ethics of, 202
 on evil, 144
 Ferguson and, 102–103
 problems, 115
 teacher credibility, 131
 views of self, 132
A New Earth (Tolle), 134
new earth, Tolle on, 138
New York, 42
New York Times, xii, 69
Newsweek, 44, 120
Newton, Thandie, 59, 61
Nicolet High School (Fox Point), 11
Nine Satanic Statements, 94–95
Nineveh, 130
nirvana, 182
Nissan, xv
"noetic science," 195
Noor (queen of Jordan), *Leap of Faith*, xvii
Norman, Philip, 98

O
Obama, Barack, xiv, 11, 172, 180
objectivity, xxi
occult, 94, 99–105

Occult America
(Horowitz), 100–101,
111–112
Olorum (divine
creator), 166
On Becoming Human
(Rogers), 82
On the Road (Kerouac),
79, 80
oneness of universe, 136
Operation PUSH, 30
"Oprafication" of
America, 53
"Oprah Effect," xiv, xvi,
123
"Oprah," origin of
name, 5
The Oprah Phenomenon
(Harris and Watson),
198
Oprah Winfrey Show,
204
  Chopra as guest, 150
  critics of topics, x–xi,
  53
  guest selection
  process, 157
  impact on viewers,
  49, 158, 178
  May ratings decline
  in 1994, 54–55
  need for new
  thinking, 64
  planning future of,
  62–63
  program themes, x,
  49–50, 51
  suggestions for
  change, 54
  syndication of, 44,
  47
  talk shows as topic,

55
  Tolle as guest, 138
  transition to religion
  topics, xi
  Vanzant as guest,
  163, 165, 167
  viewer statistics, xiv
  vision of "Change
  Your Life"
  television, 66–68
  Williamson as guest,
  56, 109, 123
  Zukav as guest,
  141–142
"Oprah's Favorite
  Things," xiv
original sin, 122
Orman, Suze, 68
orun rere, 166
Osteen, Joel, xv
OWN network (cable
  television), xv, 112–113

P
pagan religions, 93
"pain-body," Tolle on,
  139–140, 141
pain, Chopra on, 155
Pasadena Weekly, 161
past-life recall, 143
peace of God, Tolle on,
  136
People Are Talking,
  36–39
  Oprah's objection to
  being co-host, 38
personal God, 193
personality traits, and
  talk show, 38
Phil Donahue Show, 49,
  96, 155
Philadelphia Inquirer,

interview with, 43–44
Philosophical Research
  Society, 123
philosophy, Williamson
  interest in, 121–122
physical healing, Tolle
  on, 138
podcast series, xvi
Poitier, Sidney, 52, 118
politics
  faith-based, 108–109
  Winfrey's influence,
  xiv
"politics of meaning,"
  108
positive thinking,
  power of, and
  economics, 127–128
poverty, Williamson
  on, 129
power, 64
prayer
  to ancestors, 61
  in public schools,
  Supreme Court
  on, 85
  as show theme, 56
  suggested weekend
  of, 54
  in Yoruba
  spirituality, 166
"A Prayer for America"
  event, ix–xii
pregnancy, 13–15
priestess, Winfrey as,
  xiii
prime time, Oprah's
  lack of readiness, 27
privacy, of religious
  views, xx–xxi
Proctor & Gamble, xv
prophets of alternative

Index

spirituality, Winfrey's
impact on careers, xv
prosperity, spiritual life
connection to, 209
psychic, 68
Psycho-Cybernetics, 48
Punahou School
(Honolulu), 11
pure consciousness, 135

Q
Quimby, Phineas, 102

R
race, and Oprah's
decision to move to
Chicago, 42–43
rape, 14
Reagan era, 103
reality, 136
as illusion, 125
as "thin," 190–192
thoughts to shape,
194–196
recall of past life, 143
Redbook, 54
"regression therapy," 92
reincarnation, 88, 184
Christianity and, 177
East vs. West views,
92
and *karma*, 145–146
Zulav on, 142–143
religion
creating new,
untested, 185
defining, 175–176
exclusivity in, 181
fame vs. truth, xvii
flexibility to
redefine, 182–185
ignorance and, xx

LaVey questioning
of traditional,
93–94
man-made, 73–74
Oprah's blending of
traditions, 112–113
Oprah's impact, xix
Oprah's views after
anchor job loss, 29
OWN network role
in change, xv–xvi
risk from reworking,
207
vs. spirituality,
173–179
talk show transition
to, xi
Tolle on corrupted,
137
religions of world
Oprah's education
in, 157–158
teaching on spiritual
development, 73
religious revolution, 66
"Remembering Your
Spirit" techniques,
xii, 68
responsibility for
actions, 142
resurrection,
Williamson on,
125–126
A Return to Love
(Williamson), 123–124
Rich, Frank, on
Clinton, 105
Ritchie, Guy, *The Ego
Has Landed*, 159–160
rituals, 185, 210
Rivers, Joan, 44
The Road Less Traveled,

48
Robbins, Anthony, 109
Robertson, Pat, xv
Roeper, Richard, 69, 71
Rogers, Carl, *On
Becoming Human*, 82
Rolling Stones, 1969
concert in California,
97–98
Roosevelt, Eleanor,
109–110
Roosevelt, Franklin, 77
Rosemary's Baby, 96, 99
Ruth, Daniel, on
Oprah's ego, 50–51
Ryan, Meg, 133–134

S
"sacred space," 190
sadness, 24–25
Salinger, J. D., *Catcher
in the Rye*, 107
salvation
Tolle on, 138
Williamson on, 125
samsara, 184. *See also*
reincarnation
Sanders, Al, 28
Satan. *See* Lucifer
The Satanic Bible
(LaVey), 94–95
Saudi Arabia, women
in, xviii
Schucman, Helen, *A
Course in Miracles*,
122–123, 130
and understanding
of Jesus, 133
Schwarzenegger,
Arnold, 52
The Seat of the Soul
(Zukav), 67, 141

Index

Second Great
 Migration of southern
 blacks, 8
The Secret (Byrne),
 70–71, 91, 194
secular faith, 76
secularization, 85
seeker generation,
 77–78
self, 186–187
 conceptualized,
  159–160
 devotion by Church
  of Satan, 97
 divine, 192
 enhancement of,
  185–189
 Tolle and, 135
 as universe center,
  evidence for
  believing, 188
self-centeredness, 188
self-empowerment,
 religion of, 92–93
self-esteem, vs. failure,
 29–30
self-help, 48, 102
 Zukav and, 143
self-importance, 45–46
self-perception, 50
self worth, 68
selfishness, 160
September 11, 2011
 attacks, ix, 198
service to others, 186
*Seven Habits of Highly
 Effective People*
 (Covey), 109
*The Seven Spiritual Laws
 of Success* (Chopra), 154
sexual promiscuity,
 11, 14

The Shack (Young), 115
Shales, Tom, x–xi,
 55–56
Sher, Richard, 39
Shriver, Maria, 52
sickness
 faulty thinking as
  cause, 127
 Tolle on, 138
Siddhartha (Hesse), 99
sin, 122, 182
 vs. *karma*, 143
 Tolle on, 137
 Williamson on,
  126–127
Singh, Inberjit, x
slave on Underground
 Railroad, Oprah's
 reenactment of
 experience, 59–61
Smith, R. C., 45–46
social being, Winfrey
 as, 118–119
soul
 Bacon on, 162
 ultimate, 144
 Zukav's concept of,
  142
South Africa, leadership
 academy for girls,
 197–198
Spielberg, Steven, 44,
 52
"Spirit Series," xvi
spirits
 contact with, 206
 of slaves, efforts to
  connect, 61
spiritual being, man as,
 208
spiritual community,
 211

spiritual family of
 Oprah, 168–169
spiritual matters,
 decision making by
 Oprah, 33
spiritual partnerships
 to replace marriage,
 146–147
spiritual
 transformation,
 39–43
spirituality, 44
 alternative, 68
 "Best Life" series
  about, 159–161, 173
 of Christians,
  176–177
 defined in U.S., 101,
  175
 guidance in, 34
 invitation to explore
  alternative, 174
 vs. religion, 66,
  173–179
 talk show transition
  to, xi
 television shows on,
  70
 Winfrey and, xiii,
  112, 119, 172
 Winfrey's journey
  toward, 31
Springer, Jerry, 64
Stanford University, 18
Starr, Ringo, 87
stock options in King
 World, 65
success, 48
 belief in, 71
 in Chicago, 45
 and learning, 11
 mantras of, 45

suicide thoughts
of Oprah, 40–41
of Tolle, 135
supernatural, 97
supernatural living,
alternative stream, 66
Symbionese Liberation
Army, 22
sympathy, 23
syndication, of *Oprah
Winfrey Show*, 44, 47

T
Taoism, 81
Tate, Sharon, murder,
98–99
television
Oprah's interest as
child, 10
racial makeup of
personalities, 20
talk show. *See also
Oprah Winfrey
Show*
temptation, 144
humans response
to, 143
Tennessee
State Forensic
Tournament, 18
Tennessee State
University, 19
Teresa of Calcutta, 54,
89, 145
Tesh, John, 24
theodicy, 198
"thin" reality, 190–192
Thompson, Marian,
155
thought, 192, 211
and illness, 138
power from, 71

to shape reality,
194–196
Time, 108, 150, 154
"To Make a Poet Black
and Beautiful and Bid
Her Sing," 30
Tolle, Eckhart, xi, 70,
133–141, 169, 180
background,
134–135
and corrupted
religions, 137
A New Earth, 134
on physical healing,
138
Tonight Show, 44
toughness of Oprah, 22
traffic accidents, pain-
body as cause, 141
tragedy, 196
Transcendental
Meditation, 83, 87–91
Chopra and, 151
Travolta, John, 118
Triguna, Brihaspati
Dev, 151
Trine, Ralph Waldo,
102
trust, loss of, 14
truth, 33–34, 216
vs. experience,
205–207
vs. fame in religion,
xvii
Turner, Jerry, 26, 28
Turner, Tina, 52
TV Guide, 45–46

U
ultimate reality, 81
ultimate soul, 144
uncertainty, 194

Underground Railroad,
Oprah's reenactment
of slave experience,
59–61
understanding,
surrendering to god
of, 67–68
United States
Eastern spirituality
in, 111
focus on economic
issues in 1980s, 103
U. S. armed forces
chaplains, 96
U. S. Constitution,
First Amendment, 85
U. S. Supreme Court,
Engel v. Vitale, 85
Unity movement, 102
universe, 186, 194–195
Chopra on, 154
Christian
perspective,
177–178
intention of only
good, 196–199
oneness of, 136
self as center,
evidence for
believing, 188
untouchables in India,
89, 145
Upward Bound, 10
urna (Hindu Third
Eye), 125

V
valid experience, 205,
207
Vanity Fair, 46
Vanzant, Iyanla, xi, 70,
163–168

Acts of Faith, 67, 164
background,
   163–164
In the Meantime, 164
on Oprah, 163, 165,
   167
Yesterday I Cried, 164
Varma, Mahesh
   Prasad, 83
Vaught, W. O., 106
vibrations, efforts to
   feel, 69
vision, change in, 52–57
visualization, xi, 30
vocabulary, Winfrey
   on Baltimore TV
   news, 28
Vogue, 53

W
Walker, Margaret,
   Jubilee, 18, 30
Walpurgisnacht
   (European spring
   festival), 94
Walters, Barbara, 163
Washington, Booker
   T., 7
Washington D.C., 42
Washington Post, 71, 106
Watson, Elwood, *The
   Oprah Phenomenon*,
   198
Watts, Tim, 40–41
wealth, xiv, 46–47
   accumulation by
   baby boomers in
   1980s, 103
Weekly Standard, 151
Weil, Andrew, 70
Weir, Peter, 59
welfare mother,

Williamson's advice
   to, 128
Weller, Robb, 42
Werner Erhard
   (Bartley), 104
Wesley, John, 107
Wiesel, Elie, 51
Williamson, Marianne,
   xi, 51, 70, 120–129,
   169, 191
background,
   120–121
*Emma and Mommy
   Talk to God*, 128
and God, 193
on *Oprah Winfrey
   Show*, 56, 109, 123
question of evidence
   for beliefs, 129,
   131–133
A Return to Love,
   123–124
reworking Christian
   terms, 132–133
Winfrey, Oprah
   birthday celebration
   at age 40, 52–54
   in Chicago, 43–46
   father, 5
   foundations, 213–214
   grief after child's
   death, 15
   impact on viewers,
   216
   lack of preparation
   for international
   news reporting, 27
   lack of research
   on biblical
   scholarship, 32–33
   loss of Baltimore
   anchor role, 28

Mississippi years,
   3–8
   new qualities in 40s,
   66
   origin of personal
   name, 5
   philosophy
   principles, 190–207
   as Prayer for
   America host, x
   pregnancy, 13–15
   rumors of odd
   behavior, 68–70
   spiritual family,
   168–169
   success of, 73
   tarnished story,
   215–216
   turning point for,
   1–2
Winfrey, Trenton, 14
Winfrey, Vernon, 5,
   9–10, 12, 32
   and Oprah in
   college, 19
   rules for Oprah, 13
   on second chance,
   15–16
WJZ-TV (Baltimore),
   1, 25–29, 42
WLAC (Nashville CBS
   affiliate), 20–21
women, in Saudi
   Arabia, xviii
Wonder, Stevie,
   "Superstition," 35
Woodstock, 98
Woodward, Bob, *The
   Choice*, 110
WTVF-TV, 22
WVOL (Nashville
   radio station), 18, 21

Index

X

XM Satellite Radio program, xvi

Y

Yasgur, Max, 98

Yesterday I Cried (Vanzant), 164

yoga, 90, 184

Yoruba priestess, Vanzant as, 166

Young, William P., *The Shack*, 115

youth counterculture in 1960s, 80

Z

Zen Buddhism, Erhard and, 104

Zukav, Gary, xi, 70, 141–149, 191, 197

  The Dancing Wu Li Masters, 148–149

  libertinism, 146

  messianic mission of, 148

  on *Oprah Winfrey Show*, 141–142

  The Seat of the Soul, 67, 141, 149

  transformation of humankind, 147–148

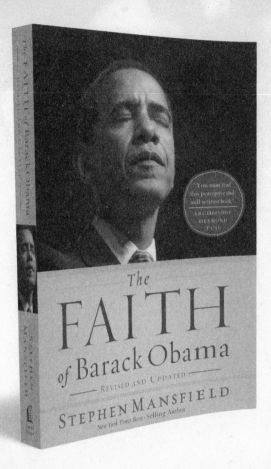

The 2008 election is only a memory now, but what happened to all those promises Barack Obama made to the American people?

In this **updated** and **revised** book, Stephen Mansfield again dives into the controversial faith of President Obama. With two new chapters devoted to the first two years of this historical presidency, Mansfield continues his exploration into Obama's faith without religious or political bias.

"You must read this perceptive and well-written book. Then you will know why Barack Obama has such a passion for justice and equity, such a gift for filling people of different generations with a newfound hope that things can and will change for the better."

—Archbishop Desmond Tutu

Available wherever books and ebooks are sold.